# AN A TO Z OF ATLANTIS

Simon Cox is the internationally bestselling author of *Cracking the Da Vinci Code* and *Illuminating Angels and Demons*. He is a full-time writer-researcher in the ancient mysteries/alternative history genre and has worked alongside some of the biggest names in this area. Simon has appeared on the BBC and ITV in the UK as well as on numerous international television and radio networks. He lives in Bedfordshire, England.

Mark Foster is a writer and historical researcher whose website Rostau.com has garnered critical acclaim within the alternative history genre. He is also a freelance graphic designer and has worked on *Phenomena* magazine as well as being creative director for *DUAT* Magazine.

# SIMON COX'S A TO Z SERIES

# AN A TO Z OF
# ATLANTIS

# SIMON COX
## AND MARK FOSTER

### with additional material by
### Ed Davies, Susan Davies and Jacqueline Harvey

MAINSTREAM
PUBLISHING

EDINBURGH AND LONDON

First published in Great Britain in 2006 by
MAINSTREAM PUBLISHING COMPANY (EDINBURGH) LTD
7 Albany Street
Edinburgh EH1 3UG

ISBN 9781845962630

A catalogue record for this book is available from the British Library

Typeset in Apollo and Hamilton

Printed in Great Britain by
Cox & Wyman Ltd, Reading

# ACKNOWLEDGEMENTS

**S**imon would like to applaud and tip his hat to: Susan Davies, project manager extraordinaire, ass-kicker and all-round brilliant person. Irreplaceable. Ed Davies for the additional research and continued help and support; Mark Foster, my co-author on this and many more books to come – light at the end of the tunnel at last! Jacqueline Harvey and family for the tireless effort and great work. The American crew: Jennifer Clymer, brilliant, brilliant, brilliant; MJ Miller – you know what? It's still all about me, baby! Jason Melton – what book? Ma and Pa on Gozo, Mark and Claire in Yorkshire. Gemms and Sam in Bicester.

Mark and Jill, Ian and Viv, the Scottish crew, for long evening chats, a wee dram or two and cheesy peas! Also in Scotland, Gordon Rutter, Bob and Lindsey Brydon (is Bob really Fulcanelli?). Iain Grimston for the lively chats. Everyone who made the last two years at the Fringe such a success, especially Naomi Hare. Rick at Joystick Junkies for the great T-shirts.

In Cairo, Ahmed and Salah for their continued friendship, support and good humour. Abdallah Homouda, TGLE. Richard Belfield of Fulcrum.

At PFD, Robert Kirby, agent, friend and top chap. Catherine Cameron, quite simply fantastic! At Mainstream: the indefatigable Fiona Brownlee; Ailsa Bathgate; our hard-working editor, Claire Rose; and Bill Campbell for the kick-start.

Jane and Alexander – hope the archery continues well. The Roberts clan, Alison, Neil, Joe and Imogen – more to come? Mark Freitag for the hot water and electricity! All the neighbours for putting up with very loud Scandinavian symphonic metal bands! Kamelot, Epica, After Forever, Within Temptation, Sonata Arctica, Nightwish, Journey, Opeth for the incredible musical backdrop. Apple for continuing to release shiny new things that I have to buy!

Mark would like to thank: Ali Russell for all your love and support and for turning my life around. My mother, Susan Foster, for the English lessons long ago and much more besides. My brother, Simon Foster, for always being there when it counts. Simon Cox, my co-author – thanks for standing shoulder to shoulder with me for so long. Your generous support, belief and, above all, friendship mean so much. Andrew Gough for being one in a million – shine on, true friend.

Greg Taylor for the long-distance friendship. Long may you continue to be the rallying point for the genre. Craig Davis for being the Man; Borgendaal, indeed. Susan Davies for your friendship and incredible energy and efficiency. Barry McCann for believing and for the entertaining correspondence. Victor Russell for the many anecdotes and the chats; you are an inspiration. Antoinette Dax for the reading material and the intriguing discussions.

And to everyone else who has made a difference: Geoff Webb; Kate and Paul Struys and the Girls; Sonja and Andy Howells; Ralph Ellis; Adam Miller; Mark Oxbrow; Ian Robertson; Jay and Sonia. Finally, I'd like to thank everyone at Mainstream for all their hard work, and especially Emily Bland for her humour and dedication.

# CONTENTS

# INTRODUCTION

This is the second in Simon Cox's A to Z series of books, following hot on the heels of *An A to Z of Ancient Egypt* and dealing with more ancient and mysterious historical enigmas. Future instalments will deal with King Arthur and the quest for the Holy Grail, and with the occult.

There can scarcely be another subject that has courted as much controversy over the years as that of Atlantis. Thousands of books have been written about the lost continent, literally millions of words, and today the subject generates just as much interest as it has in the past, if not more.

*An A to Z of Atlantis* is the latest book in this long tradition. However, unlike many of the books published about Atlantis, the purpose of this A to Z is not to promote one particular theory or to argue why one location is any more likely than another to be the site of Atlantis. Rather, we gather all of the disparate strands together into one volume in order to try and present the reader with the broadest possible range of ideas. So we look at multiple potential locations for the remains of Atlantis, as well as delving into the origins of the tale. We also study the prominent characters who have helped shape the discipline of Atlantology.

There seems to be a certain taboo attached to the study of Atlantis, as if it were somehow not a subject worthy of the effort or the research. Always there is the faint whiff of ridicule and the suspicion that those who search for the truth concerning Atlantis and whether it did or did not exist are somehow a few cards short of a full deck. This academic snobbery is unfortunate and unwarranted given the enlightening and fascinating material that can be gleaned from investigating the subject. There is no doubt that some of the research into Atlantis in the past has been misguided and does not stand up under intense scrutiny but the notion that all research into Atlantis is worthless and invalid does not help us to divine the truth.

There is also the assumption that the study of Atlantis is a relatively new phenomenon, that it is a product of the so-called New Age. However, that could not be further from the truth. The story of Atlantis is a very old one. It was first recorded almost two and a half thousand years ago and people have been pondering the meaning, the location and the importance of Atlantis ever since.

It was the Ancient Greek philosopher Plato who first introduced the idea of Atlantis to the world, apparently merely repeating what other Greeks had learned in Egypt of the legendary nation. It is not hard to imagine that even in Athens several hundred years before the birth of Christ scholars would have been debating whether Atlantis had really existed or whether Plato had made the whole thing up. So we see that this particular question is not unique to our modern age and that there really is nothing new under the sun.

With the spread of the Roman Empire, the story of Atlantis lived on and historians from Rome speculated on the location of the legendary nation. This continued long after the fall of Rome and into the Middle Ages; as the Renaissance flourished, so did the ideas concerning Atlantis. Individuals such as Athanasius Kircher and Sir Francis Bacon helped keep the idea of Atlantis alive.

We have to be aware, too, that in the intervening centuries, many documents and sources that mentioned Atlantis have been lost to us, and so it is that our knowledge of the vanished island is very likely inferior to that of those who have trod this path before us. Even so, our current knowledge of Atlantis relies heavily on those written accounts that we do have, those rare fragments that contribute to our understanding.

In the 1800s, there was an upsurge in studies into the lost kingdom and, kick-started by the writings of the American Ignatius Donnelly, the subject fell into the hands of the founders of the New Age movement, and occultists such as Madame Blavatsky wrapped their ideas around that of Atlantis. Perhaps this is why Atlantis has become tarred with the brush of pseudoscience but, beneath the wilder ideas and way-out theories, there is a kernel of truth, a persistent reality that refuses to go away.

Why, for example, do so many cultures from around the world

share the same myth of a great deluge and of the survival of certain individuals who sought refuge in boats and arks? It does indeed seem that there is some folk memory present in these tales of destruction and salvation. The question is whether these myths and legends speak of a global deluge that affected the entire world or whether all these tales speak of one place that was ruined and destroyed – a place we have come to call Atlantis.

What are we to make of the recurrence in seemingly isolated and disparate cultures of similar themes? Why, for example, did the civilisations of the Middle East and Mesoamerica both build pyramids? Why do we have multiple tales of gods appearing on the shores of the early developing world, bringing knowledge and wisdom with them, teaching the natives wherever they were encountered how to grow crops and to form laws by which they should live and build societies. Again, are these tales somehow related and do they in fact refer to a lost race of people who somehow survived the destruction of their homeland? In other words, were the 'gods' of numerous cultures around the world merely enlightened individuals from Atlantis?

Then there are the legends of tribes and races all of whom claimed to have come from a place that sounds very much like the Atlantis of Plato's dialogues – people who often share racial characteristics such as fair skin, blond or auburn hair and blue eyes. The now extinct Guanches of the Canary Islands, the Lucayans of the Bahamas (also vanished), the Basques of the Iberian peninsula, the Quiché of Mesoamerica, the Frisians of northern Europe – all these peoples either made claims that they originated from Atlantis or tell tales contain unanswered enigmas about their origins.

Is it the case that a real and tangible Atlantis existed long ago in our past? Could this answer many of these puzzling historical riddles and is this a cold, hard fact of history or a convenient mystery on which to lay our hopes?

One of the most intriguing notions concerning Atlantis is the idea that it was a veritable Garden of Eden, a paradise where mankind first built a great civilisation, a place where life really was heaven on earth. This theme crops up time and time again, and many of the places where the ruins of Atlantis are thought to exist also have independent associations with such a paradise.

The timeless allure of Atlantis clearly has a lot to do with our hopes and desires, our wish to live in an age different from our own, one that truly was a paradise on earth. This is one of the reasons the story remains powerful to this day. We believe in Atlantis because we are enthralled by the idea of such an idealised history, of a literal Garden of Eden where things were better, where people lived glorious lives. Perhaps there are so many variations on the Atlantis story and so many proposed locations for the fabled island simply because each of us has our own personal vision of just what this utopia once was.

It certainly says something about human nature that all of our myths and legends, both old and new, concerning this lost world always depict Atlantis as superior to our modern-day world. People lived longer lives, harvests were more frequent, wisdom was greater, society was more altruistic and individuals were less self-obsessed.

Therefore, the question is: have we not just collectively created a perfect world that we all would like to believe once was? Or did Atlantis truly exist?

Of course, the truth lies somewhere in the mists of time, but one thing must be remembered: Plato tells us that the fall of Atlantis was the result of the corruption of power, how absolute power corrupts absolutely. Surely the lesson of Atlantis is this very fact.

In *An A to Z of Atlantis*, we hope that we can help the reader to answer these myriad questions for themselves.

Simon Cox and Mark Foster
September 2006

# AELIAN

**A**elian, or Claudius Aelianus in full, was a Roman sophist – a teacher of wisdom, at least in theory. Born at Praeneste, he lived from around 170 to 235 AD and should not be confused with the slightly earlier, Greek, military writer, Aelianus Tacticus, who also lived in Rome. He worked as a teacher of rhetoric (persuasion through the use of speech) at Rome and took up a career as a writer, producing *The Nature of Animals* (*De Natura Animalium*), tales having curious or moralising themes (described in the Loeb Classical Library introduction as 'an appealing selection of facts and fables about the animal kingdom that invites the reader to ponder contrasts between human and animal behaviour') and *Historical Miscellany* (*Varia Historia*), similar moral fables but drawing on human history, legends and life. His works were all in Greek and received high praise at the time of their production, though they appear to some more modern critics to lack substance and depth. From the sweetness of his style he acquired the name Meliglossus, or 'honey-tongued'.

Some other works of his have survived, including *Twenty Rustic Letters*, which may be best described as interesting, and fragments of works – *On Providence* and *Divine Manifestations* – of a mainly Stoic philosophical nature. Stoic philosophy provided the principles that governed the life of the great emperor Marcus Aurelius, during whose reign Aelian was born. Elements of Stoicism developed into Neoplatonism, which was the supreme philosophy of the ancient world for over two centuries from around AD 250.

It may surprise us that, as a Roman, Aelian preferred to write in

13

the Greek language. Traditional, conservative Romans of his day still sometimes professed considerable contempt for the Greeks, who were often regarded as effete, decadent and unmanly by their warlike conquerors. However, particularly since the reign of the Emperor Hadrian (117–38 AD), who greatly admired their achievements and learning, the Greeks had become recognised as having qualities which civilised, cultured citizens might properly value. Educated Romans wishing to research the wisdom of the past found it preferable to read the ancient books in their original language and Greeks were employed to teach their masters' sons how to read, write and appreciate their much older culture. Clearly, Aelian subscribed heavily to the favourable view of this conquered but increasingly influential nation. It may be noted that Greeks eventually became Roman emperors and that Greek was accepted as the predominant language of the Empire. By the time of the writer's death, emperors originating in North Africa and Syria had already occupied the throne and men from races once looked upon as barbarian sat in the Senate. In the probable year of Aelian's demise, a gigantic Thracian peasant, Maximinus, who had risen to power in the army, was hailed as emperor. As far as is known, he never set foot in the city of Rome.

Aelian's style has been described as often lacking in purity and eloquence, and he had a taste for tales so improbable that they have sometimes been dismissed as lightweight, though others have recognised that he was deliberately adopting the eclectic manner of the great historian Herodotus. Aelian's contemporary Philostratus, a Greek sophist, nevertheless said that he possessed a style superior to that which might be expected from a writer neither Greek nor educated in Greece, a remark which could be taken to be either praising or patronising. Perhaps Philostratus was not so much surprised that Aelian did it well but that he did it at all! Followers of the ancient philosophies inevitably debated the merits of their own beliefs and teachings with those of other persuasions and, unsurprisingly, this often led to sharp disagreements. The Epicureans, who believed that pleasure was the beginning and end of living happily, were particular targets of Aelian's scorn.

One of his sources was the famous Pliny the Elder (died AD 79), and he found the works of Sostratus, who had been a surgeon versed in zoology, and the writings of several others, valuable for much of his research. Through these intermediaries scholars have been able to gather information about even earlier writers. It should be understood that much of the learning of the ancient world is now lost to us, often because of the antipathy of the early Christian fanatics, who hated the association with paganism and destroyed libraries containing books of which they did not approve. However, Aelian's writings found favour with Christians, who sometimes drew upon his learning, and as a consequence a considerable portion of his works survive.

Aelian would have been well acquainted with the philosophy and teachings of Plato (c.429–347 BC) and it would have been at least partly from the latter's *Timaeus* that he became aware of the legend of Atlantis.

In *The Nature of Animals* Aelian reports that:

> The inhabitants of the shores of the Ocean tell that in former times the kings of Atlantis, descendants of Poseidon, wore on their heads, as a mark of power, the fillet of the male sea-ram, and that their wives, the queens, wore, as a sign of their power, fillets of the female sea-rams.

It has been suggested that the sea-rams he refers to are either dolphins or narwhals. It is not possible to tell whether Aelian used any sources other than Plato for his description.

**SEE ALSO:** Plato; Pliny the Elder

# AMMIANUS MARCELLINUS

**A**mmianus Marcellinus (c.330–c.395 AD) was probably born in Antioch, in present-day Syria, into a prosperous Greek family. He became a soldier in the Roman army and fought in Gaul and in Persia, serving under the Emperors Constantinius II, Julian II ('the Philosopher') and his short-lived successor Jovian. After his military service, he travelled to Egypt and Greece, eventually settling in Rome to write his Latin history of the Empire, covering the period from the end of the first century AD to his own time. He thus continued the work of the great historian Tacitus, whose style he clearly admired and attempted to follow. It is not always remembered that the work of Ammianus was designed to be read out loud to a gathering of people, which would naturally have some effect upon style. He has been described as the most significant literary figure between Tacitus (c.55–c.120 AD) and Dante Alighieri (1265–1321).

Ammianus was the last major Roman historian of the ancient world and revived a moribund genre. His history, *Rerum gestarum libri* (confusingly sometimes referred to, since there is a better-known work by that title, as *Res gestae*), or *Chronicles of Events*, consisted of 31 books but unfortunately only the last 18 survive. These cover the years between 353 and 378. Edward Gibbon's valediction to Ammianus in his *History of the Decline and Fall of the Roman Empire* runs:

> It is not without the most sincere regret that I must now take leave of an accurate and faithful guide, who composed

the history of his own times without indulging the prejudices and passions which usually affect the mind of a contemporary.

Ammianus used his own notes in compiling his books but also made extensive use of references to the works of other writers. He wrote carefully, using a style calculated to appeal to the educated men of his day, but it seems that he felt rather on the fringe of literary society. As a result, perhaps, of not being an 'insider', he eschewed the fashion for 'bite-sized' works and went instead for an old-fashioned monumental history. This included accounts of treason, corruption and intrigue in past administrations, painting a 'warts and all' picture of the Empire rather than a patriotic but false encomium.

Rather like the much earlier historian Herodotus, Ammianus tended to pursue subjects that particularly interested him, describing peoples, wonders of science such as rainbows and earthquakes, taxation, army morale, military siege engines and that ever-popular theme throughout the ages, the dishonesty of the legal profession.

Drawing on work which has not survived by the Greek historian and rhetorician Timagenes, who lived in the first century BC, Ammianus writes that the Gaulish priests (*drasidae*, or Druids) believed their race had long before arrived there from distant islands. This has been interpreted as a belief that these Gauls were the survivors of the destruction of Atlantis. However, Ammianus's works may be understood as indicating that while some inhabitants of Gaul were indigenous to the land, they were joined by others who had migrated there from across the River Rhine, to the north-east. He says he was also told by Gauls that local women had given birth to children after dalliances with the hero Hercules; from others he had the story that they had fled from the destruction of Troy. There were other conflicting tales of Gaulish origins.

Ammianus also records that in Alexandria in Egypt Atlantis was believed by some to have been historical, not a mere legend, stating that some earthquakes are capable of swallowing parts of the earth and that a huge island in the Atlantic Ocean had been destroyed in this way.

Ammianus's history was first printed as early as 1474 and it proved so popular that, according to journalist and historian Adrian Murdoch, 'by the end of 1533 there had been at least five editions'. Nearly all of the text we have today comes from a ninth-century manuscript which has been amended in various ways by other hands, though the original meaning is generally quite clear.

Altough Gibbon comments on Ammianus's reliability, the ancient author is not completely objective. He has a taste for the dramatic and his favour or dislike for those he writes about colours his work. Yet it is extremely difficult for even modern authors to approach historical characters in an unbiased way, as anyone reading a few biographies of, say, King Richard III of England will quickly realise: he is painted as a maligned, unfortunate, talented ruler by some or, alternatively, as a murderous, greedy, wholly unreliable monster. It seems clear that Ammianus was widely read and well able to form and express his own judgements. His military training and education had prepared him to do this with style. Ammianus was a man of his time, caught up in the politics and dangers he lived through and recording events as he saw them. Although he was tolerant of religious differences, he was a pagan at a time when Christianity was gaining ever-increasing influence in the Empire, which meant that he was less critical of Emperor Julian II (reigned 360–363 AD), sometimes known as 'the Apostate' because he had chosen to reject Christianity, than other writers have since been. It should be emphasised, however, that Julian does not escape criticism from Ammianus for some of his actions. The *Encyclopaedia Britannica* notes that: 'A comparison between the Christian historians and an outstanding pagan writer, such as Ammianus Marcellinus . . . who was very ready to admire those Christians who merited it, brings out the intolerance and narrowness of outlook of his Christian contemporaries.' We owe him a debt of gratitude for his history and can forgive his incongruities and occasional absurdities since they are admixed with striking narrative and description. Whether or not his observations about Atlantis are correct is, of course, impossible to say.

# ATHENS

It is no accident that the great Athenian Plato should have written about Atlantis, as he did in his dialogues *Timaeus* and *Critias*. In a city which in his day prided itself on being blessed with an advanced system of government and had an enormous sense of superiority, it would be natural to be interested in a fabulous land lost to history which might have lessons to interest the philosophers of the period.

Athens is the capital of the modern country of Greece. The city has a history stretching back to ancient times, when the Greek peoples lived in city states which were generally self-governing, not only in what we think of today as Greece but also in modern Turkey, Italy, Sicily and much of the area bordering the Mediterranean Sea. They were great colonisers, spoke various dialects, made shifting alliances with one another and were constantly fighting among themselves. Some states had kings, others were ruled by dictators, magistrates and oligarchies, but for most of the period before Greece was swallowed into the Roman Empire, the Athenians were proud to live in a democracy dating from 508 BC. Each citizen had the right to propose and vote upon measures designed to benefit their city.

To most modern minds, this is the perfect concept of true democracy. In practice, the Ancient Athenian system was somewhat limited. No females participated in the decision-making process (unless they could find a means of persuading their male relatives to see things their way). Only adult males were eligible, and then only if they had citizen status. Slaves and foreigners were totally excluded. Well-to-do men were trained in public speaking and their rank was respected; poor, uneducated artisans and labourers found it harder to persuade an audience to accept their views and proposals. Practically, therefore, a comparatively small number of prosperous, senior males made the decisions. Today, the uncritical view is still that the Athenians 'invented' democracy, which may be true as far as it goes. An examination of most modern democratic systems reveals that some of the imperfections of the Athenian model persist. Status and power still generally speak more loudly than poverty and low rank. However, the Athenians had a personal democracy rather than one based on elected representatives, a system perhaps superior to those of today.

The people of Athens had not always enjoyed democratic government, however. Around 560 BC Peisistratos became tyrant (which merely signified 'ruler') of the city. He was overthrown twice but each time came back with renewed strength. He died as ruler of Athens in c.527. Athens benefited from his rule and its people became increasingly proud of their city. Hippias inherited the post of ruler from his father and despite increasing opposition held on to the leadership until the year 510, when the Spartans deposed the tyrant and, despite considerable disagreement about how to proceed, one Cleisthenes persuaded the Athenians to adopt a more democratic system of government. By the end of the century, the Athenians had seen off a Spartan expedition against them and defeated the Boeotians and the Khalkidians, who were hoping to annex land from their neighbours.

The Ancient Greek peoples, with a few prominent exceptions such as the Spartans, greatly valued culture and learning, and it is generally accepted that the finest period of their cultural achievements was between around 500 and 336 BC. The Athenians, with their great commercial wealth protected by a powerful fleet, were at the centre of this flowering.

In the 490s BC, the Persians recognised the importance of Athens. At that time, King Darius I of Persia was demanding at least nominal sovereignty over the Greek cities, which were expected to give tribute of earth and water to the king in token of his superiority. The independent Greeks, including the Athenians, refused to comply with the wishes of the 'King of Kings'. It is said that King Darius employed a servant whose duty it was constantly to remind his master, 'Do not forget the Athenians.'

The Parthenon in Athens still attracts visitors from around the globe. This temple to the patron goddess of the city, Athena, once housed an 11 metre high chryselephantine (made of gold and ivory) statue of the maiden goddess presenting Nike (Victory) to her people. The sculpture was created by Pheidias to replace the earlier statues of Athena which were destroyed when the city was sacked by the Persians in 480. The Athenians believed that she, like them, loved the virtues of wisdom and appreciated the arts. Her powers were believed to be equal to those of her father, the supreme god Zeus, from whose head she had sprung. The Parthenon even in its present condition, inevitably worn and damaged by more than 2,000 years of weather, wars and neglect, can hardly fail to give a hint of the greatness of the ancient inhabitants who worshipped there and gloried in their civilisation. Its creation lifted the population after the Persian invasion (c.480–479) had threatened them, though conflict between the Greeks and Persians dragged on until 449. An all-too-rare instance of cooperation among the Greeks against a foreign enemy led to victory at the Battle of Marathon (490) by a combined Athenian and Plataean force and the great sea triumph, the Battle of Salamis, a decade later, which was won only after Athens had been evacuated and sacked, its temples burned by the Persian invaders. After that victory, the golden age of Athens began, lasting almost until the end of the century.

One of the greatest Athenian figures was Pericles (c.490–429 BC), the famed orator who was elected general of Athens on 20 occasions. He organised the fleet and built strong defences for the city. City pride was epitomised in the temples and monuments he had erected and he attempted to involve less powerful citizens in government. Perhaps inevitably, though, he overreached himself when he led his people against the military might of Sparta. The Athenians were forced to shelter within the city walls while their farmlands were burned by their enemies. Their reaction was to turn against Pericles, who was removed from office, tried and fined. Such was Pericles' stature, however, that the fickle Athenians returned him to office just before his death.

A very different but equally significant Athenian figure was the philosopher Socrates, who was known as 'the gadfly' because he often annoyed people by asking them questions in return for those they asked him. He was attempting to get people to use their own brains to discover the answer to the age-old problem of how to live a good life. He was finally accused of disbelief in the gods, of introducing new gods and of corrupting the young with his ideas, and he was condemned to die in 399 BC by drinking the poison hemlock. His last days were recorded by his great admirer Plato and it is mainly through Plato's work that we know about Socrates' philosophy. Aristotle described Socrates' 'inductive argument and general definition'. There appears to have been nothing vague or woolly about Socrates.

If the works of Socrates and Plato represented a pinnacle of Athenian achievement, the plays written for the religious festivals of the Lenaia in January and the Dionysia in March were another. These were much more than simple entertainments, often commenting on current affairs, morality and philosophy. Playwrights from around the Greek world competed for prizes for the finest works of tragedy and comedy. The plays were performed at the Theatre of Dionysus below the Acropolis in Athens. Most of the scripts are now lost, but modern audiences are still able to attend performances of some tragedies, such as Aeschylus's *Oresteia* trilogy and Euripides' *Bacchae*, and the comedies of Aristophanes, for instance *Birds*, set above the earth in a city called Cloud Cuckoo Land.

It should not, however, be thought that the Athens of poets and artists was a perfect society in which to live, as Aristophanes so humorously pointed out. Women were very restricted in their activities. Unwanted babies were left out in the open to die of exposure or starvation, girls being more likely to meet this fate. A citizen falling into debt might have to sell himself and his family into slavery until, if he was very lucky, he could buy his freedom again. Most male citizens had to be prepared to go to war for their city, if necessary.

The citizens of Athens could be lacking in gratitude towards their greatest men. Pericles was not the only one to fall foul of their inconsistency. In 483 BC, large quantities of silver were discovered in a mine owned by the state, at Laurion. Immediately, the citizens had visions of sharing out the spoils but one Themistocles had the foresight and the oratorial skills necessary to persuade them to spend this new-found wealth on building a fleet of 200 ships. Earlier, he had also persuaded them to develop Piraeus into a well-defended dockyard and port for the city. Consequently, with his naval tactical skill, he was in a position to win at Salamis against the Persians. Later, Themistocles organised the building of the defensive Long Walls between the city and the port. Only a few years later, his compatriots turned against him. He was ostracised and forced into exile, ironically enough ending his life under the protection of the Persian king. Such was the gratitude of the Athenians.

The Peloponnesian Wars broke out in 464 BC between Sparta and its supporters, who were wary of the increasing power of Athens, and the Athenian allies. Fighting rumbled on intermittently for many years until finally Athens lost the empire it had acquired.

The Delian League, a confederation of Greek states formed in 477 to counter the continuing Persian threat, was originally conceived as an alliance of equals. However, by the 450s the Athenians were referring to their allies as 'the cities which Athens rules'. In 454, the treasury of the League was moved to Athens on the grounds that it would be 'safer' there; the truth was that the Athenians had come to think of contributions to the treasury as tribute.

It was not easy for lesser states allied to Athens to relinquish their allegiance. The people of Mytilene on Lesbos decided in 427 to withdraw their allegiance to Athens. Promises of help from Sparta were never fulfilled and a year later they surrendered to the Athenian forces blockading their island. The Athenians voted to kill the men and make slaves of the women and children. Almost too late, the vote was narrowly reversed and the population of Mytilene saved. This was not only an example of the fickleness of the people but also of their courage in admitting to a change of heart and their humanity, contrasting with their initial brutality. However, in 415 the Athenians forced the neutral island of Melos to surrender to them and actually carried out the atrocities which they had earlier spared the people of Mytilene.

After humiliation at the hands of Sparta, Athens suffered political problems, enduring the rule of the 'Thirty Tyrants' who carried out a reign of terror while a garrison of 700 invited Spartan troops provided their security. Though Spartan mismanagement allowed Athens to regain some of its pride and, to a more limited degree than before the war, its democratic government, the city never again enjoyed its old glory. Along with the rest of Greece, Athens became subject to the Macedonian King Philip II, father of Alexander the Great. Eventually, it became just a small part of the Roman Empire.

**SEE ALSO:** Critias; Plato; Timaeus

# ATLANTIS, CITY OF

According to Plato, the Atlanteans lived in a vast city that was constructed in a unique and very impressive fashion. Originally, the god Poseidon had fashioned the land into a series of concentric rings, creating alternate zones, two of land and three of water. After this, the Atlanteans themselves, under the rule of their king, Atlas, proceeded to shape the landscape to their own ends and a great city rose up.

The first thing they did was to bridge the water-filled rings and then, at the centre, they constructed an incredible palace, which was added to by successive generations, becoming ever more grandiose and lavish as the years passed. A vast canal was carved into the earth so that the city would be connected to the sea. This canal was said to be some 9 km in length:

> They began by digging a canal three hundred feet wide, a hundred feet deep and fifty stades long from the sea to the outermost ring, thus making it accessible from the sea like a harbour; and they made the entrance to it large enough to admit the largest ships. At the bridges they made channels through the rings of land which separated those of water, large enough to admit the passage of a single trireme, and roofed over to make an underground tunnel; for the rims of the rings were of some height above sea level.
>
> *Critias*, Plato

Next, they constructed great walls and towers around the central island, and the stone that they quarried to build these and other buildings within the city were of three colours, white, red and black, so the buildings would have looked striking.

It has been pointed out that these three colours of stone were also used at Giza in Egypt to construct the pyramids that dominate the plateau. They were constructed in black and red granite as well as white Turah limestone. It has been suggested by more than a few writers that the high culture of Egypt began as a colony of Atlantis, so the question that arises is whether these three colours of stone were considered sacred in some way and so used in certain building projects.

The walls of the city itself were covered with metal: the outermost was coated in brass, the next with tin and the third wall that guarded the innermost citadel was encrusted with orichalcum, which, according to Plato, was a metal lost to the later world that was considered almost as precious as gold and was reddish in colour.

As well as the palace of the king, which sat at the centre of the city, beyond these blinding, metal covered walls, the temple of Poseidon was built. From the description that Plato gives in *Critias*, it sounds the most impressive of all the buildings in Atlantis:

> The outside of it was covered all over with silver, except for the figures on the pediment which were covered in gold. Inside the roof was ivory picked out with gold, silver and orichalc, and all the walls, pillars and floors were covered with orichalc. It contained gold statues of the god standing in a chariot drawn by six winged horses, so tall that his head touched the roof.

The bulk of the city of Atlantis was said to sit outside the outermost ring, and it stretched across the plain for a considerable distance. The plain was vast – roughly 550 km by 370 km – and crossed by canals. It was here that the Atlanteans tended their crops. It was said that the climate was so benevolent that they were able to harvest twice during a single year, once in winter because of the rain and once in summer due to the irrigation of the canals. The mountainous land on the edge of the plain was inhabited too and it, like the plain itself, benefited from a wondrous abundance and natural bounty. It contained 'numerous villages and a wealthy population, as well as rivers and lakes and meadows, which provided ample pasture for all kinds of domesticated and wild animals, and a plentiful variety of woodland to supply abundant timber for every kind of manufacture'.

The city of Atlantis as described by Plato is a paradise, a place where no man or woman wanted for anything, a place where even the gods themselves would surely have been content to live.

With this in mind, there is one curious note to end this account of the city of Atlantis. A plan of the city drawn according to Plato's description when viewed from above reveals what has been called the 'Cross of Atlantis', formed by the concentric rings of land and the canals that cut through them. The shaft of this cross is shown clearly as the wide canal that led to the sea from Atlantis. It has been claimed that this cross has been found in megalithic stone circles and on standing stones and altars across prehistoric Europe and that the carving of this symbol was a way of keeping alive the legend of Atlantis and mankind's past. Furthermore, this is not the only place we see circles in the design of a cross. The Egyptian *ankh* has a similar shape, if not identical, and many Celtic crosses bear a striking resemblance to this symbol.

Furthermore, the Cross of Atlantis has been associated with the Garden of Eden. It has been suggested that the cross within the circles in this instance could represent the four rivers flowing into Eden, each from one of the four cardinal points. This is fitting, because the description of the city is itself a depiction of utopia. So is this the original meaning of the cross, pointing to our origins long ago in history? Does it hark back to the place where man first rose up from barbarism and became truly civilised? The first city, the first land where we flourished and lived in paradise? It is certainly a tempting thought.

**SEE ALSO:** Atlas; Plato; Poseidon

# ATLAS

There are several figures in Greek mythology called Atlas, the most prominent being the Titan who supported the heavens on his shoulders. However, according to Plato there was another Atlas who was central to the story of Atlantis and it is to this Atlas that we refer here.

Atlas was the son of the sea-god Poseidon. According to Egyptian priests who lived at the time of Plato, the gods decided to divide up the Earth amongst themselves. The island of Atlantis was apportioned to Poseidon and it was left to his children to create the sophisticated civilisation that would flourish on the island. Atlantis itself was actually named after Atlas and the mountain that sat at the centre of the island was called Mount Atlas.

In the myth of Atlantis, Poseidon was said to have met a native inhabitant of the island, a woman called Cleito, at the most sacred site on Atlantis, right at the centre of the island. From their union, Atlas was conceived, just one of ten sons, five pairs of male twins, to whom Cleito was to give birth. Plato described their meeting in *Critias*. It is worth quoting the entire passage, because in it some of the details of the island itself are revealed, features that seem to have been created at this time when Poseidon met Cleito:

> We have already mentioned how the gods distributed the
> whole earth between them in larger or smaller shares and
> then established shrines and sacrifices for themselves.
> Poseidon's share was the island of Atlantis and he settled
> the children borne to him by a mortal woman in a particular

district of it. At the centre of the island, near the sea, was a plain, said to be the most beautiful and fertile of all plains, and near the middle of this plain about fifty stades inland a hill of no great size. Here there lived one of the original earth-born inhabitants called Evenor, with his wife Leucippe. They had an only child, a daughter called Cleito. She was just of marriageable age when her father and mother died, and Poseidon was attracted by her and had intercourse with her, and fortified the hill where she lived by enclosing it with concentric rings of sea and land.

Poseidon is often characterised as a jealous and possessive god and here we see direct evidence of this. It is intriguing to discover that the most famous feature of the island of Atlantis, the great concentric circles of land and sea, were said to have been created for no other reason than to imprison the object of Poseidon's affections. Later, this island within an island was to became the great city of Atlantis and the strips of land between the water were filled with palaces and temples.

It was Atlas, the first-born of Poseidon and Cleito, who became the first ruler of the island state in this new era brought about by the sea-god. Plato detailed, again in *Critias*, the events which led to Atlas becoming King of Atlantis:

> [Poseidon] begot five pairs of male twins, brought them up, and divided the island of Atlantis into ten parts which he distributed between them. He allotted the elder of the eldest pair of twins his mother's home district and the land surrounding it, the biggest and best allocation, and made him King over the others; the others he made governors, each of a populous and large territory. He gave them all names. The eldest, the King, he gave a name from which the whole island and surrounding ocean took their designation of 'Atlantic', deriving it from Atlas the first King.

Atlas was said to be a benevolent ruler and along with his brothers he was responsible for creating the great civilisation of Atlantis. The island nation never lacked for anything and its power and wealth grew beyond anything ever seen before or since. According to Plato, the descendants of Atlas were many and the kingship passed always to the eldest son.

In those early days, all was well and the kings ruled with the blessing of the gods. In *Critias*, Plato described the altruistic rule of the descendants of Atlas:

> For many generations, so long as the divine element in their nature survived, they obeyed the laws and loved the divine to which they were akin. They retained a certain greatness of mind, and treated the vagaries of fortune and one another with wisdom and forbearance, as they reckoned that qualities of character were far more important than their present prosperity. So they bore the burden of their wealth and possessions lightly, and did not let their high standard of living intoxicate them or make them lose their self-control.

In time, though, it seems that the Atlanteans grew greedy and the rule of the line of Atlas came to an end. Plato's *Critias* is unfinished, ending abruptly just as Zeus is about to address the other gods on the matter of what to do with the civilisation, which seemed to be turning away from its divine beginnings and, in Plato's words, was in a 'wretched state'. We can guess the ending, however, because a deluge was unleashed and Atlantis destroyed.

We mentioned earlier the Titan Atlas. One of the Greek myths tells how the Titan was turned into Mount Atlas after Perseus, one of the first mythic heroes, held up the severed head of the Gorgon Medusa to show him. This is worth noting because the mountain on Atlantis was also called Atlas. It could be that these stories of two apparently different characters called Atlas do in fact share some similarities. Atlas the Titan was said to hold up the heavens on the far western edge of the world, after being condemned to the task by Zeus himself. It is interesting that Plato places Atlantis in the far west as well. Are we to deduce that Atlas the King of Atlantis and the island itself were thought to hold up the heavens and the world? It is not by any means certain but it is an intriguing possibility.

Atlas had equivalents in many cultures, particularly in societies which also possessed flood myths. According to Frank Joseph's *Atlantis Encyclopedia*, the Guanches worshipped a deity known as Atuaman or Ataman, which meant 'supporter of the sky', a title with clear links to Atlas. The Pawnee Indians of North America believed in the existence of a sky-god called Atius Tirawa, who had similar attributes to Atlas. Other possible candidates are Atao of the Minoans, Amaiur of the Basques and Atri of the Hindu myths, along with many others.

Finally, with all of the controversy surrounding ancient maps such as the Piri Reis Map and the Oronteus Finaeus, and the fact that they are sometimes said to have been based on maps which belonged to the Atlantean sea kings, it is worth noting that the name 'atlas' has today been appropriated to mean a collection of maps bound into book form. Whether by chance or intention, this is a fitting tribute to the first of the kings of Atlantis, ruler of what was said to have been the greatest nation on earth and one which in time came to contain surely the finest sailors and navigators the world has ever seen. If those sailors truly did map the world first, then giving the name of Atlas to such collections of maps is the perfect dedication.

**SEE ALSO:** Basques; Critias; Minoans; Piri Reis Map; Plato; Poseidon; Guanches

# AZORES

The Azores are a chain of islands that sit isolated in the middle of the Atlantic Ocean. There are nine main islands in the archipelago and they lie some 1,500 km from Portugal and 3,400 km from the eastern seaboard of the United States. The Azores were discovered in 1427 by the Portuguese and at the time of their discovery they were uninhabited. They were quickly populated by the Portuguese and today almost a quarter of a million people live on the islands.

The Azorean islands were all born from volcanic activity and the highest peak in the islands is Pico Alto on Pico Island. The last volcanic eruption in the island chain was in 1957. The Azores are actually merely the tips of enormous mountains that rest on the Atlantic seabed. If the Atlantic Ocean were suddenly to disappear, Pico Alto would be one of the tallest mountains in the world.

It was Ignatius Donnelly, author of *Atlantis: The Antediluvian World*, who suggested that the site of the real Atlantis could be found exactly where it had been said by Plato to exist, right in the middle of the Atlantic. His research on Dolphin's Ridge in the Atlantic led him to the conclusion that the Azores were the remnants of Atlantis, the peaks of a mountain range that had once existed on the island-continent.

If the Azores are the remnants of Atlantis then they certainly fit Plato's description, in his *Critias*, of the location of the island nation:

> a great power [the Atlantean nation] . . . arrogantly
> advanced from its base in the Atlantic Ocean to attack the

cities of Europe and Asia. For in those days the Atlantic was navigable. There was an island opposite the strait which you call (so you say) the Pillars of Heracles, an island larger than Libya and Asia combined; from it travellers could in those days reach the other islands, and from them the whole opposite continent which surrounds what can truly be called the ocean.

The Azores do in fact sit opposite the Pillars of Hercules, which form the entrance to the Mediterranean – exactly where we would expect to find Atlantis, following Plato's description. Another correspondence with *Critias* is the existence of hot springs in the Azores. Plato said that Atlantis had an abundance of both cold and hot springs and this matches what we find in the Azores. Furthermore, Ignatius Donnelly believed that the rocks that the islands are formed from offer a clue to their identity as Atlantis:

> Another corroboration of the truth of Plato's narrative is found in the fact that upon the Azores black lava rocks, and rocks red and white in color, are now found. He says they built with white, red, and black stone. Sir C. Wyville Thomson describes a narrow neck of land between Fayal and Monte da Guia, called 'Monte Queimada' (the burnt mountain), as follows: 'It is formed partly of stratified tufa of a dark chocolate color, and partly of lumps of black lava, porous, and each with a large cavity in the centre, which must have been ejected as volcanic bombs in a glorious display of fireworks at some period beyond the records of Azorean history, but late in the geological annals of the island.' He also describes immense walls of black volcanic rock in the island.

Evidence from the geological structure of the islands, both above and below the water level, does seem to indicate that there were once river systems that drained a much larger landmass. Channels now submerged beneath the ocean contain rocks that seem to have been smoothed by the flow of rivers, indicating that this region was once above the waters of the ocean. However, because there has been so much volcanic activity in the area in the last few thousand years, much of the evidence is gone, as the landscape has reshaped itself many times. It is thought that any remains of cities or other evidence of human inhabitation from many thousands of years ago could now be buried under millions of tons of lava.

That the Atlantic is a very active and unstable volcanic region is well known. A chain of volcanoes runs from the Azores to the Canary Islands, ending with the extinct volcanoes on Madeira. The area is still in a state of flux and massive movements of the seabed have been observed in the last 100 years or so. In 1898, an American telegraph company sent ships to investigate a broken cable that ran across the region some 800 km north of the Azores and found that it had been snapped by violent geological forces that had lifted the whole seabed. To show just how volatile the region is, in 1811 a new island rose in the Azores that was claimed by the British. However, within a few years the island had sunk again and it never returned above the waves.

In *The Shining Ones* by Christian and Barbara Joy O'Brien, the authors claim to have found evidence that the area around the Azores was once a much larger landmass. Christian O'Brien is an exploration geologist with years of experience and he possesses a great understanding of the geology of the ocean floor:

> It began to look as if a large land mass, 450 miles across from east to west, and 300 miles from north to south, had tilted from north to south and had sunk beneath the waves, leaving only its mountain peaks showing above the waters – peaks which now form the ten islands of the Azores . . . It was now possible to visualise a great island about the size and shape of Spain, with high mountain ranges rising over 12,000 feet above sea level and impressive rivers running in curving valley systems. In the southeast, a feature which we have called 'The Great Plain' covered an area in excess of 3,500 square miles, and was watered by a river comparable in size to the River Thames in England. It has, as we shall see, points in common with the great plain described by Plato in his *Critias* as being a feature of the Island of Atlantis.

The O'Briens believe that this large landmass was once home to an extraordinary race they call 'the Shining Ones', people who brought about a worldwide civilisation and who were destroyed by a series of disasters.

It is clear that we still don't understand precisely the geological mechanisms at work deep beneath the surface of the Atlantic. Perhaps the same volcanic activity that has changed the landscape of this archipelago over the years will reveal the evidence we are looking for, bringing it to the surface once again. And so it could be that Pico Alto, possibly the peak of what was once the great Mount Atlas, might again be considered the pillar of Atlantis.

**SEE ALSO:** Critias; Dolphin's Ridge; Donnelly, Ignatius; Pillars of Hercules; Plato

# BASQUES

Lewis Spence, in his 1905 book *The Mysteries of Britain*, tells us that the Basques believed themselves to be descendants of the Atlanteans. They have a folk tale of how they came to live on the shore of the Bay of Biscay, arriving by boat from a place they called Atlaintika, 'the Green Island', which sank into the depths of the ocean long ago. Spence also points out that the Basques are very likely of Cro-Magnon descent, which again marks them as being possible migrants from Atlantis. As we see with other races said to have been survivors from Atlantis, such as the Guanches, there are tell-tale signs that these people were Cro-Magnons, so it seems possible that Atlantis was the original home of this particular branch of human stock.

Today, the Basques occupy a region in the borders of France and Spain. As a people, they have a history of oppression and both countries have tried to impose limits on their culture. The majority of Basques live on the Spanish side of the border and now occupy an autonomous region ruled by a Basque government. Many people still speak the Basque language and it is this tongue, known as Euskara by the Basques, which is one of the most fascinating facets of these people, and one that points to clues regarding their past and origin.

Euskara is a language that is completely unique in the world and bears no similarity to other European languages. It does, however, have elements that are thought by some to be related to the extinct language of the Guanches of the Canary Islands as well as that of the Berbers of North Africa, although this is still a highly controversial subject. The uniqueness of Euskara is one of the prime reasons why proponents of the story of Atlantis believe that the Basque people truly did originate from that island. It has been pointed out that certain elements of Euskara bear a resemblance to the languages of tribes in the Americas. Again, this has fuelled speculation that the Basques colonised Spain from Atlantis. Similar theories have been proposed about the Quiché people of Guatemala. Peter Stephen Duponceau, a linguist of the nineteenth century, had this to say about the Basque tongue:

> This language, preserved in a corner of Europe by a few thousand mountaineers, is the sole remaining fragment of, perhaps, a hundred dialects constructed on the same plan, which probably existed and were universally spoken at a remote period in that quarter of the world. Like the bones of the mammoth, it remains a monument of the destruction produced by a succession of ages. It stands single and alone of its kind, surrounded by idioms that have no affinity with it.

To add to the intrigue, the eighteenth-century abbot Dominique Lahetjuzan believed that the Basque tongue was actually the language that was spoken in the Garden of Eden. He claimed to have traced the etymology of all the names of the characters in the Book of Genesis and found that their origins were in the Basque language. It was an idea that flourished in the following century, with other abbots and bishops agreeing with Lahetjuzan's line of reasoning. Ignatius Donnelly, in his work *Atlantis: The Antediluvian World*, posited that the Garden of Eden was located on Atlantis.

Some scholars maintain that the Basques once occupied all of Spain and the Iberian peninsula and that slowly, over the centuries, they were pushed back until they came to inhabit just the small region where they live today. Clearly, if we agree with the theory that Atlantis was located in the Atlantic Ocean, this adds weight to the myth that survivors of its fall landed on the shores of Spain.

The links between the Basques and the now extinct Guanches of the Canary Islands could be considered further proof of such a diaspora. Similarities are thought to exist between the languages of these two peoples and it is said that they shared an otherwise unique goat cult. Many of the Basques have auburn hair, a characteristic also noted in Guanches.

The exact origins of the Basque people are still shrouded in

mystery. If they were migrants fr▓▓▓
that their journey is far from over▓▓▓
to call their own and instead livin▓▓
between France and Spain, many Bas▓▓▓
to establish outposts as far away as t▓▓
and Uruguay. And so it is that the uniq▓▓
Euskara, the very tongue that may hav▓▓
all those thousands of years ago, contin▓▓
globe.

**SEE ALSO:** Canary Islands; Donnelly, Ignatius;

# BIMINI

**B**imini is a chain of islands that form a small part of the Bahamas in the Caribbean. They sit some 90 km east of Florida and are well known as a diving and fishing hotspot. As well as the abundance of sea life, divers also hunt for the many shipwrecks in the area. However, Bimini is not just known for fish or sunken ships. In 1968, a stone formation, the 'Bimini Road', was discovered in the shallow waters surrounding North Bimini island roughly a kilometre and a half offshore. It was first identified by Dr Mason Valentine, a palaeontologist, geologist and zoologist, who made his discovery while diving the waters around Bimini.

The word 'road' is actually misleading. The name Bimini Road was used to describe the formation by its first observers because it appeared to resemble a paved road under the water. It is now thought that the stones could once have formed a series of walls that, if above sea level, might resemble some of the walls found at Sacsahuaman, near Cuzco in Peru. At Bimini, we find beneath the water several parallel walls as well as an elongated feature that looks like a reversed letter 'J'. Each of the stones found in the formation appear to be some 3 m by 4 m by roughly 70 cm thick.

When the Bimini Road was discovered, it was found that the large blocks were actually formed from beach rock and it is thought by many that the features we see today were constructed by shaping and heaping these blocks upon one another. French Oceanographer Dimitri Rebikoff pointed out that the structures bear a remarkable similarity to ancient harbours found in the Mediterranean and he suggested that this was exactly what the Bimini Road was – the remains of a harbour that had been used long ago in antiquity. The Mediterranean harbours to which he referred were also constructed from beach rock, so there are clear similarities. Beach rock is by no means a friable, unusable rock, as is sometimes inferred. Around the Bahamas, the beach rock in question is limestone – the same material that was used to construct the Great Pyramid, which has stood for well over 4,000 years.

A harbour built in such a location in ancient times would make perfect sense. Bimini stands on the verge of an Atlantic current which flows northwards across the ocean towards the Azores, and ultimately Great Britain and Europe. One section of the walls clearly shows a very regular curve, which does not look natural at all, seeming to indicate that the formation could very well be man-made.

In the 1970s, a historian, Dr David Zink, went to Bimini to examine the stone formation and concluded after much study that the stones might once have formed a Megalithic temple much like Stonehenge in Great Britain. The famous Frenchman Jacques Cousteau, star of the hit TV series *The Undersea World of Jacques Cousteau*, even got involved in the action, visiting the underwater formation in the '70s and filming his adventures. However, Cousteau would not commit himself as to whether he felt the Bimini Road was an ancient, modern or even a natural formation.

There are claims that many of the rocks that once made up the Bimini Road were dredged from their original positions sometime during the 1920s and transported to Florida, where they were used to construct breakwaters. If this is true, it is clear that the original shape and nature of the formation could be very different from that which we see today. For example, it is claimed that before the '20s some of the stones were visible above the waves, the inference being that the dredging that took place stripped these ancient walls right back so that only their foundations now remain.

Other mysterious features have been reported in the waters surrounding Bimini – stone columns, marble objects, even stone circles – though it is thought that many of the latter are composed of nothing more than living sponges. Despite all these claims of man-made structures beneath the waves, many geologists and oceanographers insist that the feature known as the Bimini Road is a natural formation, created, they say, by volcanic activity, which squeezed the lines of rock we see today through cracks in the ocean floor.

It is likely that all of this controversy would have raged

quietly, purely within the confines of geology conventions and oceanographers' conferences, if one man had not thrust it very firmly into the public gaze. The Bimini Road would surely have attracted very little of the world's attention had it not been for the 'Sleeping Prophet' himself, Edgar Cayce.

Cayce was known for giving psychic readings and reporting on his patients' so-called previous reincarnations, often claiming that the individuals had lived lives in Ancient Egypt or in Atlantis while the legendary nation was still above the waves. One such reading, given in 1933, mentioned Bimini specifically as a site once connected with Atlantis:

> As indicated, the records of the manners of construction
> of same [the Tuaoi Stone, or firestone] are in three places
> in the earth, as it stands today: in the sunken portions of
> Atlantis, or Poseidia, where a portion of the temples may
> yet be discovered, under the slime of ages of sea water; near
> what is known as Bimini, off the coast of Florida . . .

Cayce believed that Bimini had once been an ancient outpost of Atlantis and had been known in ancient times as Alta. However, numerous researchers have made much of Cayce's words, believing them to be an assertion that Bimini itself formed part of a greater area under Atlantean control known as Poseidia. According to Cayce, Poseidia was formed when the large island continent of Atlantis split into three separate landmasses after cataclysmic geological changes, dividing the homeland into three sections: Og, Aryan and Poseidia.

So when Cayce indicated that this portion of Atlantis, Poseidia, would rise from the depths of the sea and be discovered once again, many people considered this to be a prophecy concerning an important find in the vicinity of Bimini. It is in Reading 958-3 that we find the now famous quote said to herald the discovery of the Bimini Road: 'Poseidia will be among the first portions of Atlantis to rise again. Expect it in '68 and '69; not so far away!'

However, there is now some doubt, even amongst Cayce supporters and members of his Association for Research and Enlightenment (ARE), that Cayce himself ever associated Bimini with Poseidia. In another reading, Cayce gives a very telling answer:

> Q: Is this [the area surrounding Bimini] the continent known
> as Alta or Poseidia?
> A: A temple of the Poseidians was in a portion of this land.

Here he seems to be saying that the Poseidians occupied the Bimini Islands but that this was not their homeland. If we remember that Cayce actually predicted that it was parts of Poseidia that would rise in 1968 or 1969 and not specifically Bimini, we have a problem; because if Cayce himself did not associate Bimini with Poseidia, then he was obviously not referring to the discovery of the Bimini Road. Furthermore, it must be stated that the Bimini Road did not 'rise', it was simply discovered by divers and was still, to all intents and purposes, an underwater feature. Much has been made of the fact that its discovery occurred in '68 – the year Cayce earmarked for a discovery – but this may be nothing more than coincidence.

So if Bimini is not Poseidia then where could this ancient part of Atlantis be located? Well, several researchers at ARE put forward the case that, according to Cayce's readings, a large portion of Atlantis once situated around the area that we know today as the Sargasso Sea fell beneath the waves and what was left above the water became known as Poseidia. This area is thought to be what we know today as the islands of the Azores, in the middle of the Atlantic. Now, it is known that the area surrounding the Azores is particularly unstable and that parts of the seabed in that region are in fact rising. What is more, in the last 100 years there have been accounts of islands in the area rising suddenly out of the sea and then sinking a few years later – further evidence of the unpredictable nature of the geology of this region of the Atlantic.

The seabed around Bimini, on the other hand, is certainly not rising. So could Cayce have been referring, when he gave his famous reading predicting that Poseidia would rise again in '68 or '69, not to Bimini or the Bimini Road but to sections of the Azores? It would seem much more likely. However, some proponents of the Sleeping Prophet seem determined to prove that Cayce meant Bimini and in so doing bring credence to his prophecy of a find being made in 1968 or 1969.

Having looked into the predictions of Cayce, is there any other evidence that might suggest that Bimini had connections with Atlantis or was even the site of the fabled island itself? A lot of knowledge has been lost over the centuries. The original inhabitants of Bimini were decimated, resulting in the destruction of their beliefs and history. The native people of the Bimini Islands were known as the Lucayans, a branch of the Arawak Indians who had settled the entire Bahamas chain centuries – if not millennia – before the Europeans discovered the New World. When Columbus landed in the Bahamas in 1492, the Lucayans' fate was sealed. For years, they had been hounded by the Caribs, an extremely aggressive and warlike race who had invaded the Caribbean in the years before Columbus's arrival and who were also known to be cannibals. The Lucayans had retreated to the northern Caribbean islands to escape from the Caribs. When the Spanish landed and enquired about the many scars that marred the bodies of the Lucayans, they were told that the Caribs ceaselessly hunted them – wishing to consume them.

However, it was only after Columbus landed that the Lucayans began dying in great numbers. The Spanish enslaved the native population and many died as a result of overwork in gold mines or pearl fisheries. Many more died of European diseases to which they had no immunity and others either killed themselves or were victims of the invaders' cruelty and propensity for murder. Within a few years – some estimates put it at less than 30 – the native population had been completely devastated and the Lucayans were all but extinct. Today, everything we know about these people comes from archaeological evidence, because not a single Lucayan survived and no one alive today can claim to have Lucayan ancestry.

In *The Atlantis Encyclopedia*, Frank Joseph tells us that the Lucayans possessed many skills and crafts. He also remarks that their appearance was unusual in that they had light skin, auburn hair and, in some cases, blue eyes. This description sounds remarkably like the Guanches of the Canary Islands, who, incidentally, were also decimated by the Spanish. Joseph goes on to suggest further links between the Lucayans and these distant people who lived far away, off the coast of Africa:

> The Lucayans knew Bimini as 'Guanahani', another curious connection with the Ancient World, because the name translates as 'the Island (hani) of Men (guana)' in the language of the Guanches. These were native inhabitants of the Canary Islands, off the northwest coast of North Africa, until their utter demise at the hands of the Spanish in the 15th and 16th centuries. Although no monumental buildings were found on Bimini, in Arawak, Guanahani meant 'the Place of the Encircling Walls'; in Arawak, hani was also synonymous for 'crown' or 'wreath'. This oldest known name for the island may have referred to a large stone platform lying in 19 feet of water less than two miles off Bimini's northernmost point.

These connections are intriguing and, again, with the obliteration of the Lucayans, it seems that we may have lost many tales of Atlantis that could have helped us divine the truth about the location of this mysterious vanished land.

In direct opposition to the claim that the underwater features found around Bimini are the remains of Atlantis, author Gavin Menzies, in his book *1421: The Year China Discovered America*, puts forward the idea that the Bimini Road was in fact built by the Chinese and that the remains we see today were once a harbour and dry dock. Menzies claims that these were built so that the Chinese sailors could repair ships damaged in storms around Bimini. He also documents other features that the Chinese left around the world during their early voyages.

In 2003, another underwater feature was discovered just 160 km from Bimini, just off the coast of the largest of the Bahamian islands, Andros. Known as the Andros Platform, this feature is very similar to the Bimini Road. The Andros Platform comprises an area some 400 m by 50 m and is formed of three tiers of huge, rectangular stone blocks, roughly ten metres by eight metres and over half a metre thick.

Are these underwater ruins in the Caribbean the remains of Atlantis or are they simply buildings constructed by a modern culture? Perhaps more to the point, are they man-made at all or are they formations created by natural processes occurring over millions of years? Whatever the answer, the area around Bimini and Andros has always been ripe with mystery and remarkable tales. It must be remembered that the Bahamas are inside the legendary Bermuda Triangle, about which there have been incredible accounts of missing boats and aircraft, and unusual phenomena have been reported for years. In his 1984 book *Atlantis: The Lost Continent Revealed*, Charles Berlitz recalls one such story, told to him by Dr Ray Brown. Brown was diving off the Berry Islands in the Bahamas, looking for Spanish wrecks on the seabed, when events took a strange turn:

> We saw that our compasses were spinning and our manometers were not giving readings. We took off north-east from the island. It was murky but suddenly we could see outlines of buildings under the water. It seemed to be a large exposed area of an underwater city. We were five divers and we all jumped in and dove down, looking for anything we could find. As we swam on, the water became

clear. I was close to the bottom at 135 feet and was trying to keep up with the diver ahead of me. I turned to look toward the sun through the murky water and saw a pyramid shape shining like a mirror. Thirty-five to forty feet from the top was an opening. I was reluctant to go inside.

What are we to make of such descriptions? While some may be nothing more than figments of people's vivid imaginations, it is clear that not all accounts can be brushed aside so easily. The Bimini Road is real and so is the Andros Platform. Hopefully, through more testing and exploration, we can persuade these enigmatic features to reveal their life histories to us.

**SEE ALSO:** Azores; Canary Islands; Cayce, Edgar; Guanches

# BLAVATSKY, MADAME

**H**elena Petrovna Blavatsky was an esoteric writer and thinker, as well as the chief founder of the famous Theosophical Society. She is often labelled as the architect of what we now know as New Age thinking and many believe that she herself was the herald of this so-called New Age.

She had a unique vision and trod her own path, as is clear from this quotation from her letters:

> Nothing can make me falter on the path, once I have started on a journey. Do you want to know why? Because some twenty years ago I had lost faith in humanity as individuals, and love it collectively, and work universally instead of working for it individually. To do so I have my own way. I do not believe any longer in perfection; I do not believe any longer in infallibility, nor in immaculate characters.
>
> Each of us is a piece of charcoal, more or less black and, excuse me, stinking. But there is hardly any piece so vile and dirty that it has not atoms wherein lie the germ of a future diamond. And I keep my eyes fixed on these atoms, and do not see the rest, and do not want to see. As I work for others and not for myself, I permit myself to use these atoms for the common cause.

Blavatsky was born in Ukraine in 1831, the daughter of Russian nobles. Her mother died when she was eleven years old and her father, realising that his army life was not conducive to rearing his daughter, sent her to be brought up by her wealthy maternal grandparents in Saratov in Southern Russia. At the age of just seventeen, Blavatsky was married to a forty-year-old vice-governor, but after three unhappy months she ran away and instead began a life of adventure, travelling first to Constantinople and then, over the next ten years, to Egypt, England, France, South America and many other locations.

It was during her travels, especially in India and Tibet, that she began to formulate the ideas that would later be revealed to the world through her writings and work with the Theosophical Society. She founded the Society in 1875, at the age of 44. By this time, she was living in New York and the psychic abilities that she had developed as a child were impressing many people and enhancing her reputation.

At the heart of theosophy is the belief that all of the world's religions contain a fragment of the whole truth. It is this adherence to the belief that all religions are, in essence, part of the same whole that underlined the theosophical movement. Theosophy also deals with any practice that enables the individual to acquire a direct knowledge of God, through meditation, revelation or other means.

Madame Blavatsky did not invent theosophy; it had been around for centuries and some of the ideas it promotes can be found in the writings of Plato himself, as early as the fifth century BC. However, it was probably Blavatsky who first voiced what theosophy actually embodied and she crystallised the movement when she formed the Theosophical Society, providing a focus for the beliefs of herself and others in one organisation that could spread the word around the globe.

Blavatsky is known for her esoteric writings but her most famous work must surely be *The Secret Doctrine: The Synthesis of Science, Religion and Philosophy*, published in 1888. It is in this book that we find her beliefs on Atlantis and the people she claimed once lived there. Arriving in the wake of Ignatius Donnelly's *Atlantis: The Antediluvian World*, Blavatsky's work was clearly inspired by the ideas in Donnelly's book. *The Secret Doctrine* was an important book in its own right, though, furthering the case for Atlantis and keeping the subject in the public gaze. She claimed, as others had before her, that Atlantis had been the ancestral home of many of the high cultures of ancient times:

> What was this nation? The secret doctrine teaches that it
> was the latest, seventh sub-race of the Atlanteans, already

46

swallowed up in one of the early sub-races of the Aryan stock, one that had been gradually spreading over the continent and islands of Europe, as soon as they had begun to emerge from the seas. Descending from the high plateaux of Asia, where the two Races had sought refuge in the days of the agony of Atlantis, it had been slowly settling and colonizing the freshly emerged lands. The emigrant sub-race had rapidly increased and multiplied on that virgin soil; had divided into many families, which in their turn divided into nations. Egypt and Greece, the Phoenicians, and the Northern stocks, had thus proceeded from that one sub-race.

As well as Atlantis, Blavatsky also discussed the existence of another submerged landmass called Lemuria. In one passage of *The Secret Doctrine*, she describes her belief that at some point in the past the legends of Atlantis and Lemuria had merged into one:

> The myth of Atlas is an allegory easily understood. Atlas is the old continents of Lemuria and Atlantis, combined and personified in one symbol. The poets attribute to Atlas, as to Proteus, a superior wisdom and an universal knowledge, and especially a thorough acquaintance with the depths of the ocean: because both continents bore races instructed by divine masters, and because both were transferred to the bottom of the seas, where they now slumber until their next reappearance above the waters . . . For Atlas is Atlantis which supports the new continents and their horizons on its 'shoulders'.

Blavatsky had a huge influence on her peers and those who were to come after her, including the infamous occultist Aleister Crowley, the philosopher Rudolf Steiner, the esoteric writer Dion Fortune and James Churchward, who was to champion the existence of another vanished world in his book *The Lost Continent of Mu*.

Despite the criticism and cynicism that is today directed towards some of the writings of Blavatsky, it must be remembered that she made an outstanding contribution to philosophy in general and her work with the Theosophical Society is still bearing fruit today. In defence of her life's work, she wrote:

> The Secret Doctrine is the common property of the countless millions of men born under various climates, in times

with which History refuses to deal, and to which esoteric teachings assign dates incompatible with the theories of Geology and Anthropology.

She also contributed greatly to the advancement of the discussion regarding Atlantis and furthered the study of the vanished race of Atlanteans. One of Blavatsky's predictions was that we might at some future point find a treasure-trove of Atlantean artefacts that would dazzle the world and prove once and for all that the nation had in fact existed. The truth is we are still waiting. But it is an appealing thought, and perhaps that is the allure of Atlantis – that our enduring belief in a land that was once both a paradise on earth and the home of our earliest ancestors allows us to dream and to hope.

> Who shall say that one hundred years from now, the great museums of the world may not be adorned with gems, statues, arms, and implements from Atlantis, while the libraries of the world shall contain translations of its inscriptions, throwing new light upon all the past history of the human race, and all the great problems which now perplex the thinkers of to-day.

**SEE ALSO:** Atlas; Donnelly, Ignatius; Lemuria; Mu; Plato; Steiner, Rudolf

# BRASSEUR DE BOURBOURG, ABBÉ

**A**bbé Charles-Étienne Brasseur de Bourbourg is probably best known for his writings on the Mesoamerican world and for bringing to light ancient documents that have helped us understand the world of the Aztecs and the Mayans.

Brasseur de Bourbourg was born in 1814 and after studying philosophy and theology he became a Roman Catholic priest at the age of 30. In 1848, he travelled to Central America as a missionary, a calling that would occupy him on and off for the next 15 years. It was in Mexico that he fell in love with the pre-Columbian civilisations that had created the ancient Mesoamerican world and the ruins of which were scattered throughout the region. He collected a large number of manuscripts and went to great lengths to understand the cultures that had lived in Central America, staying with indigenous tribes and learning Nahuatl, one of the main Mexican languages, as well as Cakchiquel and Quiché.

This fascination culminated in the publication in 1859 of a history of the Aztecs. He also translated local languages into the Latin alphabet and played a large part in increasing knowledge of 'de Landa's alphabet', an undeciphered Mayan alphabet recorded by the Spanish priest Diego de Landa in 1556. This document would, after Brasseur de Bourbourg's day, prove to be the key that unlocked the Maya glyphs.

Brasseur de Bourbourg, along with Carl Scherzer, was also the discoverer of the *Popol Vuh*, the four-volume book that contains the famous creation myth of the Mayan Quiché people. He found it in a library in Guatemala City and published one of the first translations, in French, in 1861.

The *Popol Vuh*'s captivating accounts of a long-lost homeland where the Quiché had originated sparked Brasseur de Bourbourg's interest in Atlantis. He found other texts and codices that seemed to support this view of a vanished motherland. One such text, the Codex Chimalpopoca, seemed to be detailing a legend of a great deluge:

> This is the sun called Nahui-atl, '4 water.' Now the water was tranquil for forty years, plus twelve, and men lived for the third and fourth times. When the sun Nahui-atl came there had passed away four hundred years, plus two ages, plus seventy-six years. Then all mankind was lost and drowned, and found themselves changed into fish. The sky came nearer the water. In a single day all was lost, and the day Nahui-xochitl, '4 flower,' destroyed all our flesh . . . Even the mountains sunk into the water, and the water remained tranquil for fifty-two springs.

Brasseur de Bourbourg became convinced that Atlantis had sat out in the Atlantic and that this was the original homeland of the Mayans. He also believed that if such concepts as boats, spears and legal institutions like marriage, as well as legends of a great deluge in ancient history, existed on both sides of the Atlantic, then they must have shared a common origin. In his introduction to the *Popol Vuh*, he explained his belief that the kingdom of Xibalba that was mentioned in the text bore a striking similarity to Atlantis itself:

> Both countries are magnificent, exceedingly fertile, and abound in the precious metals. The empire of Atlantis was divided into ten kingdoms, governed by five couples of twin sons of Poseidon, the eldest being supreme over the others; and the ten constituted a tribunal that managed the affairs of the empire. Their descendants governed after them. The ten kings of Xibalba, who reigned (in couples) under Hun-Came and Vukub-Came (and who together constituted a grand council of the kingdom), certainly furnish curious points of comparison. And there is wanting neither a catastrophe — for Xibalba had a terrific inundation — nor the name of Atlas, of which the etymology is found only in the Nahuatl tongue: it comes from atl, water; and

we know that a city of Atlan (near the water) still existed on the Atlantic side of the Isthmus of Panama at the time of the Conquest.

However good Brasseur de Bourbourg's intentions, he does seem to have fallen into a trap that was prevalent in his day: he allowed pre-conceived ideas to influence his beliefs and to have a profound effect on his writings and translations. One classic example is his translation of a Mayan document known at the time as the Troano Codex, a text that now forms part of the larger Madrid Codex, having been reunited with its missing half, the Cortesianus Codex. At the time, Brasseur de Bourbourg believed that the Mayan glyphs formed an alphabet, but it was found out much later to be a syllabic script — one composed of signs for every syllable, not individual letters. It was de Landa's alphabet that had provided the key, Brasseur de Bourbourg claimed, acting like a Rosetta Stone for the glyphs he had in front of him. However, he had no idea that his understanding of de Landa's Alphabet was completely false. Therefore he firmly believed that what he was reading was an account of the destruction of Atlantis when he offered his translation:

> On the sixth day of Can, in the eleventh Mulac in the month of Zac, occurred dreadful earthquakes and continued until the thirteenth Chuen. The land of Clay Hills Mu and the land Moud were the victims. They were shaken twice and in the night suddenly disappeared. The earth crust was continually raised and lowered in many places by the subterranean forces until it could not resist such stresses, and many countries became separated one from another by deep crevices. Finally both provinces could not resist such tremendous stresses and sank in the ocean together with 64,000,000 inhabitants. It occurred 8,060 years ago.

Brasseur de Bourbourg's work greatly inspired writers like Ignatius Donnelly, who used Brasseur de Bourbourg's translation as proof positive that Atlantis had existed, and upon this unstable foundation they went on to build even greater claims. It was also used by writers such as James Churchward, who would give the world tales of Mu, another ancient lost continent.

Unlike some other Mayan scholars with radical ideas, such as Augustus Le Plongeon, Brasseur de Bourbourg seems to have retained a fair amount of credibility, and he is recognised as having made a lasting contribution to the study of ancient cultures. He was never completely ridiculed in the way that Le Plongeon was. Brasseur de Bourbourg has certainly played an important part in the development of Mayan studies: his uncovering of such works as the *Popol Vuh* and de Landa's alphabet has helped us understand the history of Central America. Whether these works really do offer proof of Atlantis is another matter entirely and one that is still open to interpretation.

**SEE ALSO:** Donnelly, Ignatius; Le Plongeon, Augustus; Mu; *Popol Vuh*; Poseidon

# CANARY ISLANDS

This group of seven islands sits in the Atlantic Ocean a hundred kilometres off the north-west coast of Africa. They are often cited as a possible location for Atlantis and it has been suggested that the islands are the tips of mountains that formed the original landmass. Plato himself believed that Atlantis sat just outside the Pillars of Hercules which mark the beginning of the Strait of Gibraltar, so their location certainly fits the theory.

The islands were home to a unique race of people known as the Guanches, who believed that their homeland had sunk beneath the waves, leaving them stranded on the islands. Unfortunately, the Guanches became extinct after the Spanish conquest of the islands in the fifteenth century, so their stories and tales are lost to us today.

Greek and Roman travellers landed on the islands and writers from these two empires revealed that the native inhabitants of the Canary Islands kept alive legends of the fall of Atlantis. They were said to be illiterate and to pass down their history orally, so we have no written records to verify these claims. The entire history of the Guanches vanished with their death.

It has been suggested that the Canary Islands were home to the Garden of the Hesperides of Greek myth. This was the fabled orchard tended by nymphs called the Hesperides, said to be found in a far corner of the world, in the west. According to the legend, it was here that Hera grew golden apples that could confer the gift of immortality. To protect her crop, Hera placed in the garden a dragon with one hundred heads, called Ladon. Hercules, as one of his labours, was instructed to steal three of Hera's apples and so he set off on a long journey to discover the location of the Gardens. When eventually he found them, he did manage to steal the life-preserving golden apples but only after he had slain Ladon.

Where the dragon's blood flowed, trees sprang up from the earth and these, it is claimed, were the ancestors of the rare Dragon Tree (*Dracaena draco*), a species that is found on the Canary Islands. These trees have multiple clumps of branches and it is easy to see how they could be thought of as the descendants of the hundred-headed Ladon. The Dragon Tree also happens to have bright-red, resinous sap, which was used by the Guanches to aid the process of mummification. The sap was also used in the Middle Ages in alchemy and magic, the practitioners of which considered it to be the dried blood of dragons. It was long believed, and is still argued by some, that the Dragon Trees are of immense age. One specimen destroyed in 1867 was thought at that time to have been over 6,000 years old.

If the Canary Islands were thought of as the location for the Garden of the Hesperides by the Greeks, this ties in neatly with theories that such earthly paradises as the Garden of Eden were located on Atlantis. Certainly, Ignatius Donnelly in *Atlantis: The Antediluvian World* thought that this was the case. Therefore the identification of the Canary Islands with the Garden of the Hesperides adds further weight to the possibility that the Canary Islands are the remains of what was once Atlantis.

It is interesting to note that the Elysian Fields, the part of the Greek underworld where warriors went to find solace after death, were also said to be located in the far west of the world – in other words, outside the Pillars of Hercules, precisely where the Canary Islands are situated. In fact, Homer himself connected the Canary Islands with the Elysian Fields. There is this curious passage in the *Odyssey*:

> . . . down the dank
> mouldering paths and past the Ocean's streams they went
> and past the White Rock and the Sun's Western Gates and
> past
> the Land of Dreams, and soon they reached the fields of
> asphodel
> where the dead, the burnt-out wraiths of mortals make
> their home.

This certainly seems to be describing a journey past the Pillars of Hercules and it is surely no coincidence that the plant asphodel is a native of the Canary Islands and that it flourishes there. Were the Canary Islands thought of as the Elysian Fields, the place where the dead go?

We shouldn't forget either that, according to Dante's *Divine Comedy*, purgatory existed beyond the Pillars of Hercules out in the Atlantic Ocean. Was it located on one of the Canary Islands? Certainly the barren and sulphurous upper slopes of Mount Teide on Tenerife resemble Mount Purgatory, fitting the description of a place where the dead might reside.

Some researchers have claimed that the Egyptians too placed their underworld in the west. According to Donald Mackenzie's 1907 work *Egyptian Myth and Legend*, this place was called Aalu:

> The Paradise of Aalu is situated in the west. Bleak and
> waterless deserts have to be crossed, and these are infested
> by fierce reptiles; boiling streams also intercept the pilgrim,
> who is ever in danger of being compelled to turn back.

In *The Atlantis Encyclopedia*, Frank Joseph describes Aalu as 'Ancient Egyptian for "The Isle of Flame", descriptive of a large, volcanic island in the Distant West (the Atlantic Ocean)'. This sounds suspiciously like the Canary Islands.

In yet another instance of the Canary Islands as mythological afterworld, it is thought today that the Fortunate Isles or the Isles of the Blessed, the paradise of Celtic myth, were in fact the isles of Macaronesia, the group of islands that includes the Canary Islands.

If the Canary Islands are in fact the location for all these myths and legends concerning the dead and the underworld, then it is curious given their association with Atlantis. Is there more behind these tales and stories? Did the ancient races of the world realise that the Canary Islands were once part of the landmass known as Atlantis and did they place their mythical underworld on the islands because of a belief that their ancestors had once lived there?

The Canary Islands are certainly a good candidate for the site of a lost continent destroyed in a devastating cataclysm. The islands still harbour active volcanos and the island of La Palma is one of the world's most volatile volcanic regions – the last eruption took place in 1971.

The region's instability has even provoked scientists to warn of a possible world disaster, known as a mega-tsunami, originating in the Canary Islands. An eruption on La Palma in 1949 caused the western half of the island's Cumbre Vieja ridge to drop several metres towards the Atlantic Ocean. If during a future eruption the western side of the island broke free and slid into the ocean, it would generate a giant wave hundreds of metres in height. This wave would race across the Atlantic and strike the eastern seaboard of the USA as well as the Caribbean. It has been estimated that the height of the wave by the time it reached the Caribbean could be as high as 90 m.

Such predictions are awe-inspiring as well as terrifying. Did such an event happen in the Canary Islands' past, and is this where the legend of the deluge originates from? Plato clearly believed so.

**SEE ALSO:** Celts; Donnelly, Ignatius; Guanches; Pillars of Hercules; Plato

# CAYCE, EDGAR

Edgar Cayce is probably more famous today than he ever was in his own lifetime. He could be thought of as a precursor to the New Age movement and certainly remains one of its greatest influences more than 60 years after his death.

Born in 1877 in Kentucky, Cayce had a limited education as a result of the financial position of his parents. However, at the age of thirteen, three years before leaving school, he found that he was able to absorb the contents of a book just by sleeping on it. His education over, Cayce began the first of many occupations that saw him labouring on a farm, working in bookshops, selling insurance and oil prospecting amongst other things. Then, at the age of 21, he lost his voice for a long period of time and, giving up on the doctors who could not seem to cure him, he sought help from a hypnotist, who suggested that he put Cayce into a trance and that Cayce then prescribe a cure for himself. Much to the young man's surprise, the results were successful and he regained his voice. It was this hypnotist, Al Layne, who suggested that Cayce use his powers to help others.

So it was that Cayce began to give readings for patients who required cures for their ailments and in 1901 he took up a new and bizarre career as a hypnotic healer. At the beginning, he refused to see his patients face to face and instead he would use only their name and address. His results were said to be incredible and during the next ten years of his life the success of his many diagnoses brought him new clients and, after national newspapers took an interest in the incredible story of Edgar Cayce, the psychic, more than a little celebrity.

He was popularly known as 'the Sleeping Prophet', this name given to him because he closed his eyes and seemingly fell into a trance whenever he gave one of his readings. However, the title he gave himself was 'psychic diagnostician' and this was what he had printed on his business cards.

The majority of Cayce's readings were these so-called health readings – they form some 70 per cent of the total of all his recorded readings. However, from 1923 onwards other topics that did not concern the patient's health and instead covered many esoteric subjects began creeping into his readings. The main themes were Jesus Christ, especially his early life and previous incarnations, astrology, ESP (extrasensory perception), reincarnation and meditation. However, of prime importance to us here are the topics of Atlantis and Ancient Egypt, the latter being an age-old colony made up of Atlanteans, according to Cayce.

Cayce maintained that he could discern details from the subject's previous-life incarnations and the readings seemed to show that many of his clients had lived either in Atlantis or in Ancient Egypt. Over the years, he documented their lives and activities. Through the readings, Cayce claimed that Atlantis had experienced three periods of violent upheaval during its history. Around 50000 BC, a major geological event destroyed the island's power source. In 28500 BC, Atlantis broke up into three smaller islands known as Poseidia, Og and Aryan. Then, in 10500 BC, the greatest disaster occurred, causing all three of the islands of Atlantis to sink.

Atlanteans had been migrating to Egypt well before this final destruction, according to his readings, and it was said that the high culture that had developed in Egypt flourished and reached the pinnacle of its greatness just as Atlantis sank below the waters. It was under a high priest called Ra-Ta that Egypt achieved this, and as in the stories of Osiris and Quetzalcoatl becoming great civilisers and leaders of men, so Ra-Ta took on a similar mantle and was said to have transformed humanity across the world. Becoming a beacon for other cultures, Cayce's Egypt of 10500 BC was the high water mark for mankind, surpassing any scientific achievements in all of history, including the modern era – or at least Cayce's era, the early to mid-1900s.

One of the most sensational themes that developed over the course of the readings was the existence in Egypt of a so-called Hall of Records, a depository of information that contained 'a record of

Atlantis from the beginnings of those periods when the spirit took form or began the encasements in that land'. He gave further details in other readings:

> They extend through the first destructions of that ancient civilization, the exodus of Atlanteans to other lands, and the final destruction of Atlantis. They contain a description of the building of the Great Pyramid, as well as a prophecy of who, what, where, would come [to make] the opening of the records.

However, Cayce did on several occasions allude to the fact that there was not just one Hall of Records on the earth and he spoke of another in South America during many readings, including the following one, given in 1933:

> As indicated, the records of the manners of construction of same [the Tuaoi Stone, or firestone] are in three places in the earth, as it stands today: in the sunken portions of Atlantis, or Poseidia, where a portion of the temples may yet be discovered, under the slime of ages of sea water; near what is known as Bimini, off the coast of Florida. And in the temple records that were in Egypt, where the entity [the soul channelled in the reading] later acted in cooperation with others in preserving the records that came from the land where these had been kept. Also the records that were carried to what is now Yucatan in America, where these stones (that they know so little about) are now – during the last few months – being uncovered.

So do these multiple halls of records exist? Certainly, to date, none have been found. However, Cayce's mention of Bimini as one of the possible locations is intriguing, because at the time the island had not been considered a candidate for the remnants of Atlantean civilisation. It was not until 1968 that the now-famous Bimini Road was found in shallow waters just off the coast of the island. Coincidence, or proof that Cayce was relaying the true history of Atlantis in his readings?

While information on these other halls of records is fairly scant, we know much more about the Egyptian Hall of Records from Cayce. During subsequent readings, he went into much more detail, as in this one, also from 1933:

In the record chambers there were more ceremonies than in calling the peoples at the finishing of that called the pyramid. For, here those that were trained in the Temple of Sacrifice as well as in the Temple Beautiful were about the sealing of the record chambers. For, these were to be kept as had been given by the priests in Atlantis or Poseidia (Temple), when these records of the race, of the developments, of the laws pertaining to One were put in their chambers and to be opened only when there was the returning of those into materiality, or to earth's experience, when the change was imminent in the earth.

During a main reading Cayce would sometimes offer the sitter the chance to ask questions, which he would attempt to answer. In the course of the above reading, the following was revealed:

Q: If the King's Chamber [inside the Great Pyramid] is on the 50th course, on what course is this sealed room?
A: The sealed room of records is in a different place; not in this pyramid.
Q: Give in detail what the sealed room contains.
A: A record of Atlantis from the beginnings of those periods when the Spirit took form or began the encasements in that land, and the developments of the peoples throughout their sojourn, with the record of the first destruction and the changes that took place in the land, with the record of the sojournings of the peoples to the varied activities in other lands, and a record of the meetings of all the nations or lands for the activities in the destructions that became necessary with the final destruction of Atlantis and the building of the Pyramid of Initiation, with who, what, where, would come the opening of the records that are as copies from the sunken Atlantis; for with the change it must rise again.

Time and time again, we find Cayce referring to individuals who would have a bearing on the finding of this Hall of Records, souls that would reincarnate at a future time to play a significant role. Cayce predicted that 1998 would be the year that the discovery of this treasure trove of information would occur, but that date has come and gone, leaving many to argue that, far from this proving that Cayce was wrong, the year of 1998 was just the beginning of a chain of events that will lead to the eventual discovery of the Hall of Records.

However, it turns out that this is not the only prediction that Cayce made that has not come true. Another prophecy was that we would discover an Atlantis 'death ray' by 1958. Yet another claim was that by the end of the twentieth century the cities of New York, Los Angeles and San Francisco would all be destroyed and Japan would be completely submerged beneath the waves: 'the greater portion of Japan must go into the sea.' Perhaps more alarming, the earth was supposed to experience an axis shift by 2001, resulting in a reversal in the world's climate. Finally, he also said that China would convert to Christianity and become a beacon for the religion – although, to be fair, on this occasion Cayce didn't actually give a date, so there is still time.

Cayce always felt torn concerning the readings. On the one hand, he was a firm believer in the Christian faith, yet he believed that the individuals he was channelling during the readings were previous incarnations of the subject's soul. As Cayce knew only too well, reincarnation was not accepted within the Christian canon and was at odds with his faith. It appears that Cayce was able to reconcile this paradox, or at least he didn't allow it to affect his work. Although he was sometimes doubtful, when the readings told Cayce to continue what he had started, he felt compelled to carry on.

Some of Cayce's claims and those made on his behalf by his descendants and the Association for Research and Enlightenment (ARE) – the organisation he set up in 1931, which continues to work to understand Cayce's readings – seem slightly more dubious when we discover that as a young man Cayce worked for several years in a shop called Hopper's Bookstore in the town of Hopkinsville. This bookshop specialised in esoteric works and especially the occult, so there is no doubt that it would have contained books on Atlantis such as Ignatius Donnelly's *Atlantis: The Antediluvian World*. In fact, the Atlantis described by Cayce in his readings sounds almost identical to that presented by Donnelly. Other books that could have been an inspiration include *A Dweller on Two Planets* by Frederick Oliver, a book that the author claimed he channelled and which proposes America as a modern-day Atlantis, surely an incredible revelation for the young Cayce. The novels of Marie Corelli could clearly have been another inspiration for Cayce and, interestingly, one of the themes found in her work is reincarnation and in particular how this might be reconciled with Christianity, an issue that, as we have seen, Cayce would often wrestle with in later life.

Despite this propitious placing of Cayce in an occult bookshop during his formative years, his son Hugh Lynn Cayce flatly denied that Cayce was exposed to any of this material, saying that his father 'did not read material on Atlantis, and that he, so far as we know, had absolutely no knowledge of the subject'.

Eventually, the demand for the readings and Cayce's zealousness in giving them led to his death. He is said to have given some 25,000 readings over a period of 43 years (of which 14,000 were transcribed and are available to us today) and at the end of his life he was giving up to 8 readings a day to keep up with popular demand. Cayce ignored warnings that this was more than his body could cope with and he died in 1945 after suffering a stroke the previous year.

His legacy was the ARE and today the organisation is stronger than ever, represented in over 60 countries. Its members are said to number tens of thousands and, according to its own literature, it continues to 'research and explore transpersonal subjects such as holistic health, ancient mysteries, personal spirituality, dreams and dream interpretation, intuition, and philosophy and reincarnation'.

It is doubtful if the question of whether Cayce was a genuine psychic will ever be truly answered. It is a fact that Cayce was extremely consistent, giving readings on the same subject over a decade apart which showed almost no variation. However, if the claims about his phenomenal memory are true, perhaps this is not surprising. It has to be said that if he made the whole thing up, he must have had an incredible imagination and would have had to keep up the pretence over a period of some 22 years without ever making a mistake or contradicting himself.

Is it possible that his life readings, those relating to the past, were in fact true, while his attempts to tell the future failed? We will never know, but the fact remains that a whole industry has grown up around analysing his predictions and 'histories', around the remarkable phenomenon that was Edgar Cayce.

**SEE ALSO:** Bimini; Donnelly, Ignatius

# CELTS

It should be emphasised that the concept of 'the Celts' as a unified race of people is incorrect. There is little evidence for any great ethnic cohesion of the peoples who refer to themselves as Celtic today. The Romans, for instance, seem not to have regarded the inhabitants of the British Isles and Ireland as being Celtic, though they saw the 'barbarians' who attacked their city in 390 BC (or, depending on which chronology we accept, 387) as such. There is a great deal of current debate about the term 'Celtic', extending even to disagreement about whether the word should be pronounced with a soft or hard 'c'.

The picture is blurred, as it appears that the concept of invaders moving into new areas resulting in a more or less total displacement of the native population is incorrect. More likely, population movements involved a degree of integration and interbreeding of natives and newcomers. What is indisputable is that during the course of many years people who may be identified by the term 'Celtic' migrated from areas they regarded as homelands to others in search of suitable agricultural opportunities.

For instance, the people of north central Spain referred to as Celtiberians, an ethnicity which the *Oxford Classical Dictionary* describes as 'probably formed by a fusion of the Celtic invaders with the existing Iberians, whose traditions dominate the mixture', seem to be fairly typical. People thought of as Celtic populated areas stretching north of the Mediterranean Sea from Phrygia and Cappadocia in Asia Minor to north-western Spain in ancient times. They had a profound influence on the development of Europe during the first millenium BC. Daphne Nash, in her excellent *Coinage in the Celtic World*, makes the point:

> Mediterranean societies seem to have regarded Celtic Europe as a limitless reservoir of human labour, raw materials, and a range of exotic goods, while the Celts viewed the Mediterranean as an inexhaustible store of wealth, variously tapped by peaceable exchange, service as mercenary soldiers, and outright plunder.

Today, many natives of Scotland, Wales, Ireland, Cornwall, Brittany and the Isle of Man celebrate their Celtic origins and some are able to speak the various forms of the ancient languages, which comprise two main groups, Goidelic and Brythonic. This division means that while Welsh speakers may be able to understand some of the Cornish or Breton language, and a Highland Scot who has the Gaelic may converse with an Irish speaker, although there are some recognisable common origins, the Scots and Welsh will not understand much of each other's native speech. The revival and encouragement of the restoration of Celtic languages is often linked to nationalistic as well as cultural interests. The word 'Gaelic' is often used as an alternative to 'Celtic' in connection with Irish and Scottish language and culture.

The Romans recorded that their first meeting with the Celts came when, having discovered that in Etruscan Italy there was land they regarded as underused, the Senones, Celtic invaders, announced that they wished to acquire it peacefully but would fight for it if necessary. The Romans, trying to defend their Etruscan interests, angered the Celts by their duplicity and suffered the indignity of having to pay off their new-found enemies when they discovered that Celtic boasts of being fierce warriors were no less than the truth. The Romans agreed to pay one thousand pounds in gold but complained that the Celtic weights were incorrect and that the ransom they were receiving was therefore even more excessive. It is said that the Celtic chief, Brennus, in a magnificent gesture, threw his sword among the weights, increasing the amount of tribute to be paid, announcing proudly, 'Woe to the vanquished' (*'Vae victis'*). The story was recorded by the Roman writer Livy, who goes on to claim that shortly afterwards the Romans regrouped, reneged on their agreement, fought the Celts and defeated them, slaying their leader. However, earlier and probably more accurate Roman records seem to show that the Celts walked off with their plunder unmolested. No wonder the awful folk-memory of this early humiliation lingered in Roman thoughts to the extent that, when later expansion brought them into contact with other Celtic tribes, their thoughts were bent on belated vengeance on these people whom they regarded as barbarians.

These 'barbarians' differed from the 'civilised' Romans in several ways. They generally transmitted their traditions and knowledge orally, writing little down, though they had the ability to do so. Their towns were differently constructed from the Graeco-Roman ones. The Celts did not have the killing fields for humans and animals that the Romans did in their amphitheatres. Their art was also different, though accomplished. They saw the world in an alternate way, they were ruled by an aristocracy and their Druid priests were very powerful. To the Romans, they were alien. Since the Celts chose not to record their history in written form, we have to rely on those who thought them curious and barbarian for most of our information about them, although artefacts they left behind show that they were very skilful groups of people.

Celtic craftsmen interpreted what they saw around them in a quite different way from most other peoples. They loved curved and complicated designs. Celtic artisans were open to influences from other cultures, including the Graeco-Roman world, but they adapted these to their own artistic conventions, producing artefacts which remain startlingly strange and beautiful today. Their metalwork techniques were advanced. Among the Celtic artefacts in the British Museum, one which stands out is a bronze shield, originally gilt, about 78 cm high, from the second century AD. Among the many examples of coins produced by the Celtic tribes in England are those on which, in an adaptation of the wreathed portrait of Greek currency, an abstract of shapes is imprinted, of which, for those familiar with the original, only the wreath is instantly recognisable. Disjointed horses, crab shapes and objects reminiscent of porcupines all appear along with other designs. It was not that the Celtic moneyers were incapable of producing conventional pictures, they simply chose this way to distinguish between issues. It was a cultural statement.

The Greek historian Herodotus referred to the Celts as living 'beyond the Pillars of Hercules', the same location given by Plato for the lost continent of Atlantis. According to their own legends, the Celts originated from a submerged island, given various names in myth, including Ys. The destruction of Ys by cataclysmic volcanic eruptions is identical to the demise of Atlantis that Plato details in *Timaeus*.

The controversial historian William Comyns Beaumont, in his 1946 book *The Riddle of Prehistoric Britain*, wrote:

> Atlantis was drawn in one way or another into the vortex of the earliest Graeco-Phoenician myths of Oceanus, of the 'earth-shaker' Poseidon, the Gorgons, the Cyclops and others, all for definite reasons pointing to the North Atlantic Ocean. This, if correct, rules out the Canaries or Azores (as some have identified with Atlantis), or the regions of Morocco where the so-called Atlas Mountains are a misnomer altogether, but advances the British Isles and the Scandinavian mass, formerly at one with Northern Britain or separated only by a wider river and strait. In short, for a variety of reasons I was impelled to identify Atlantis with the British Isles.

Comyns Beaumont suggested that it was in Britain that advanced civilisation developed, and that the Greeks, Celts and other cultures were descended from this group. In describing the destruction of Atlantis, he wrote:

> This prodigious event was by no means local and inundation was only one of its tremendous legacies to future generations . . . It mainly afflicted directly the northern regions of Europe, but with prodigious speed flung outliers in scattered portions of America. Its epicentre lay in Scandinavia and the British Isles, commemorated since by many an epic and legend placed geographically altogether wrongly by historians and theologists, and it established among other effects the region of the Greek and Celtic Hades, the Place of Burning, which can be identified.

**SEE ALSO:** Atlas; Azores; Canary Islands; Plato; Poseidon

# CRANTOR

**T**his philosopher was born in about 335 BC. A native of Cilicia, he emigrated to Athens in search of knowledge and became a pupil of Xenocrates of Chalcedon, who was a disciple of Plato. Crantor was clearly a man who formed close ties with his colleagues, as on his death he left his possessions to his companions Arcesilaus, Polemon and Crates.

Crantor had the honour of producing the first commentary on the dialogues of Plato, no doubt inspired and informed by his master's teaching. Although the text is lost, it is referred to in the work of Proclus, who wrote further commentaries on Plato's writing. It seems that Crantor claimed to have travelled to Egypt to visit the temple of Neith, the place where the story of Atlantis was passed to Solon, Plato's source. Crantor says that he saw the columns in the temple on which the hieroglyphic inscriptions recounted the destruction of the civilisation of Atlantis. Plato's *Timaeus* had obviously made an impression on him, as it would on many men of learning after his time.

Crantor's *On Grief* became the model upon which the learned Roman Marcus Tullius Cicero, murdered in 43 BC, based his own *Consolatio* after the death, two years earlier, of his daughter, Tullia, to whom he was devoted. Cicero gave it as his opinion that every word of *On Grief* ought to be learned by heart.

Crantor's *On Grief* took the form of a letter to Hippocles, a friend whose children had died. This was a new literary concept in an age when sudden mortality, especially of the young, was commonplace. He argued that the period of a person's life is a punishment at the end of which the soul is released by death. Plato's *Phaedo*, written in connection with the death of Socrates, and Aristotle's *Eudemus*, subtitled *On the Soul*, may well have been his sources of inspiration.

Cicero was not the only man of letters who admired Crantor's style. It may not be said that Crantor was a particularly original thinker, but in the classical world the ability to use words in the approved manner of the time was of the utmost importance, and this he had. Matters which Crantor considered to be among the good things of life included virtue, health, pleasures and wealth, in that order.

**SEE ALSO:** Plato; Proclus; Solon; Timaeus

# CRETE

**C**rete is located in the Mediterranean and is the fifth-largest island found there. Today, it belongs to Greece but it was once the home of what is claimed to be the oldest Mediterranean culture, the Minoans, who are thought to have lived there from around 2600 to 1500 BC.

Many commentators on Plato's *Timaeus* and *Critias* believe that the Greek philosopher was retelling the story of Ancient Crete and its destruction after the volcano Thera erupted with tremendous fury in the Mediterranean some time around 1500 BC. There are certainly many parallels between the culture of the Minoans and that described by Plato. However, it is possible that Plato did not himself know the identity of the island whose tale he was telling. If, as has been suggested, he was merely recounting the story that the poet Solon had learned during his travels in Egypt, then the details of the legend could have been long forgotten. It was, after all, 1,000 years after the fall of the Minoans that Plato came to write his account. So it is a possibility that what Plato was recording was a memory of how the volcano Thera had erupted and destroyed the culture of the Minoans on their island of Crete.

The Minoans were at the peak of their power when Thera erupted with disastrous consequences, the volcano being just 100 km to the north of Crete. Today, the remains of Thera form the island of Santorini. We have no way of knowing just how powerful an eruption of Thera this was, but judging by the geography of Santorini, it has to have been one of the largest volcanic eruptions to have taken place in the past 20,000 years: the island was almost totally destroyed in a series of explosions that literally ripped it apart.

All we have to compare it to in modern times is the eruption of the Indonesian volcano Krakatoa in the nineteenth century. In 1883, Krakatoa finally blew her top, resulting in an explosion that is estimated to have been as large as would be caused by 13,000 atomic bombs the size of the one dropped on Hiroshima in 1945. The incredible explosion was so loud that it was heard as far away as Australia and has been documented as the loudest sound ever heard in recorded history. Krakatoa caused devastating tidal waves and spewed out clouds of superheated gas and ash that scorched much of the land for many miles around. In total, some 36,000 people were killed and many more injured by the eruption.

There is evidence to suggest that Thera was a much bigger eruption than Krakatoa, and its position at the heart of the Mediterranean, at a time when many cultures were growing up on the shores of that sea, should give us some idea of how catastrophic the event must have been.

It is now thought that the Minoans would have been unable to survive the fury of this volcano that sat literally on their doorstep, and so it is that Thera is credited with the murder of the Minoans. Not only would their ports and coastal cities have been pummelled by a series of disastrous tsunamis but the millions of tons of ash and volcanic rock that would surely have been released into the atmosphere would have led to crops failing for several years after the volcano itself had fallen into the sea. Even where fields and crops were not covered in ash, the climate would have been altered for years afterwards. This would mean that any survivors from the flood that must have swept over Crete would have died of starvation in the aftermath.

So here we have present certain elements that we also find in Plato's account of Atlantis. We have the death of a high culture, we have a deluge in the form of the tsunamis and we have the sinking of an island, in this case not Crete but Thera itself: Santorini today is only a third of the size it was when the volcano of Thera sat above it.

Furthermore, certain practices described in Plato's *Timaeus* seem to correspond with those which we know took place on Crete. In particular, the bull rituals that Plato describes taking place in Atlantis seem to echo the beliefs of the Minoans. Plato wrote that bulls had the run of the Temple of Poseidon, meaning that they must have been considered sacred. At certain times, the kings of Atlantis would be left alone in the temple and would offer prayers before hunting the bull without weapons, using only ropes and staves. When they captured the animal, it was led to a sacred pillar. This tale of hunting a bull in the temple could certainly be seen as a mirror of the tale of Theseus and the Minotaur, in which the Greek hero stalks the monstrous creature, half man and half bull, in the labyrinth at Knossos, Crete – the home of the Minoans.

It certainly seems possible, then, that Crete was indeed the island of Atlantis as described by Plato. To add further weight to the argument, we only have to look at the name Atlantis itself. This word is not found before Plato's account. This, according to Plato, is because:

> Solon intended to use the story in his own poem. And when, on inquiring about the significance of the names, he learned that the Egyptians had translated the originals into their own language, he went through the reverse process, and as he learned the meaning of a name wrote it down in Greek.

So is it possible that accounts of the place we call Atlantis were in existence before Plato but we simply fail to recognise them as such because the island goes by a different name? It turns out that Atlantis, or at least a place very much like it, had appeared in Egyptian texts before Plato wrote about it, but here it was known by the Egyptian name of Keftiu. However, according to many scholars, Keftiu refers to Crete, as Charles Pellegrino explains in his book *Unearthing Atlantis*:

> There are papyrus documents that make references to early contacts between Egypt and a place called Keftiu, which is generally accepted to be Minoan Crete. Keftiu is first mentioned in Egyptian writings dating back to the third millennium BC.

The Egyptians traded with the Minoans and called them 'the men of Keftiu'. It is thought that the name Keftiu itself is derived from a shorter word, *keft*, that essentially means 'pillar'. The Egyptians thought of the island of Keftiu as containing a 'sky pillar', one of four ancient pillars upon which the sky was supported – in other words, a large mountain. The writer J.V. Luce makes the following important point in his 1969 book, *Lost Atlantis: New Light on an Old Legend*:

> It is even possible that the Egyptian priests had some recorded material about the worship of sacred pillars which was so prevalent in Minoan Crete . . . Imagine Solon's reaction when confronted with this sort of information about ancient Keftiu. He could not have failed to associate it with the myth of Atlas, 'the Titan' who held the sky on his shoulders.

However, there are some facts that do not fit. The Egyptian legends maintained that elephants were present on Keftiu, as they were on Plato's Atlantis, and we know that there were no elephants on Crete. So is this place that the Egyptians described as Keftiu really Crete or is it a description of Atlantis itself? Could it be that Atlantis existed before the Minoan culture came to Crete; that the Minoans were refugees from Atlantis who brought much of their culture, including their worship of bulls, from the other island? In short, was the sunken island of Plato's tale the original homeland of the Minoans?

Whether Atlantis was Crete or not, it must be remembered that the story of Crete and the culture of the Minoans was considered to be just a myth until, at the beginning of the twentieth century, the archaeologist Arthur Evans found evidence that it was historical fact rather than mere legend. Could it be that one day we will find hard evidence to confirm that Atlantis was much more than just a story?

**SEE ALSO:** Atlas; Critias; Minoans; Plato; Santorini; Solon; Timaeus

# CRITIAS

**C**ritias (*c*.460–*c*.403 BC) was an Athenian philosopher who acquired a reputation as an orator, and his rhetorical skill gave him a head start in that society in being recognised as a statesman. His ability with words was also valuable for the poetry that he produced. Fragments of three tragedies and a satyr play written by him survive, while a collection of elegies and other works by him are referenced by later writers.

Critias was a leading thinker of his day and a man of many talents but little is known, though much is argued, about his life and works. He was an admirer of the wisdom of the great Socrates (*c*.470–399 BC). Critias was related to Plato's mother, and it is through the reminiscences of Plato that we learn something of the life and death of Socrates. He seems to have lived mainly in the open air, chatting to high and low, to artists, fellow philosophers, workmen and politicians, influencing at least some of them in their choice of lifestyle. Socrates was interested in getting people to think for themselves, to consider what constituted a good life.

One of Socrates' dislikes was untruth; he spoke about 'the god of Falsehood'. He had great difficulty in getting people to justify considering themselves to be wise. He decided that he must be wiser than those he conversed with, if only because he at least knew that he was ignorant. He believed it was his god-given aim in life to make people realise how little they really knew and how they could improve their conduct. While he had served, as was the Athenian citizen's duty, as a soldier, and with some distinction, Socrates tried to avoid taking any political role, claiming that to do so would be against his principles. As a prominent citizen and follower of the controversial Socrates, Critias was frequently the butt of the contemporary comedians' wit.

Critias's admiration for the great philosopher did not extend to standing up against tyranny, as Socrates himself did in 404. In that year, Socrates disobeyed the Thirty Tyrants, of whom Critias was one, when instructed to help arrest an enemy of the regime. He might have paid for this with his life had the Thirty themselves not fallen. At the end of his life, Critias played a leading role in Athenian politics, becoming involved with the Spartans and the rule of the Thirty in 404 and 403. The Athenians had finally had their military and naval power whittled away by their enemies, the Spartans and their allies. Under blockade, the citizens were starving, but a cessation of hostilities was finally agreed and the Athenians had to come to terms with the realisation that what they saw as their collective creative genius and superior intellect had been overcome by an unimaginative, unyielding, tough, oligarchic nation. Pausanias (second reign 408–394 BC), the Spartan king, was diplomatic enough to believe that the utter destruction of their old enemies would be unhelpful if a balance was to be struck among the Greek states and a lasting peace created.

The people of Corinth and Thebes, Spartan allies, wished at that time to see Athens wiped from the map, but the Spartans, though severe, would not go to such lengths. They insisted, however, that the Athenians give up their remaining ships, that the walls defending the port of Piraeus as well as the Long Walls between the port and the city be demolished, that Athens's foreign possessions be yielded and its exiles, including some regarded as enemies of the state, allowed to return. Further, Athens must conclude an alliance with Sparta as part of the Peloponnesian League. Having been forced to agree to these terms, the Athenians then had to see their fortifications destroyed under the supervision of Lysander, the brilliant but unscrupulous Spartan general and statesman, who despised the Athenians. They had little alternative but to agree to the appointment of thirty of their citizens to rule them.

The Thirty Tyrants cut the number of men entitled to be citizens and established absolute rule. Their government was extremely harsh, amounting to a reign of terror. Lysander kept a baleful eye on their regime. Some 1,500 who opposed the Thirty were executed and they attempted to have the exiled former leader, Alcibiades, whom they loathed, murdered by the Persian satrap who had given him sanctuary.

Lysander was called away overseas and the Thirty began to quarrel among themselves. After eight months of oppression, the desperate Athenians, encouraged by the democrat Thrasybulus, who was living in exile at the time, organised an uprising. Assisted quietly by the Thebans, Thrasybulus defeated the tyrants in a battle at Piraeus in May 403, during which Critias was killed. His fellow members of the Thirty fled and those still surviving two years later were massacred.

Further bloodshed was avoided when arbitration was agreed and over the course of the next three years or so the laws of Athens were revised and the criteria for membership of the citizen body amended. For the famous Socrates, sadly, this moderate improvement in the fortunes of the people of Athens did not extend to him for very long. He had been too outspoken and had annoyed too many powerful men. His enemies had him condemned to death and he drank hemlock.

Sadly, too, Socrates' former pupil Critias, at the end of his long and productive life, had taken a leading part in the tyrannical rule of the Thirty and his reputation has been coloured by the politics of his last few months. Despite being a highly talented man, Critias did not, in the long run, benefit from the wisdom Socrates attempted to spread. His life was summed up by Dr J. Lemprière in his *Classical Dictionary* of 1788 as follows:

> One of the 30 tyrants set over Athens by the Spartans, after the fatal battle of Aegospotamos. He was eloquent and well-bred, but of dangerous principles, and he cruelly persecuted his enemies, and put them to death. He was killed in a battle against those citizens whom his oppressions had banished.

As an epitaph, this may be accurate as far as it goes, but it is an incomplete summary of a lifetime.

Critias's name is probably most familiar today as the title of one of Plato's dialogues, in which he appears. *Critias* purports to be a conversation sparked by Socrates' vision of an ideal society. The character Critias tells what he claims is a true story about a war between the people of Atlantis and the Athenians 9,000 years before Plato's time. According to the dialogue, he heard the tale from his grandfather, who shared his name, who in turn had it from his own father. It had been handed down, Critias says, by Egyptian priests who had a reputation for knowledge which was second to none, to Solon (c.638–c.559 BC) the great statesman, traveller and poet.

**SEE ALSO:** Athens; Plato; Solon

# CRYSTAL SKULLS

Several crystal skulls have been found in Central America, the most famous being the one that Frederick Mitchell-Hedges claimed he discovered during the 1920s. According to the English explorer, he discovered it while excavating the ruins of a temple in the ancient Mayan city of Lubaantun, now in Belize. He believed the skull to be 3,600 years old, although he never clarified how he arrived at this date. Lubaantun is considered to have been founded no earlier than AD 700 but it is certainly possible that the object is older than the site where it was found.

Several authors and researchers claim that there exists an old Native American prophecy, said to originate from the group of elders known as 'Twisted Hairs', that speaks of 13 life-size crystal skulls containing knowledge about the origins of the human race and predicts that, when the time is ripe, these skulls will be discovered and come together to reveal what they hold. The question that many have asked is if the skull that Mitchell-Hedges found is one of these famed skulls or if it is a modern fake. In an effort to answer the skull's critics, Anna Mitchell-Hedges sent the artefact to Hewlett-Packard's crystal processing laboratory in Santa Clara, California, in 1970.

The first thing the testing team discovered was that the skull was carved from a single block of natural rock crystal. This, they explained, was only slightly softer than diamond, making it an incredibly hard material to work by hand. However, there are apparently no marks made by modern tools on the skull and the scientists concluded that the skull was very likely shaped by hand using abrasive methods. Furthermore, due to the particular hardness of the crystal from which it is carved, the amount of time necessary to make the object using such techniques was estimated to run into generations rather than years.

Apart from the skull's tremendous light-reflecting properties – for example, a beam of light shone up into the skull from below was refracted through the eye sockets as if through a perfect prism – another remarkable discovery was made. The skull seems to have been carved from a particular form of crystal, one known as piezoelectric silicon dioxide. This unique type of crystal is used in modern electronics such as computers and precision chronographs. Therefore the question has to be asked: did the creators of the Mitchell-Hedges artefact know this and design the skull for a precise function that is now lost to us, or is this fact just a coincidence?

While this is intriguing evidence, there is one point worth considering. It is impossible to date a piece of crystal and, likewise, there is no way of discovering when the carving took place. So, as remarkable as the workmanship is, it could have been carried out a few hundred or many thousands of years ago.

What's more, there is some doubt as to the veracity of Mitchell-Hedges' story of the skull's discovery. In *The Mystery of the Crystal Skulls*, Chris Morton and Ceri Louise Thomas disclose that a note in the British Museum's archives reveals that the skull was in fact put up for auction at Sotheby's in 1944 by a Sydney Burney and that the British Museum had been thwarted in their efforts to secure the artefact because it had been removed from the auction late in the sale and purchased instead by 'Mr Mitchell-Hedges' in a private transaction. This seems clear evidence that Mitchell-Hedges did not in fact find the skull in Belize as he claimed. However, his adopted daughter and the skull's current owner, Anna Mitchell-Hedges, had a simple explanation. She told Morton and Thomas that Burney had loaned money to Mitchell-Hedges and that the crystal skull had been used as security. So when Burney had decided to sell the skull, Mitchell-Hedges had raised the money owing to Burney and the repayment of the loan had been concluded by the removal of the item from the auction and the arrangement of the private sale.

What are we to make of this tale? While we only have Anna Mitchell-Hedges' account as evidence, it is fairly convincing, because if this was not the case, why did Burney not continue with the auction? The skull was sold to Mitchell-Hedges for £400; a larger sum of money could surely have been realised at auction, especially with a keen British Museum as one of the potential bidders. The fact that Burney pulled the item from the auction and instead sold the item via a private sale does seem to back up Anna Mitchell-Hedges' claims.

Ms Mitchell-Hedges refuses to submit the skull for further testing, stating simply that the necessary data was gathered in the 1970s. While this has been seen as conclusive proof that she knows the item is not what she claims it to be, it could be indicative of nothing more than the wishes of a very old woman who feels she does not want to begin another round of experiments and controversy at this late stage in her life. Perhaps whoever the skull passes to next will take up the baton and answer the outstanding questions once and for all.

Believers in the authenticity of the crystal skull have put forward the idea that it was manufactured in Atlantis long before the island nation was destroyed. There are compelling claims that the Maya arrived in Central America after the destruction of Atlantis, or a landmass much like it, and the supposition is that such artefacts were rescued from the destruction and brought to the migrants' new home. As is the case with much of the lore surrounding the ancient civilisation, this had led to a pervasive belief amongst Atlantis adherents that the Atlanteans made widespread use of crystals and possessed some kind of advanced crystal technology. The truth is that we don't have any conclusive proof that this was the case. This does not mean that the Atlanteans, if they existed, did not make use of crystals in their everyday lives; we just don't know one way or the other. Anna Mitchell-Hedges herself actually went one step further and claimed that the skull originally came from outer space and that it ended up in Atlantis before being transported to Belize.

Many other skulls have been found, all reportedly originating in Mesoamerica, but, again, there is doubt surrounding these objects and it has been suggested that some of them were manufactured in Europe. Whatever their origins, none are as impressive as the Mitchell-Hedges skull. However old the skull turns out to be, it is an impressive display of the stone-carver's art and will no doubt continue to epitomise everything that is mysterious in the world for many years to come.

Chris Morton, in *The Mystery of the Crystal Skulls*, describes the occasion when he first picked up the Mitchell-Hedges skull, and perhaps his words sum up the humble yet heady power of these crystal objects:

As I examined the skull, its smooth contours and hollow eye sockets, I thought about how I would one day die and that I too would be little more than an empty skull. Not only me, but everyone I knew and cared about would go the same sad way. I wondered if perhaps that was the purpose of the crystal skull, to remind each of us of our own mortality and of the very short time that each of us has as a living being on this Earth.

If the skull could teach that lesson to every one of us, it would be a very potent object indeed.

# DELUGE MYTHS

Surprisingly, there are over 500 deluge myths worldwide and many of these, even those from distinct and unconnected areas, are thematically very similar to the best-known account: that of Noah's Flood, as outlined in Genesis. Ignatius Donnelly suggested a reason for this in his 1882 book *Atlantis: The Antediluvian World*, in which he speculated that the flood myth was so widespread because it related to the sinking of Atlantis, with the survivors of the Atlantean flood fleeing to all parts of the world and taking their tale of disaster and survival with them. For that reason, certain themes and common elements occur again and again, speaking of a universal point of origin.

A frequent pattern in deluge myths that is followed by the Noah story is of a flood sent from God (or the gods) as a punishment for the iniquities of the human race, survival by boat of a chosen few, the inclusion of pairs of animals and landing on a mountain-top, with no survivors except the hero of the story and his entourage. In Genesis, the deluge is a punishment from God because of humanity's wickedness, but God decides to give Noah seven days to prepare for the event and save his family. Noah is told to build an ark to house himself, his family and a pair of all earth's creatures. At the given time, it begins to rain for 40 days and 40 nights. The flood covered the entire planet and when the rain stopped 110 more days were to pass before the ark came to rest on Mount Ararat. In order to test whether the flood was over, Noah sent out a raven then a dove. After its second flight, the dove returned to the ark with an olive branch. Seven days later, Noah sent out the dove once more and this time it did not return. At this, 'Noah removed the covering of the ark, and looked, and, behold, the face of the ground was dry.' In total, Noah's ordeal had lasted an incredible 12 months and 10 days.

Although this was once thought to be the only account of the Flood, biblical scholars were extremely excited when a number of very similar accounts were found on cuneiform tablets from Mesopotamia. The Sumerian version, which dates to the third millennium BC and is earlier than the biblical description, has as its hero a priest king called Ziusudra. His father, Ubartutu, is actually attested on the Sumerian king list as the last of the semi-mythical 'rulers before the flood', which, according to the king list, occurred in Sumeria around 3000 BC. At that time, the Sumerian god Enki, Lord of the Earth, instructed Ziusudra to build a boat to escape the deluge that 'raged over the land' for seven days and seven nights. When the sun came out again, Ziusudra found that his boat was now on a mountain.

The later, Akkadian version from Babylonia (modern Iraq) appears in *The Epic of Gilgamesh* and dates to around 2000 BC. This is an adaptation of the Sumerian epic, with the leading role taken up by a man called Utnapishtim. Once again, the flood had been sent by the gods to punish humankind for its sins. One god, Ea, whispered to Utnapishtim to build a boat 200 ft wide and 200 ft high, into which Utnapishtim took his family, craftsmen, sheep, goats, gold and silver, food and drink. A dreadful storm ensued and it rained for six days and nights. When the sun shone on the seventh day, the boat was stuck high on a mountain-top. Utnapishtim then sent out a dove, a swallow and finally a raven, and when the raven did not return, Utnapishtim and his followers left the boat. Another later version, starring Atrahasis, states that because humankind was making too much noise, the gods tried to decrease its number by epidemic and drought. However, still 'the people multiplied, the earth was bellowing like a bull; the gods got distressed with their uproar' (*Atrahasis Epic*), and so they eventually sent down a flood, which proved successful in culling the world's population.

If, as the Bible states, Abraham was born in Ur, it is easy to see how there might be parallels between the Babylonian and Old Testament versions of the deluge. However, it is not so easy to explain why similar accounts can be found further afield. From India, the Vedic tradition, dated to 1000 BC, relates how the wise man Manu was warned by the god Vishnu of an impending flood. In this tale, Vishnu sends Manu a boat and tells him to 'load it with two of every living species and the seeds of every plant'. As soon as the task was completed, the sea rose and soon everywhere was flooded. Vishnu now appeared to Manu as a golden, one-horned fish and towed the boat to a mountain peak, where it stayed until the waters receded. The flood was so violent and widespread that it 'carried away all creatures and Manu remained alone' until a woman emerged from waters a year later.

From Greece, the story of the Flood of Deucalion relates how Zeus wanted to destroy the world with a great flood because of his disgust at humans eating the flesh of boys. The Titan Prometheus, father of Deucalion, warned his son and told him to build a boat. Deucalion and his wife, Pyrrha, floated for nine days before reaching Mount Parnassus. The flood wiped humanity out and, as the only people left, Deucalion and Pyrrha went to the oracle at Delphi to find out what to do. There they are told that, in order to repopulate the earth, they must throw the bones of their mother over their shoulder. Luckily, they were able to guess that this referred to Gaea – Mother Earth. Grabbing up stones, Deucalion threw a handful and they became men, while Pyrrha's became women.

On the other side of the Atlantic, the concept of humankind being purged can be seen in the flood myth of the Haida tribe from Canada, whose tale features the common theme of people escaping in boats and landing on a mountain. From the Aztec account found on the Axayacatl Sun Stone (AD 1479), we learn that 'torrential rains and floods' destroyed the Fourth Sun. The survivors, Coxcoxtli and his wife, Xochiquetzal, had been forewarned of a forthcoming flood by the gods and told to build a huge boat, which eventually came to rest on a mountain peak. Likewise, the Mechoacanesecs of Central America state that God wanted to destroy all humanity by a flood. Only Tezpi, his wife, children, animals, birds, grain and seed were saved, as Tezpi built a huge boat that came to rest on a mountain-top after God ordered the waters to recede. To test whether or not it was safe to disembark, Tezpi released a number of birds but time after time they did not return, until eventually the hummingbird came back, carrying a branch in its beak.

Other legends, from Vietnam, Burma, Malaysia and Laos as well as China and Thailand, also relate how a mighty flood covered the entire earth, with only a few people surviving, often having saved two of each species. Considering the widespread parallels seen here, it is arguable that the similarities between accounts are more than just coincidence.

Not so common, but nevertheless of importance, are those deluge myths that refer to a hole in the sky. A Rabbinic Hebrew account states that the Flood was caused by God removing two stars from the Pleiades, the resultant hole allowing water to rush through and engulf the earth. Interestingly, China has a similar account. In this, a hole in the sky is caused when an angry prince shakes one of the eight columns that support the sky, causing the column to collapse and the southern corner of the sky to tear. It was through this hole that water poured and flooded the land of Chi (around the area of the Yellow River). Chinese chronology dates this event to c.2953 BC.

As with the legend of the sinking of Atlantis, earthquake, volcanic eruption and flood also feature, particularly in accounts from the Americas. The Creek Indians relate how great monsters were released when the mountains cracked open and how the monsters were drowned in a flood that also destroyed all humankind. The Araucanians of Chile recount that a volcanic eruption followed by a massive earthquake caused a flood that drowned the world, while, according to a Brazilian legend, a fight between two brothers produced an earthquake which caused a great cascade of water to surge up. The water spewed higher than the mountains and reached up to the clouds until the whole world was flooded. The only survivors were the two brothers and their wives, who clung to the trees. This theme also appears in the Scandinavian legend of the wolf Fenrir, which broke free from its chains and shook itself so violently that it caused mountains to tumble and the earth to tremble. Humankind was swept away by the overflowing rivers and seas, and eventually 'the earth sank beneath the sea'. Not all died, however, as the survivors began a new world.

The idea of a lost island or city also appears in some deluge myths, such as in the Okanagan tradition, from the Appalachian Mountains in America, which states that a lost island situated in the middle of the ocean was associated with a great flood. Similarly, the Irish legend of Tir-na-n-oge tells of a great city that sank beneath the waves, and, according to the Haida, their original homeland was a faraway land where they lived in a wonderful city, from which they were forced to flee when God sent a great flood down on them as a punishment.

Other versions of the myth come from sources as far-flung as the Inuit of north Canada – who speak of a time when the earth was flooded by the sea coming in too fast, leaving only a few survivors – and the Australian Aborigines, who tell a tale concerning a medicine man, Gumuduk, who had the power to bring rain by use of a magic bone. Kidnapped by a rival tribe, Gumuduk eventually escaped and buried the bone, casting a spell so that wherever he walked salt water would rise up, inundating and choking the plain. When the flood subsided, the region had become a desert, unable to support man or beast.

Concerning the worldwide deluge myth, is there any geological evidence to prove that such a massive flood happened in antiquity? Archaeological excavations in Iraq show that there were a number of floods in the region during the fourth millennium BC, although there appears to be no break in the material cultural record, suggesting that the flood was not as disastrous as the accounts imply. At Ur, layers of deposited silt are between 2.5 and 3 m deep, and although there are signs of floods at other sites, these do not all date to the same period, effectively ruling out a universal flood even in that relatively small region.

However, glacial action and melting polar ice caps could have resulted in serious flooding much earlier than the fourth millennium BC. The flood that caused Atlantis to sink could have been due to ice melting and the corresponding rise in sea level. In *The Sunken Kingdom*, Peter James mentions the work of Professor Cesare Emiliani, a geochemist at Miami University who studied the radiocarbon dates of core samples taken from the Gulf of Mexico. The salinity levels in these samples showed that around 9600 BC (using an average date) there appears to have been a sudden melting of the North American Valders readvance ice sheet. From his findings, published in the journal *Science* in 1975, he reasoned that 'this event, in spite of its great antiquity in cultural terms, could be an explanation for the deluge stories common to many Eurasian, Australasian and American traditions'. Emiliani said that the date given by Plato for the sinking of Atlantis, 9600 BC, 'coincides, within all limits of error, with the age of both the highest concentration of ice melt water in the Gulf of Mexico and the Valders readvance'. Other scientists do not agree, however, believing this was a gradual event that would have been barely perceptible to people living in the area at that time. James also states that Emiliani's date of 9600 was a rough average and the event could have occurred any time between the radiocarbon dates of 10360 and 8720 – or the ice sheet could have taken that long to melt. The reality is that we are unable to ascertain if the glacial melting was gradual or not. But examination of coral near Barbados suggests that the ice melt was sudden and that from 10500 the sea level rose 24 m in 1,000 years or less.

An alternative theory is that the end of the ice age was due to an asteroid hitting the Atlantic, thus disturbing the ice and causing a massive flood. (This could be hinted at in the Ancient Egyptian 'Tale of the Shipwrecked Sailor', the protagonist of which ends up on a magical island whose inhabitants, bar one, were all killed by a star falling to earth. The island eventually disappeared into the sea without trace.) The Aztecs mention that the First Sun ended with a flood and they date this event to 11600 BC (Codex Vaticano-Latino, written in 1533). Another sea-level rise occurred around 3000 BC, which ties in with the date of the Sumerian flood and hence, presumably, Noah's Flood, as well as the date of 2953 for the flooding of the land of Chi.

The Egyptian historian Manetho mentions that the Flood of Deucalion occurred during the reign of the sixth king of the 18th Dynasty. Based on Egyptian chronology, this would date that flood to around 1500 BC, which ties it in with the eruption of the small Mediterranean island of Thera. The priests of Sais in Plato's *Timaeus* considered this deluge to be the most recent of a series of substantial floods. They stated that: 'You remember only one deluge, though there have been many.' Obviously, they were privy to information that we no longer possess.

**SEE ALSO:** Donnelly, Ignatius; Plato; Prometheus; Timaeus

# DENDERAH ZODIAC

The Temple of Hathor at Denderah in Egypt contains two zodiacs: a rectangular one on the ceiling of the Hypostyle Hall and a circular one on the ceiling of a chapel on the temple roof. It is this circular one that is the most famous and which is generally meant when reference is made to the Denderah Zodiac. The zodiac currently *in situ* at Denderah is a copy of the original, which is in the Louvre Museum in Paris.

The Denderah Zodiac depicts the night sky as seen from Denderah, with the Pole Star situated in the centre of the zodiac in the paws of a jackal. The signs of the zodiac encircle this in a fairly erratic fashion. Intermingled with these are symbolic representations of the five planets Jupiter, Mercury, Saturn, Mars and Venus, and the constellations of Orion, Hydra, Leo and Centaurus. The planets are easily identifiable, as they each hold a *was* sceptre, symbolic of prosperity and happiness, as well as having a possible link with the celestial measurement of time. Around the outer rim of the disc are the 36 decan gods, each representing a specific star that could be seen above the horizon at dawn for a 10-day period. The round zodiac itself is supported by the goddesses of north, south, east and west, as well as eight falcon-headed deities.

Although the temple as seen today dates from about 100 BC, with later restorations in the Roman period, it is thought by some that the temple was built on the site of an earlier structure. This is because of its unusually deep foundations and the inscription that states that the temple was built 'according to the plan laid down in the time of the Followers of Horus'. However, this alone is not an indication of the temple's true date and many cultures of the ancient world, Egypt included, often predated sacred sites as a way of amplifying their sanctity.

Of the Egyptians, Diodorus Siculus said in his *Library of History* that 'they have preserved to this day the records concerning each of these stars over an incredible number of years, this study having been zealously preserved among them from ancient times'. In fact, the Ancient Egyptians' knowledge of astronomy was so 'zealously preserved' that academics and researchers are still unravelling the mysteries of the Denderah Zodiac. In 1846, French mathematician Jean-Baptiste Biot noted that Sirius is depicted twice on the Denderah Zodiac: in alignment with the axis of the temple and Gemini, thus giving its correct position in the sky; and in between the Isis cow's horns in alignment with Cancer. Biot asserted that this must signify that at the time of its construction the temple was orientated towards the rising of Sirius when it was in Gemini and calculated this date to be approximately 700 BC. However, the significance of the second mention of Sirius was thought by the scholar René Schwaller de Lubicz to indicate that Sirius is 'marked . . . in relation to its rising at the time of the summer solstice', which, according to Biot, shows the 'uncommon skill' of the Egyptian astronomers.

Schwaller de Lubicz asserted that the Denderah Zodiac clearly points towards the Ancient Egyptians having knowledge of the precession of the equinoxes, as shown by 'a line passing through Gemini and Taurus, indicating a precessional date about 4000 BC' (John Lash, quoted in *The Atlantis Blueprint*). The precession of the equinoxes is caused by the earth's 'wobble', whereby the constellations move about the sky over a 26,000-year cycle, with the zodiacal houses changing every 2,160 years. Not only does the observation of this phenomenon necessarily take place over an extremely long period of time but the precession is also 'difficult to observe and measure', as Graham Hancock remarks in *Fingerprints of the Gods*.

The researcher John Anthony West sees the sign of Cancer as having special significance within the Denderah Zodiac because of its 'curious placing'. In *Serpent in the Sky*, he notes that 'whatever the scheme directing the arrangement, it is certain that the sign of Cancer has been singled out for special treatment'. Unfortunately, without the key to this zodiac, it is extremely hard to figure out what the Egyptians were trying to say. With reference to precession, West is uncertain as to whether we can attribute knowledge of this occurrence to the Ancient Egyptians based on the evidence of the Denderah Zodiac alone.

What may be of importance is a fifth axis that has been discovered by John Lash, an astrologer and mythologist, as discussed by Rand Flem-Ath and Colin Wilson in their book *The Atlantis Blueprint*. Lash, who does believe that the information displayed on the Denderah Zodiac shows that the Egyptians knew about precession, has identified an axis in addition to the north—south, east—west axes, one which 'marks the moment of precession when one full cycle ends and a new one begins'. This axis, which he calls axis E, begins from the decan at the outer rim with four rams' heads surmounting an altar, passes through Pisces, where the spring equinox occurs today, and on to the feet of Virgo. Lash sees this as highly significant, stating: 'We are currently living through the last two centuries of the full 26,000-year cycle . . . axis E signals this moment of epochal transition in a vivid, intentional way.' Lash also notes that the Denderah Zodiac has two North Poles, so the Ancient Egyptians knew about magnetic north and true north. He concludes by saying that 'the entire cycle of 26,000 years was understood in its formal organisation' by the Egyptian astronomers. The Denderah Zodiac also marks the half-cycle, which expresses a date of 10500 BC.

Due to the date of its creation, many of the constellations are represented by their Mesopotamian symbols, although others are typically Egyptian, such as Virgo, which is depicted as the Egyptian corn goddess, and Aquarius, symbolised by the Nile god Hapy. What is interesting, however, is that the Egyptian zodiac consisted of 12 signs, with the sun spending 2,160 years in each sign – exactly as the Inca zodiac. In his book *The Lost Realms*, Zecharia Sitchin noted a number of similarities in names and depictions of the zodiac signs between the Incas of Peru and the Mesopotamians. However, this is also relevant to the Egyptian signs. Thus Aquarius for the Incas was Mother Water and Lord Water, whilst for the Egyptians it was Hapy the Nile god pouring water from out of two jars. Likewise, the Incas represented Virgo as Maize Mother, with the Egyptian zodiac using the grain goddess holding a sheaf of wheat. These similarities must confirm a common heritage.

The complexity of the information contained within the Denderah Zodiac and the extremely long period that astronomers would have needed to be able to make such detailed observations and develop knowledge of the precessional cycle are astounding. The astronomical information required must have been known well before the date of the temple's foundation and the date when the Zodiac was made. Our modern zodiac is thought to have its roots in Mesopotamia but considering the length of time the Egyptians were studying the stars, as suggested by their calendars (which could date to 4240 BC), it is just as likely that the Egyptians were the first astronomers and astrologers. Indeed, there is a school of thought according to which the survivors of Atlantis came to Egypt and brought with them their knowledge of the stars, this information being preserved by a group called the Followers of Horus. It may well be, therefore, that the Atlanteans were ultimately responsible for the Denderah Zodiac.

**SEE ALSO:** Followers of Horus; Diodorus Siculus

# DIODORUS SICULUS

As his name suggests, Diodorus Siculus was a native of Sicily ('Siculus' simply means 'Sicilian'), a member of the Greek community residing in Agyrium during the first century BC. He was probably born around the year 80 BC, or a little before, and died c.21 BC. He wrote his *Library of History* (*Bibliotheca Historica*) intending it to be an account of the whole of world history up to his own era. Although he visited Egypt in c.60–56 and seems to have been well travelled, the main thrust of his writing concerned the areas he knew best, therefore Greek, Roman and Sicilian themes predominate. Nevertheless, he dealt with subjects from the history not only of Egypt but also of Mesopotamia, Scythia, Arabia, North Africa and India. Fifteen of the forty books of the *Library* survive intact and more books are extant in fragmentary form.

He gives us a slant on the Peloponnesian Wars to compare with that of Thucydides and information about Alexander the Great and his father, King Philip II of Macedonia. He was not at all particular about ensuring that his information was accurate (not atypically for his day), with the result that we cannot entirely rely on him. In the 1911 edition of the *Encyclopaedia Britannica*, he is harshly criticised:

> The faults of Diodorus arise partly from the nature of the
> undertaking, and the awkward form of annals into which
> he has thrown the historical portion of his narrative. He
> shows none of the critical faculties of the historian, merely
> setting down a number of unconnected details. His narrative

contains frequent repetitions and contradictions, is without
colouring and monotonous.

He does have particular value for modern scholars, though, in that
it is often only as a result of the material he carefully copied from
even earlier authors whose works are lost to us that we are able to
have even a vague idea of their writings. One of his major failings,
on the other hand, is that he clearly has more of a fascination for
the unusual and unlikely tale than for what we might regard as
history.

Diodorus Siculus's monumental work, which in its modern
translations runs into twelve volumes, may be divided into three
sections: first, a history of many peoples, which includes a great deal
of myth and the story of the Trojan War; second, the subsequent
period until the demise of Alexander the Great in 323 BC; and third
and finally, the next nearly three centuries, which include the Gallic
Wars of Julius Caesar. The last famous figure mentioned is Octavian
Caesar (better known today as Augustus).

Diodorus Siculus claims that the people of Atlantis had no
knowledge of the fruits of Ceres, the ancient Roman corn goddess.
This deity, whose name is perpetuated in our modern word 'cereal',
was responsible for the growth of plants, and especially of grain
crops. What the author is alleging, therefore, is that the Atlanteans
did not have the benefit of cereals, which perhaps implies that they
would not have known bread or cakes, and beer would not have
been consumed by them. It must be borne in mind by those who
favour an Atlantis situated somewhere towards the Americas that
although the natives of North and South America did not yet have
possession of Old World cereals, they had other crops which have
since been eagerly seized upon by peoples across the globe. Potatoes
and maize are just two of the gifts of food which the American
continent has made available to the rest of the world. Diodorus, of
course, like his contemporaries, could have had no knowledge of
those continents. But what of Atlantis?

Diodorus, like Herodotus, described some Libyan tribes as
'Atlantean'. He records that they lived near the 'shore of the ocean'.
He claims that the Titans, who populated Atlantis, were the sons
of the union between Ouranos (Uranus) and Titaea. Cronos, their
child, deposed his father and succeeded him in the kingship. Plato
thought that the Atlanteans were ruled by kings; Cronos, however,
has the status of a god and the Titans were considered to be demigods. This suggests that Diodorus Siculus was not using Plato's

impression of Atlantis as his principal source, if at all.

For Diodorus, the race of warrior women known as the Amazons was real. They ruled and fought while their men carried out the domestic tasks usually associated with women. He wrote that their queen, Myrina, took her forces to Atlantis and dominated the Atlanteans. After their victory, the Amazons faced up to dealing with the monstrous Gorgons, who were a threat to Atlantis, and after risking danger and death at the hands of the still resentful Atlanteans, they fought the horrible Gorgons. They did not meet with total success, however, and the hero Perseus later had to complete their task.

Diodorus's story was a parable warning men of the consequences of allowing women freedom outside their own homes; the thought of warrior women was laughable, the idea of them dominating their menfolk unthinkable, unnatural and uncivilised. Diodorus was demonstrating the value of the patriarchal society in which the Greeks, even more than the Romans, lived. Perhaps he was also demonstrating his own insecurities, bringing into the open his fear of what life would be like if females were allowed to exercise the power which men enjoyed. As his Amazons cannot really cope with their unnatural role and fail to put an end to the threat of the Gorgons, Diodorus sets his own fears at rest and rejoices that it is a man, Perseus, who is the ultimate victor.

It is a feature of Minoan art that women are depicted as participating in sport. This is atypical of Ancient Greek women (with the notable exception of the Spartans), but Minoan females can be seen wrestling, boxing and bull-leaping. They often appear larger than male figures in the same picture and there are examples of females being hailed by men and of goddesses carrying weapons. Women appear to have participated in Minoan life on at least an equal footing with their male counterparts. Is it possible that these unusual features have their origins in the distant past, in the Atlantis of Diodorus Siculus?

The *Dictionary of Ancient History* neatly sums up Diodorus thus: 'His inaccuracies, confusions, and doublets astound, but without him knowledge of Greek history would be gravely diminished.'

**SEE ALSO:** Minoans; Plato

# DOGON TRIBE

The Dogon people came to the world's attention in the mid-1970s, after Robert Temple placed them at the centre of his controversial book *The Sirius Mystery*. He claimed that the tribe's worship and knowledge of the star Sirius backed up his theory that ancient astronauts had visited earth long ago in antiquity.

The Dogon occupy a region in Mali, in Western Africa, and number some 300,000. They live in a region dominated by the Bandiagara Escarpment and many of the Dogon villages are on the cliffs which themselves extend for some 150 km. Before the Dogon, the Tellem inhabited the cliffs. They were evicted by the Dogon and today many Dogon search the steep cliffs for Tellem relics, which they sell to the West. The Dogon practise an animist religion, although today some have converted to Islam and a few even to Christianity. Despite this, the dominant religion is still the one they have always adhered to, a system of beliefs that is widely acknowledged to have developed over thousands of years. Their belief that every creature and object possesses a soul is vividly brought to life by elaborate rituals and dances in which entities and objects are revered, the participants wearing lavish masks and accompanied by the beating of drums. The Dogon also believe in totem animals that protect each individual. Originally, some of the villages of the Dogon people were shaped in the form of the human body, a further manifestation of the importance in their religion of living beings and their links with supernatural powers.

Together with ancestor worship and spirit communication, the Dogon religion involves very detailed knowledge about the cosmos.

Central to their complex belief system is the star Sirius. Sirius is the brightest star in the night sky and for millennia has been held in great esteem across the world, its presence in the sky indicating to the Ancient Egyptians, for example, when the Nile would flood. So perhaps it should not be too surprising to discover that an isolated tribe should revere such a star. However, when two French anthropologists, Marcel Griaule and Germaine Dieterlen, visited the Dogon in the 1930s, they were intrigued to find that the tribe held some very curious beliefs concerning Sirius. It took them 15 years working with the tribe before they reached their conclusions and in the late 1940s they published their findings.

They revealed that the Dogon believed that Sirius had a companion star, an invisible star that was extremely heavy and orbited Sirius itself every 50 years. This star they called *po tolo*, which means 'smallest seed'. Its heaviness was something that they drew particular attention to and Griaule and Dieterlen reported that the Dogon said that every person on the earth put together could not lift it. They also described this second star as being white in colour, despite the fact that this was impossible to ascertain from earth.

Far from this being a myth, it turns out that Sirius is in fact a binary star system – in other words, one consisting of two stars. The second star is known today as Sirius B. In the 1840s, the existence of this stellar object was guessed at from the gravitational effect that its orbit had on Sirius A. Then, in 1862, its faint image was discovered by telescope, proving that it really did exist. However, it was not adequately photographed or documented until 1970 because of the brightness of its companion. Furthermore, as the Dogon had claimed, Sirius B, while very small, was found to be incredibly heavy, being a very dense white dwarf. To many, including Temple, this revelation was staggering. How could the Dogon possibly know of the companion star's existence if we did not have the technology to see it clearly until the 1970s?

Interestingly, the Dogon told Griaule and Dieterlen that there was a third star, *emme ha tolo*, or the 'Star of Women'. Scientists are still puzzling over whether Sirius might be a trinary and not a binary system and a paper written in 1995 suggested that anomalies in the orbit of Sirius A could be caused by a third star, Sirius C. If this was conclusively proved, it would be strong evidence that the Dogon do possess detailed knowledge of the star system, knowledge that we ourselves do not yet have.

Temple proposed that the Dogon people learned all of their

secrets from a North African tribe called the Garamantes, who in turn had picked up their sacred knowledge from the Egyptians. Temple claims that the Garamantes passed through the area that the Dogon inhabit in the eleventh century and that this is when the dissemination of information began.

This connection with Egypt is worth looking into. One of the core beliefs of the Dogon is that the souls of the dead on earth end up in the vicinity of Sirius. This sounds very similar to the beliefs of the Ancient Egyptians, who thought that their dead became stars in the heavens and that the Duat, the Egyptian underworld and realm of the dead, was a region in the stars. Sirius was very important to the Egyptians, being closely linked with Isis, the wife of Osiris, lord of the dead.

Furthermore, the Dogon version of the creation of the universe bears a strong resemblance to the creation myth of Egypt. The Dogon describe a single creator of the universe known as Amma, who made a creature called Nommo. Nommo then multiplied to become four pairs of twins. This sounds very much like the Heliopolitan cosmogony of the Egyptians, which describes the appearance of Atum, followed by the gods Shu, Tefnut, Geb, Nut and their offspring Osiris, Isis, Seth and Nephthys. According to the Dogon, one of the twins of Nommo caused great imbalance in the universe by going against the word of Amma and so, in an effort to restore balance, Amma sacrificed one of the Nommo. The body of the dead Nommo was cut into pieces and scattered across the whole of the universe. This story bears a remarkable similarity to the tale of the Egyptian god Osiris, killed by his brother Seth, who then proceeded to dismember Osiris's body and distribute the parts throughout Egypt.

The existence of Sirius's companion is not the limit of the Dogon's knowledge of the universe: they are also aware that the moon with which we share our orbit is lifeless; they know that Saturn has rings; they know that the Milky Way follows a spiral course through the universe; they describe the four major moons of Jupiter; they know that the earth spins upon its axis and that we orbit our sun; and finally, they know that stars are really suns, just like the one at the centre of our solar system.

While many, including Robert Temple, have posited the idea that the Dogon people could only have received their knowledge of Sirius and other cosmic bodies such as Saturn from aliens who landed on the earth, there is another possibility. If Atlantis possessed such an advanced culture as is suggested by Plato and other writers, then it is clear that they would have held detailed knowledge of the stars and the cosmos.

The Dogon told Griaule and Dieterlen that they were taught their precise knowledge of Sirius by a race of beings that they call the Nommo (perhaps believed to be either descendants of the original Nommo gods or the gods themselves). However, despite Temple's interpretation, it is certainly not true that the Dogon ever believed that the Nommo came from Sirius itself. It has been assumed that the Dogon were talking about alien visitors when they describe the Nommo descending to earth in an ark. However, this could be a memory of the deluge and could in fact refer to ships reaching dry land after the flood had passed – similar, in fact, to the story of Noah's ark settling on Mount Ararat. Was this the knowledge that the Dogon had held sacred for so many years? Were they describing survivors of Atlantis who taught the Dogon in vivid detail all about the stars? It is interesting to note that the Dogon described the Nommo as 'water spirits', beings that could be found in every body of water. The name Nommo actually translates as 'masters of the water'. Again, this could relate to a folk memory of a race of people who were known as great navigators and who had sailed the entire world.

Temple offered up the possibility that it was the god Oannes who taught the Dogon their precise knowledge of Sirius and the companion star. This is interesting because Oannes is described in very similar terms as Osiris and Quetzalcoatl by ancient tribes, in that he was thought of as an educator and a civiliser of barbaric races. He was also, like Quetzalcoatl, linked with the sea, and, according to Babylonian tales, he emerged one day from the waters of the ocean clad in fish scales and proceeded to teach the Babylonians wisdom.

Was such a character responsible for instructing the Dogon people about Sirius and was this visitor from Atlantis? It is certainly a possibility and in fact it is one that is, to most at least, a lot more palatable than the story that it was aliens who taught the Dogon all they know. It would certainly appear on the face of it that the tales of the Nommo could stem from a memory of visitors or survivors from Atlantis who took refuge in Africa after their home was destroyed in a great flood.

**SEE ALSO:** Plato; Quetzalcoatl

Images of *moai*, the enigmatic statues that are scattered across Easter Island.
(© Anna Tatti)

*Above*: The volcanic landscape of La Palma, the Canary Islands.

*Below*: The coast of La Palma. Are these islands remnants from Atlantis?

*Above*: The only remaining Guanches on the Canary Islands;
statues on Tenerife.

*Below*: Guanche carvings on La Palma.

*Above*: The pyramid of Kukulkan at Chichen Itza in Mexico. Kukulkan was another name for the god Quetzalcoatl, the *plumed serpent*.

*Below left*: Carved serpent head on the stairs that climb the pyramid.
*Below right*: Inside the pyramid of Kukulkan.

Mayan ruins at Coba in Mexico. The Popol Vuh, a Mayan codice, seems to possess themes consistant with the tale of the fall of Atlantis and could describe the migration of the Mayans to their new home in Mesoamerica.

*Above*: Looking into the volcanic caldera of Thera on Santorini.

*Below*: Minoan murals on the island of Crete.
Were these people the true Atlanteans?

*Above*: View from the Acropolis over modern Athens.

*Above*: The man responsible for the birth of Atlantis; Plato.

# DOLPHIN'S RIDGE

It was in Ignatius Donnelly's *Atlantis: The Antediluvian World* that Dolphin's Ridge first received mainstream attention. Studies carried out in the 1870s by HMS *Challenger* and USS *Dolphin* found a large body of undersea land, roughly 2,000 km wide and at a depth of almost 5.5 km. The Azores are connected to this sunken landmass, being merely the tips of huge underwater mountains. In his book, published in 1882, Donnelly put forward the theory that this structure was once Atlantis and that it had sunk below the ocean after a series of violent convulsions. Furthermore, there were some unexpected finds connected with Dolphin's Ridge:

> Evidence that this elevation was once dry land is found in the fact that 'the inequalities, the mountains and valleys of its surface, could never have been produced in accordance with any laws for the deposition of sediment, nor by submarine elevation; but, on the contrary, must have been carved by agencies acting above the water level.' (*Scientific American*, 28 July 1877)
> Ignatius Donnelly, *Atlantis: The Antediluvian World*

In 1915, an eminent French geologist, Pierre Termier, wrote an article for the *Annual Report of the Smithsonian Institution* in which he discussed core samples that had been brought up to the surface from a depth of 3,000 m. These samples were found to contain fragments of vitreous lava that contained crystalline formations that could only have been formed under atmospheric pressure, and not deep below the oceans.

The question is, how long ago was this submerged landmass to be found above sea level? Termier tackles this issue as he ends his article:

> We are here on a line which joins Iceland to the Azores in the midst of the Atlantic volcanic zone, in the midst of the zone of mobility, of instability, and present volcanism. It would seem a fair conclusion, then, that the entire region north of the Azores and perhaps the very region of the Azores, of which they may be only the visible ruins, was very recently submerged, probably during the epoch which the geologists call the present because it is so recent, and which for us, the living beings of today, is the same as yesterday.

So it would seem possible, based on this evidence, that Dolphin's Ridge could once have been the lost continent of Atlantis, although it has to be stated that the mechanism by which such a large landmass could sink to such a depth in a relatively short period of time – geologically speaking, at least – is yet to be understood. In fact, it is this assumption that such a disaster is impossible that has led most scientists to conclude that it never happened.

There have been tentative theories put forward to try to explain how such an event might happen, the most vivid being the idea of the existence of large caverns deep below the ocean floor that contain nothing but gas. It has been proposed that if this gas were to be vented suddenly due to volcanic activity or some other geological movement, large masses of land above would sink as these caverns collapsed in on themselves.

Science fiction or science fact? Until we have conclusive scientific proof that such a natural phenomenon has happened in the past, Dolphin's Ridge will remain an enigma, a possible candidate for Atlantis and one whose secrets lie some 5,000 m below the ocean's surface.

**SEE ALSO:** Azores; Donnelly, Ignatius

# DONNELLY, IGNATIUS

Ignatius Donnelly is best known today for his book on Atlantis, published in 1882, *Atlantis: The Antediluvian World*. It was a groundbreaking work which brought Atlantis firmly into the focus of popular culture for the first time in many years. Many of the ideas that still prevail today concerning Atlantis were first formulated in Donnelly's book. He was born in Philadelphia in 1831 and, having initially studied law, he later became a Republican congressman, first entering politics in the 1860s.

After leaving public office in 1878, Donnelly turned again to practising law but he also continued his writing and research, and it was during this period in his life that he wrote *Atlantis*. Twenty years earlier, Donnelly had stumbled upon Plato's account of Atlantis. Deeply inspired, he charged himself with the task of bringing to light a new vision of Atlantis, but it took him all that time to collect together a body of evidence that he felt was large enough to prove his case and was ready for public consumption.

When his work was finally complete, Donnelly was in a precarious financial state, yet in 1882 he travelled to New York confident that he had a major work on his hands. And so it was to prove; Harper & Brothers immediately agreed to publish his manuscript and the book was an overnight sensation. In fact, it was so successful that there were twenty-three printings in its first eight years and it has never been out of print since.

It was not just the general public who were inspired; the British Prime Minister, William Gladstone, read the book in that very first year of publication and so taken was he by the story and by

Donnelly's arguments that he is said to have ordered the Royal Navy to search for the lost continent, only to be confounded when the Treasury refused him the funds that would have been necessary for such an expedition.

Donnelly had always possessed a passion for history and in particular the origins of modern man. He had noticed that many of the great civilisations around the world bore remarkable similarities to one another and he proposed that this was not down to chance but rather because they had all been seeded from one place: Atlantis. As we still do today, Donnelly went back to Plato's account of Atlantis and rather than treat the story as pure legend, he took it as unadulterated history.

Donnelly proposed that Atlantis was exactly where Plato sites it, outside the Mediterranean and the Pillars of Hercules, smack bang in the middle of the Atlantic Ocean. This was the reason, Donnelly declared, why so many of the world's civilisations grew up around the Mediterranean:

> How comes it that all the civilizations of the Old World radiate from the shores of the Mediterranean? The Mediterranean is a cul de sac, with Atlantis opposite its mouth. Every civilization on its shores possesses traditions that point to Atlantis . . . The Mediterranean has been the centre of the modern world, because it lay in the path of the extension of an older civilization, whose ships colonized its shores, as they did also the shores of America. Plato says, 'the nations are gathered around the shores of the Mediterranean like frogs around a marsh.'

However, critics have used this point against Donnelly, arguing that if Atlantis had instead once been inside the Mediterranean itself, then many of these puzzles of the origins of civilisation would be answered more satisfactorily. Donnelly was not swayed, though. The Atlantic floor was beginning to be explored at the time he wrote the book and it was this research that he used to convince the public that the true location of Atlantis was the Atlantic, and in particular a feature known as Dolphin's Ridge.

Another of Donnelly's firm beliefs was that Atlantis truly was the original, antediluvian world, the world, described in the Bible, that existed before the Great Flood that Noah survived. Therefore, to Donnelly, Atlantis had once been the actual location of the Garden of Eden, the Garden of the Hesperides, the Elysian Fields,

Mount Olympus, Asgard and many other places held sacred in local traditions around the world. In his own words, it was the source of 'a universal memory of a great land, where early mankind dwelt for ages in peace and happiness'.

· As if this was not radical enough, Donnelly then proceeded to claim that Atlantis was the place where humankind originally rose from barbarism to civilisation. Donnelly was the first researcher ever to suggest this idea; Plato himself makes no such claim. Donnelly believed that great cultures such as Dynastic Egypt began as colonies of Atlantis before the continent disappeared beneath the deluge. He cites similar traits in disparate civilisations such as the Egyptians, the Mayans and the Guanches as evidence that this was the case.

Over the years, many criticisms have been levelled at Donnelly, not least that he single-handedly created the genre of 'pseudoscience'. Is this justified? There is no doubt that Donnelly made mistakes along the way but, at the time, in the burgeoning field of comparative mythology, somebody had to blaze a trail; overall, Donnelly did a good job in beginning the debate, and much of what he wrote still stands up. How many works of today could we say the same of in 120 years' time?

Norman Wolcott, the man who prepared the text of Donnelly's most famous work for the Project Gutenburg website, and who has long studied Donnelly, has this to say on the subject:

> One must not be too critical of Donnelly; Atlantis was the product of the science of his time. The discoveries of Schliemann at Troy and Mycenae showed that the ancient Greek legends were to be taken seriously as real history. Where better then to start than with Plato's Atlantis? Little was known then of new world geology or ethnology which the next century would reveal. And Donnelly's hyperbolic oratory makes for a fun read. His phoenix may yet rise from the ashes of history.

I suppose we should end this section with the words of Donnelly himself, taken from the final chapter of his great book. They do indeed sum up the school of thought that he gave birth to over 100 years ago when he first published *Atlantis: The Antediluvian World*:

> Science has but commenced its work of reconstructing the past and rehabilitating the ancient peoples, and surely there

is no study which appeals more strongly to the imagination than that of this drowned nation, the true antediluvians. They were the founders of nearly all our arts and sciences; they were the parents of our fundamental beliefs; they were the first civilizers, the first navigators, the first merchants, the first colonizers of the earth; their civilization was old when Egypt was young, and they had passed away thousands of years before Babylon, Rome, or London were dreamed of. This lost people were our ancestors, their blood flows in our veins; the words we use every day were heard, in their primitive form, in their cities, courts, and temples. Every line of race and thought, of blood and belief, leads back to them.

**SEE ALSO:** Dolphin's Ridge; Guanches; Pillars of Hercules; Plato

# EASTER ISLAND

**D**iscovered by the Dutch Admiral Jacob Roggeveen on Easter Day 1722, Easter Island was known to the Pacific Islanders as Rapa Nui. An inhospitable, small, triangular-shaped volcanic island, it is situated in the Pacific Ocean some 3,600 km from the Chilean coast, its nearest neighbour being the Pitcairn Islands, 2,092 km away. Since its discovery, Easter Island has been a source of fascination and debate because of the giant statues, known as *moai*, which can be found throughout the island. Theories abound that these mysterious statues – enigmatic, brooding giants – were erected by aliens, Atlanteans or Lemurians. According to the American psychic Edgar Cayce, the statues and *rongorongo* script unique to Easter Island were the product of the lost continent of Lemuria, the culture of which spread to a number of islands and peoples of the Pacific. In one of his trance-state readings, Cayce stated that Lemuria 'began its disappearance' in 8700 BC. If he was correct, the statues and script would necessarily have been created during a period prior to this date.

There are 887 moai on Easter Island, although it is believed there are probably more to be discovered. Of these moai, some 230 statues were erected on platforms (*ahu*) that held up to 15 standing silently in a row. The remainder are scattered around the island. Although at first glance they appear to be alike, each statue is actually different, be it in design or size. However, each has an elongated, rectangular head and body, with arms held at its sides and long, slim hands positioned underneath a large abdomen. No legs were carved, although the top of a loincloth is discernible. Facially, the statues display strong brows, long noses, prominent chins and lengthy ears, many of which have a hole in the lobe where a disc of sorts was placed. Those mounted on platforms appear to have had white-and-red eyes inserted in their now empty sockets, which apparently stared slightly upwards towards the sky, and most were adorned with a stone hat. The largest statue, which was never cut away from the quarry, is 20 m long and estimated to weigh 270 tonnes, although the largest standing statue weighs 82 tonnes. Remarkably, the statues were not representations of gods but *aringa ora*, the 'living faces' of long-deceased high-ranking Easter Islanders. The statues were intended as funerary ancestor monuments to keep their memories alive. It is believed that the statues were carved when the individual was still alive and only erected on the platforms once they had died. As to the earliest dating of the statues, common opinion points towards 600–1100 AD, much later than Edgar Cayce suggested.

One of the main reasons why the Easter Island statues were thought by many to have been completed by a technologically advanced culture is their enormity; the scale of the task of quarrying, moving and erecting them would have been tremendous. However, despite the statues' immense size, it is not necessarily the case that sophisticated tools or techniques would have been required to create them. Made from tuff (volcanic ash that has been compounded and hardened), which is a relatively soft rock and easy to work using a basalt hand-tool, the statues were carved in the quarry lying on their backs with the base pointing downhill. All the basic details of the statues were carved before they were detached from the rock and moved down the slope. With the aid of grooves cut into the ground to help steer the statue, as well as ropes and hoists, the statue was moved to its site, which could be anything up to 10 km away. It is thought that this was achieved by lashing the statue onto a wooden sledge and heaving it forward by use of ropes. To aid movement, a lubricant was used – probably mashed root vegetables, or wooden rollers when there was a sufficient supply of timber. However, the islanders themselves state that the statues were usually erect when moved and experiments using a base, wooden rollers and ropes show that a statue moved well using this method when hauled by a sufficient number of people. It is thought the technique employed may have depended upon the size and weight of the statue. When the statues were erected on platforms, levers and stones were used to raise them up to the required level and they were then pushed into place. It appears that rivalry between the several clans on the island meant that each group competed to erect the largest or the most statues, resulting in their widespread distribution.

Whilst the giant statues of Easter Island have been dated with relative certainty, it is harder to put a precise date on the Easter Island script, although the late eighteenth century has been proposed. The rongorongo (meaning 'recitation') script was scratched onto wooden boards, of which only 25 survive. The writing consists of symbols that closely resemble those used in Easter Island rock art and depict objects and animals. Neither alphabetical nor syllabic in form, the rongorongo script is a mnemonic device, with the symbols acting as a prompt for the reader. As such, the 'text', which was sung, would vary depending upon who read it, so although the basic storyline was fixed, the details would have varied greatly. As can be deduced, this makes a thorough deciphering of the script almost impossible.

There has been much debate about the origins of the Easter Islanders. In 1947, the Norwegian explorer Thor Heyerdahl set out on a balsawood raft from Peru to prove his theory that the natives of Easter Island originated from South America. Unfortunately, the attempt failed, with the strong Pacific currents taking him and his small crew to Tahiti. Even so, Heyerdahl did prove that it was possible to sail thousands of miles across the Pacific in a flimsy boat, thus emphasising the courageous and exhausting feat undertaken by the first settlers of Easter Island. Today, the consensus is that these founders were Polynesians who came from the west. Local tradition states that Hotu Matua, a chief on the island of Marae Renga in the archipelago of Hiva, was defeated in battle and as a result was forced to leave, whereupon he and his kin group went to Easter Island. Another tradition states that the islands of Hiva, situated somewhere to the west of Easter Island, were swallowed up by the sea and all its inhabitants forced to flee – a story remarkably similar to the one expressed by Edgar Cayce. However, all the archaeological and linguistic evidence points to the colonisation of the island around AD 400.

With such a vast expanse of water to cross, the journey undertaken by the first colonisers would have been an almost impossible endeavour. However, the Polynesians were superb navigators who not only used the stars to steer by but were also able to read wave patterns and surface currents to discover the whereabouts of a landmass. Boys were taught from a young age how to employ this method by use of a *mattang*, an implement made of sticks woven into a cruciform shape with interlocking patterns. These patterns represented the motions of waves around an island and by learning these, the Polynesians were able to read the waves and currents by the sense of touch alone, recognising the mattang's patterns in the vibrations of the waves against the boat.

At some point in the seventeenth century, there appears to have been an eruption of violence on Easter Island that resulted in the deliberate toppling of many of the giant statues. Earthquake activity has been ruled out because there is no mention of it in the island's oral tradition or other evidence for it. The cause seems to have been 'the wars of the throwing down of statues', as described in the folk tradition of Easter Island. Clan fought clan, destroying the ancestor monuments that had taken so much time and effort to erect. The wars, the result of internal feuds and conflict over dwindling arable land and food, culminated in a major battle between two clans. Easter Island had proved to be an ecological disaster. Due to its isolation, the islanders could rely only on its own natural resources, but these were badly managed as well as being devastated by the animals introduced onto the island at the time of its initial settlement, until a point was reached when the inhabitants could no longer sustain themselves adequately. The animals initially introduced onto the island to help feed the population were a major reason for the decline, as they spread disease and destroyed the natural habitat. This caused a drop in the seabird population as their eggs were eaten by the Polynesian rats, and the birds themselves were eaten by humans. The rainforest that had once existed was completely destroyed by rats, as were other trees and shrubs, at some point between 1400 and 1640 AD. These ate the nut kernels of the palm tree, leading to its extinction on the island. Deforestation by the human population in order to obtain timber for fires, building rafts and moving statues, and to clear land for crops, amplified the problem. The destruction of the island's trees led to soil erosion and its increasingly poor quality affected the crops that the people relied upon more and more. Even fishing was affected, because the lack of wood meant that larger canoes could no longer be built.

All this in turn led to a breakdown in the cooperative system that had allowed for the distribution of resources and hence the making and erection of the giant statues. The added hardship of warfare and the ensuing deliberate destruction of crops resulted in starvation and decline for the once lush and fertile island. As the archaeologist Patrick Kirch, who made a study of Easter Island, notes, it 'temporarily but brilliantly surpassed its limits and crashed devastatingly'.

**SEE ALSO:** Cayce, Edgar; Lemuria

# EPAGOMENAL DAYS

**E** pagomenal days are literally 'days out of time'. They are the extra days that were added to ancient calendars to correct the length of the year. It is curious to note that many ancient calendars are based on a year of 360 days and not our current 365 days. Early cultures possessing a 360-day year include: the Hebrews, the Romans, the Mayans, the Chinese, the Babylonians and the Egyptians. For example, the Greek Historian Plutarch tells us in the year AD 75, 'During the reign of Romulus, they only kept to the one rule that the whole course of the year contained three hundred and sixty days.'

This worldwide adoption of a 360-day calendar has often been explained away as a device of primitive cultures, a simple calendar of peoples who did not know the true length of the year. But the Egyptians, amongst others, were known as keen astronomers and were even supposed to be aware of the phenomenon called precession, a 26,000-year cycle that describes a wobble in the Earth's axis. If the Egyptians were able to calculate precession, does it seem likely that they would miscalculate the Earth's orbit around the sun?

Staying with the Egyptians, let's examine when the change in their calendar took place and how. The later Egyptian civil calendar of 365 days was clearly based on an older calendar of 360 days, with five epagomenal days simply added to the end of the year. So they had a year of 12 months, each containing 30 days, plus the five intercalary days. This new calendar was introduced sometime around 2900 BC and we have to assume that prior to this the

Egyptians had used a calendar of just 360 days. Even with the five epagomenal days, the Egyptian calendar was not quite in sync with the true year of the Earth's orbit and because it did not include the leap day that we currently use, the calendar did not stay in time with the seasons of the year. This new calendar was therefore known as the *annus vagus*, the 'wandering year'.

So how did the epagomenal days come into being? In Egyptian mythology, it was the god Thoth who added the five extra days to the year. One of the roles assigned to the ibis-headed god was that of recorder of time, so it is no surprise to find that he is entwined with this story. According to the myth, the great god Shu was outraged to find that his daughter, Nut, had coupled with her brother, Geb, and become pregnant. As an act of revenge, he declared that she could not give birth on any of the 360 days of the year, despite the fact that she was pregnant with five offspring. To solve the problem, Thoth played draughts with the moon and, winning, he was given $1/70$ of her light. Now, $1/70$ of a 360-day year just happens to be five days, and that is exactly what he created from the moonlight. In this way, five epagomenal days were added to the year and Nut was able to give birth to her children – Osiris, Horus, Set, Isis and Nephthys – each on one of the sacred new days.

What is intriguing about this myth is the involvement of the moon. The importance of the moon is reinforced by Thoth's centrality to the myth, as he was known as a lunar deity. Is this story hiding an ancient belief that our orbit around the sun was altered somehow by the moon? Did this change take place around the year 2900 and is this why calendars across the world had to be changed?

In his controversial book *Worlds in Collision*, published in 1950, Immanuel Velikovsky proposed the idea that the shift from an orbit of 360 days to one of 365 days was indeed brought about by celestial mechanics; in other words, a large comet or planetary body passed by the Earth and altered our orbit for ever.

One side effect of such an event, according to Velikovsky, would be huge floods, which would undoubtedly ravage the surface of the world. In fact Velikovsky was not the first to examine the possibility of such an event. As early as 1799, astronomer Pierre-Simon Laplace warned of the dangers should a large comet come too close to the earth:

> The axis and the movement of rotation would be changed.
> The seas would abandon their ancient positions, in order

to precipitate themselves toward the new equator; a great portion of the human race and the animals would be drowned in the universal deluge, or destroyed by the violent shock imparted to the terrestrial globe; entire species would be annihilated; all monuments of human industry overthrown; such are the disasters which the shock of a comet would produce, if its mass were comparable to that of the earth.

Could such an event have been responsible for the destruction of Atlantis and at the same time an increase in the duration of the Earth's orbit of five days, a transition that would have required the addition of five days to the world's calendars?

One final clue lies in the circle. Researchers have asked why, if our calendar is 365 days long, should the circle be divided into 360 degrees? Is this a throwback to a time when we did in fact have a year of just 360 days? It does seem a tantalising question and it is not one that is easily answered. However, as Richard Mooney points out in his book *Colony: Earth*, the answer could lie in the historical records of the Far East:

The ancient Chinese calendar was a 12-month year of 30 days each. They added $5\frac{1}{4}$ days to the year, and also divided the sphere into $365\frac{1}{4}$ degrees, adopting the new length of the year into geometry as well.

This change reportedly came about in the fourth century BC and does indeed seem to indicate that the circle is tied to the length of the year, adding further proof that at some time in our history we did possess a true year of 360 days. Whatever did cause our orbit to alter so drastically could not have been a gentle event; in the story of the epagomenal days and our calendars changing across the world, we may be seeing evidence of a worldwide cataclysm powerful enough to destroy Atlantis.

**SEE ALSO:** Denderah Zodiac; Plutarch

# FOLLOWERS OF HORUS

According to the Egyptian priest and historian Manetho (who lived in the third century BC) and the Turin Royal Canon, a king list compiled during the reign of Ramesses II in the thirteenth century BC, the Followers of Horus (*shemsu hor*) were an undisclosed number of semi-mythical demigods who ruled over Egypt for 13,400 years before the formation of a unified Egyptian state under one mortal king. Despite the purported importance of these individuals, Egyptologists have undertaken little, if any, in-depth analysis to try to discover more about the Followers of Horus, their role and significance.

While the Ancient Egyptians saw the Followers of Horus as semi-divine Predynastic rulers, Egyptologists have written them off as merely mythical figures. Professor Henri Frankfort of the University of London noted in his 1978 book *Kingship and the Gods* that the term Followers of Horus was 'a vague designation for the kings of a distant past . . . but it would seem unwise to treat the term as primarily of a historical nature'. The accepted view is that, in order to legitimise their position, the Dynastic pharaohs associated themselves with a long line of gods and mythical beings from a bygone golden age. Professor Fekri Hassan of University College London has observed that, as Egyptian kingship was closely associated with the hawk-headed god Horus, and had been from an early period, the notion of the Followers of Horus was likely conceived by the ruling elite as a means of underpinning their right to rule. Hence the Followers of Horus were more to do with the concept of royal ancestor worship than with actual historical individuals.

Many alternative authors have, however, theorised that the Followers of Horus were in fact survivors of the Atlantean catastrophe who came to Egypt and brought with them a high level of sophistication, wisdom and technological insight. The Turin Royal Canon refers to the Followers of Horus as 'the venerable *shemsu hor*', indicating the esteem in which they were held and the reverence with which they were regarded. Despite this, little evidence remains in the textual and archaeological record to allow us to piece together a comprehensive account of these enigmatic individuals.

If the Followers of Horus were Atlantean refugees, has any archaeological evidence survived to indicate the arrival in Egypt of an exotic people? In his 1961 book *Archaic Egypt*, the Egyptologist Walter Emery stated his view that the Followers of Horus were a foreign, aristocratic 'master race' — a term that had fallen out of favour because of its associations with Nazi Germany. Emery asserted that these Followers of Horus created the civilised ruling elite of Egypt during the period either side of unification in 3100 BC. He supported his theory by citing the discovery of skeletal remains from the northern part of southern Egypt, which were taller and had larger skulls than those which Emery deemed to be of the indigenous population. Emery commented that the anatomical differences and the change in burial practices were 'so marked that any suggestion that these people derived from the earlier stock is impossible'. However, Emery stated that 'the racial origin of these invaders is not known and the route they took in their penetration of Egypt is equally obscure'. The idea of a 'dynastic race' was first put forward by the distinguished Egyptologist Sir Flinders Petrie, who excavated a number of Upper Egyptian Predynastic sites from the late 1890s to the early twentieth century. Petrie noted a sudden change in burial customs and the material culture, which he thought was due to an invading, conquering race. He concluded that changes in Egyptian culture between 4000 and 3500 BC (known as the Amratian Period) resulted from the influx of 'a fair race coming from the north', whereas the following Gerzean Period saw 'invaders' coming into Egypt from the east.

In 1956, Douglas Derry wrote an article entitled 'The Dynastic Race in Egypt', which also claimed that differences in skeletal remains showed that there was a race of superior people in Egypt, 'perhaps relatively few in number but exceeding the original inhabitants in intelligence', who entered Egypt from the east. However, Petrie and Derry had come to opposing conclusions.

Having examined 334 skulls at Tarkhan in southern Egypt, Petrie concluded that the invading ruling class had smaller skulls than the indigenous population, whereas Derry believed that the 19 larger skulls he studied were those of conquering easterners. Today, Emery's dynastic race theory has been largely discounted, as later discoveries have shown that the indigenous people of northern Egypt were taller than those to the south.

Interestingly, Predynastic palettes and maceheads depict what Egyptologists refer to as 'Follower of Horus standards'. These portray four individuals as standard-bearers to the king, each carrying a pole surmounted by an object. One object is thought to be a piece of flesh, the second is a representation of the god Wepwawet (the Opener of the Ways), and the final two figures each carry the falcon representation of the god Horus. The standards are understood to be symbols of the King's power and are always shown in association with the King. However, why these symbols were chosen and what their significance was is uncertain. It has been suggested that the standards symbolise certain areas within Egypt (called *nomes*), although a deeper, as yet unknown, meaning cannot be ruled out.

The earliest known references to the Followers of Horus are found in the Pyramid Texts. These consist of a series of spells written on the walls of a number of Old Kingdom pyramids (although not the Giza pyramids), intended to aid the King's achievement of immortality in the afterlife. Although the references in these are sparse, they suggest that the Followers of Horus were seen as having a cleansing role associated with the ascension of the King. It is they who wait on the King and recite the ascension prayers, and in this respect they take on a priestly role. Hence Utterance 471 states that:

> The Followers of Horus cleanse me, they bathe me, dry me,
> they recite for me 'The Spell for Him Who Is on the Right
> Way', they recite for me 'The Spell for Him Who Ascends',
> and I ascend to the sky.

So not only do the Followers of Horus recite specific spells but these spells are also effective, indicating that they had secret and powerful knowledge. This is underlined by a section in the Book of the Dead that lists the Followers of Horus among beings found in 'the eleventh cavern, [containing that which is] covered . . . hidden, secret'. Again, the allusion to things arcane indicates an association with knowledge that was not available to all.

So what was this knowledge? An inscription in the Temple of Denderah in southern Egypt mentions that the Followers of Horus were directly responsible for its floor plan. Although the temple dates from the fourth century BC, a six-volume study on the building by Émile Chassinat and François Daumas states that the ritual foundation bricks found at the temple recount that the layout and architecture had their roots in an earlier time. From the inscription:

> The august foundation in Dendera was found in the ancient writings, written on a roll of leather in the time of the Followers of Horus, which was found at Memphis in a coffer at the royal palace, in the time of the king of Upper and Lower Egypt, Lord of the Two Lands . . . Pepy.

This would date the discovery of these writings to around 2200 BC, although the mention of the Followers of Horus alludes to a much earlier period. Again, as with the king lists, the linking of a temple to an ancient time served to create an eternal connection between the past, present and future. Thus both king lists and foundation bricks position the gods and demigods more securely within Egyptian history.

Similarly, the Edfu Texts from the Temple of Horus at Edfu mention that 'Seven Sages' came to Egypt from an island that had been destroyed by a flood. While most had drowned, the survivors managed to get to Egypt. The texts testify that these survivors were 'the Builder Gods . . . the Ghosts, the Ancestors . . . the Senior Ones . . . who illumined this land when they came forth unitedly'. In *Keeper of Genesis*, authors Robert Bauval and Graham Hancock note that this sounds very similar to the role undertaken by the Followers of Horus, with both the Seven Sages and the Followers of Horus associated with temple plans. Bauval and Hancock have suggested that the Followers of Horus interbred with the elite of the local population and from their offspring chose the most intelligent and worthy to educate and initiate into their traditions. In their view, the Followers of Horus provided the 'spiritual force' behind the monarchy, with their role being to ensure that their ancient knowledge continued to be handed down from generation to generation. Further, Bauval and Hancock believe that the Followers of Horus were responsible for planning the three Giza Pyramids. This would have required a group of people with astronomical, technical and intellectual knowledge, who, over an extended period of time, would be responsible for mapping out astral movement and the precession of the equinoxes and for the recording of calendrical information in order to bring the vast project to fruition. Bauval and Hancock believe that the name Followers of Horus was chosen because the astronomers followed the journey of the sun (represented by the sky-god Horus) as it passed through the signs of the zodiac. The esoteric author René Schwaller de Lubicz believed the term was used because these individuals followed 'the path of Horus' and were 'superior beings' responsible for producing the pharaonic line. In his view, these individuals were the social and spiritual elite, who used their knowledge and 'sacred science' to unify the country and create the marvels of Egyptian civilisation.

**SEE ALSO:** Denderah Zodiac

# GUANCHES

The native inhabitants of the Canary Islands were a mysterious people known as the Guanches. Spain conquered the islands in the fifteenth century, but only after a long and bitter struggle — it took the Spaniards 100 years to wrest control of the Islands from the Guanches. When the conquest was finally complete, rather than governing these people, Spain chose to virtually exterminate them, and the culture of the Guanches vanished. However, clues remain that illustrate just how remarkable these people were.

The preserved remains of the Guanches have revealed that they were fair featured and had red or blond hair. They were a tall people, with males over 6 ft tall not unusual. The Spaniards noted that they resembled northern Europeans yet had a larger stature.

> All historians agree in reporting that the Canarians were beautiful. They were tall, well built and of singular proportion. They were also robust and courageous with high mental capacity. Women were very beautiful and Spanish gentlemen often used to take their wives among the population. The belief that the ancient Canarians were a people favoured by great duration of life became popular at the time of the Spanish conquest.
>
> *The Early Inhabitants of the Canary Islands*,
> Alf Bajocco

Their name comes from the longer word *guanchinerfe* which means 'man of Tenerife', the largest of the Canary Islands. This is intriguing, because the Guanches themselves supposedly held that they had once survived a great flood that had destroyed what was originally a much larger homeland, and that their race only survived by taking refuge on the slopes of Mount Teide, Tenerife's great volcano, which just happens to be the highest peak in Spain.

The origins of the Guanches are not clear and their history is one of the mysteries of ancient man. Many believe that the Guanches were true remnants of Cro-Magnon man, much like the Berbers of north-west Africa. It is interesting to note that Cro-Magnon man is thought to differ from modern man in several ways, including having a stronger physical frame and a larger brain capacity. This certainly fits the descriptions of the Guanches that have been passed down to us.

How they came to reside in the Canary Islands is also a puzzle. Indeed, if they were survivors of the destruction of Atlantis, this would answer many of the questions that trouble us today. It is worth pointing out that when the Guanches were rediscovered in the fifteenth century, it was found that they did not know how to sail the ocean that surrounded them and in fact they were terrified of the sea, fishing only in tidal pools. Each of the islands was cut off from the others and it has been noted that it was as if the locals had deliberately turned their backs on the sea. It is usually assumed that the Guanches originally arrived in the Canary Islands by boat, in which case this loss of naval expertise is astounding. However, it must be said that if instead these people were thrown upon the islands in the wake of a great deluge, then their lack of seafaring ability, or unwillingness to travel on the ocean, becomes much more understandable.

Some early travellers found tantalising clues about Atlantis preserved amongst the Guanches. The Roman writer Marcellus visited the islands in the first century AD. Frank Joseph describes the significance of this writer's findings in his book *The Atlantis Encyclopedia*:

> Perhaps the most revealing of all surviving material connecting the Canary Islanders to Atlantis is found in the Tois Aethiopikes by Marcellus. In AD 45, he recorded that 'the inhabitants of the Atlantic island of Poseidon preserve a tradition handed down to them by their ancestors of the existence of an Atlantic island of immense size of not less than a thousand stadia [about 115 miles], which had really existed in those seas, and which, during a long period of

time, governed all the islands of the Atlantic Ocean.' Pliny
the Elder seconded Marcellus, writing that the Guanches
were in fact the direct descendants of the disaster that sank
Atlantis.

The evidence provided by the preserved remains of the Guanches
has been mentioned. These people mummified their dead, in much
the same way as did the Ancient Egyptians. Further ties with Egypt
have been unearthed. The Canary Islands are so called because their
Latin name is Insularia Canaria, meaning 'islands of the dogs'. Ancient
travellers noted that the Guanches worshipped dogs, especially in
connection with the rituals associated with the mummified remains
of their dead. In Egypt, it was Anubis, the jackal-headed God, who
presided over the process of mummification.

Furthermore, it turns out that the Guanches built step pyramids
on their islands, structures similar to those found in Egypt and
South America, although on a smaller scale. In Guimar on Tenerife,
six such structures have been found. They are built from black
volcanic rock and are accurately aligned on an east–west axis. It
is possible that there were once many more of these structures
across the islands. The Roman scholar Pliny the Elder mentions that
when the Carthaginian king Hanno arrived on the islands, he was
confronted by the ruins of great buildings. Are these connections
with the culture of Egypt a coincidence or did the two peoples have
shared beginnings?

The Tenerife pyramids' resemblance not only to structures in
Egypt but also to monuments in Mexico and Peru is remarkable,
and this connection becomes even more interesting once we throw
into the equation the appearance of the Guanches themselves.

In South America, the Aztecs and Olmecs believed that their god
Quetzalcoatl had Nordic features, fair skin and red or blond hair
and facial hair. Their legends state that he came from across the sea
and taught their ancestors how to build pyramids and how to grow
corn.

When Columbus arrived in South America, he was worshipped
as a god because the locals believed that he was from the same
legendary race as Quetzalcoatl. In a curious coincidence, Columbus
actually began his voyage to the New World from La Gomera in the
Canary Islands. The Guanches of Tenerife initially refused Columbus
permission to land because the bearded European looked too much
like themselves and they were suspicious of him.

Is it at all possible that Quetzalcoatl was in fact a Guanche and did he teach the South American Indians how to build pyramids? Or were the Guanches merely the remnants of a civilisation that had once existed where the Canary Islands now sit, the remains of Atlantis itself? Perhaps the answers to these questions died when the Spanish wiped out the Guanches for ever after they had conquered the islands.

**SEE ALSO:** Canary Islands; Pliny the Elder; Quetzalcoatl

# HAPGOOD, CHARLES

Charles Hapgood was a college teacher who unleashed upon an unsuspecting world the spectacular twin theories of pole shifts – the idea that the earth's poles could move suddenly – and crustal displacement, the possibility that the earth's crust 'may be displaced at times, moving over the soft inner body, much as the skin of an orange, if it were loose, might shift over the inner part of the orange all in one piece', causing huge devastation across the entire surface of the globe in the process.

Born in 1904, Hapgood taught history in New Hampshire, USA, and it was there, inspired by one of his students, that he began the search for a satisfactory geological explanation for how Atlantis might have been destroyed. Hapgood was intrigued by the work of Hugh Auchincloss Brown, whose theory of catastrophic pole shifts can be found in his book *Cataclysms of the Earth*, which was finally published when the author was in his late 80s.

In 1953, feeling he was getting somewhere, Hapgood sent his ideas to Albert Einstein, who was so impressed with the theory that he wrote back to Hapgood stating: 'I find your arguments very impressive and have the impression that your hypothesis is correct. One can hardly doubt that significant shifts of the crust have taken place repeatedly and within a short time.' The two continued to correspond until Einstein's death in 1955. Prior to his death, Einstein wrote a foreword to Hapgood's book, *Earth's Shifting Crust: A Key to Some Basic Problems of Earth Science*, which was eventually published in 1958:

I frequently receive communications from people who wish to consult me concerning their unpublished ideas. It goes without saying that these ideas are seldom possessed of scientific validity. The very first communication, however, that I received from Mr Hapgood electrified me. His idea is original, of great simplicity, and − if it continues to prove itself − of great importance to everything that is related to the history of the earth's surface.

He went on to summarise Hapgood's theory:

In a polar region there is a continual deposition of ice, which is not symmetrically distributed about the pole. The earth's rotation acts on these unsymmetrically deposited masses, and produces centrifugal momentum that is transmitted to the rigid crust of the earth. The constantly increasing centrifugal momentum produced in this way will, when it has reached a certain point, produce a movement of the earth's crust over the rest of the earth's body, and this will displace the polar regions toward the equator.

Hapgood proposed that the earth's North and South poles had not always been where they are now and that they were likely to move over time, sometimes suddenly. Today, Hapgood's ideas are not heavily supported within the geological community, with most experts choosing to adhere to the well-worn theory of plate tectonics. However, it is possible that Hapgood's theory could sit side by side with the concept of plate tectonics, and that the two ideas together could explain long-term movements in the earth's landmasses.

Hapgood's theories had great consequences for the search for Atlantis. Clearly, his idea of crustal displacement could point to one possible reason why Atlantis was destroyed. If Atlantis had indeed been in existence when such a displacement occurred, surely it would have suffered disastrous effects. It is not hard to imagine that such a 'slip' of the earth's crust could cause exactly the type of deluge that is said to have overwhelmed Atlantis. It's not difficult either to see how a large landmass could 'sink' if the whole of the earth's crust was on the move and in a state of flux.

Hapgood modified his theory over time. Initially believing that this displacement could happen overnight, he later changed his mind, stating that the movement of the earth's crust might occur over many thousands of years. However, there is a chance that both versions of his theory are correct: that slow movements are always occurring, while sudden shifts can also take place, much in the way that Einstein explained it – triggered by a build-up of ice at the poles.

As well as pointing to a mechanism that could have caused the destruction of Atlantis, Hapgood's work also led to another, more radical solution to the question. Hapgood's theory was taken further by Rand Flem-Ath, who wrote *When the Sky Fell* with his wife, Rose, in 1995. Their ideas were in turn aired in Graham Hancock's bestseller *Fingerprints of the Gods*. Rand and Rose Flem-Ath, developing Hapgood's theories, suggested that it was not necessarily the case that Atlantis sank into the Atlantic; instead, they proposed that Atlantis was once the landmass that we know today as Antarctica.

This radical theory hypothesised that Antarctica had not always sat at the South Pole but had once occupied a temperate region on the earth's surface, where a civilisation such as Atlantis could have flourished. It was, they claimed, one of Hapgood's crustal displacements that had, disastrously, sent Atlantis towards the South Pole, where life would have been impossible, however advanced the culture that inhabited the continent. So it was not that Atlantis did not sink beneath the sea but rather was buried beneath the ice.

Hapgood's other ideas involved ancient maps such as the Piri Reis Map, and in his 1966 book *Maps of the Ancient Sea Kings: Evidence of Advanced Civilization in the Ice Age* he proposed that a civilisation advanced enough to map the entire world (including an ice-free Antarctic) must have existed long ago in antiquity, before the last crustal displacement occurred.

The publication of *Fingerprints of the Gods* by Graham Hancock in 1995 led to a resurgence of interest in the work of Charles Hapgood and many came to believe that such a crustal displacement was imminent. This fuelled pre-millennial doomsday prophecies, and a large number of people really thought that the world might end on 31 December 1999 and that we were to experience a large-scale movement of the earth's crust, resulting in the overnight eradication of our modern culture in much the same way as Atlantis was destroyed.

Thankfully, this disaster never arrived and we are still all here debating whether such a phenomenon is indeed possible and if it is likely to occur in the future. Charles Hapgood would have had a lot to say on the subject if he were here today, we are sure.

**SEE ALSO:** Piri Reis Map

# HERMES

**H**ermes was a Greek deity who was transformed in the ancient world from a mere spirit into an important god. He protected not only travellers and merchants but also shepherds. He was the inventor of the lyre, a distinctively shaped stringed instrument, which he fashioned from a tortoiseshell. Since he had a huge talent for oratory, the idea evolved that he could be influential in assisting those with literary aspirations. A poet holding forth while plucking a lyre might have cause to be grateful to Hermes. He has also been credited with the creation of the first pan-pipes and the first flute.

Hermes was a god who was able to influence the world of the living; however, he also appeared in the underworld, helping the souls of the dead by guiding them with his rod. Gods were otherwise thought of as dwelling either above the earth or below it in Hades. Hermes can be considered unique in visiting both realms. He came to be identified with the image of a beautiful young man with a perfect athletic figure and so was thought of as the god from whom an ambitious athlete might seek help, perhaps to make up for his own slight deficiencies in talent. A supplicant might pray to him for assistance, promising that if the prayer was answered, Hermes would receive a reward, presumably of sufficient worth to tempt him into answering the request positively. It sometimes worked the other way; a disappointed and disgruntled worshipper might threaten some form of retribution. Pagan worship involved making bargains with the gods. Another task assigned to this apparently overworked god was to act as a messenger, a kind of divine deliverer of oral telegrams. Hermes is often depicted wearing a brimmed hat with wings at both sides, and with winged boots, or later sandals, on his feet. He carries a *kerikeion,* or caduceus, a messenger's staff with two snakes twined around it, which has become a symbol of healing.

Perhaps remarkably, he was also the god of thieves. Only a very short time after his birth, he stole cows belonging to his fellow god Apollo, leading them backwards so that they could not be tracked. It was only when Apollo noticed that the newly invented lyre had strings fashioned from cow gut that the robbery was discovered. Apollo was as charmed by the instrument as he was annoyed by the theft. In the end, it was agreed that Apollo should keep the lyre, on which he became famously adept, while Hermes kept the herd. As a young offender himself, he therefore had much in common with thieves. The story illustrates the way the gods were viewed in the ancient world. Though divine, they could be fickle, immoral, greedy and unreliable, a concept which can be difficult for modern minds to grasp.

Hermes was also worshipped by the Romans. He was known to them as Mercury (Mercurius) and it is from him that the unique metal element sometimes known as quicksilver gets its name. The chemical mercury has properties which appear to be magical – the way it can be split into small liquid droplets, its ability to amalgamate with other metals, and so on – although it is recognised today as a highly dangerous substance which should be treated with great caution. Its chemical symbol, Hg, comes from Latinised Greek for watery silver, hydrargyrum. Mercury was also chosen by the Romans as the name of the planet which moves most quickly around the sun.

Hermes was born of an illicit union between the chief god Zeus and the nymph Maia. He was linked with fertility and was believed to have associated with various female deities with similar interests. Just one of his alleged conquests was Aphrodite, the Greek Venus. The couple had a child called Hermaphroditus.

In ancient times, boundaries were marked by pillars or stones known in Greece as herms, and in Athens these were also erected outside houses to fend off evil. The markers were carved, with a (usually bearded) head of Hermes at the top and male genitalia lower down. They were considered sacred. There was a great scandal in Athens in 415 BC, during the Peloponnesian Wars, when the herms were vandalised shortly before the Athenian fleet was due to sail to Sicily to attack Syracuse. It was generally believed that the mutilation of the herms had been carried out by men opposed to the principle of the expedition and that their action would result in bad omens and anger Hermes, who, as the god of travellers, could be expected to keep a watchful eye on those sailing to war. The expedition sailed but shortly afterwards one of the leaders, Alcibiades, was recalled, having been accused of involvement in the sacrilege. Rather than face the political enemies accusing him, he deserted to the Spartans. The expedition ended disastrously: the leaders were executed and the Athenians who remained alive were imprisoned in the Syracusan stone quarries. To this day, it is not known who was responsible for the desecration of the herms.

Around the first to third centuries AD a collection of texts written in Greek, Latin and Coptic began to appear. These were ascribed to an Egyptian god, the ibis-headed Thoth, who began to be referred to as Hermes Trismegistus, a name which translates as 'thrice-great Hermes'. The Greeks also renamed the Egyptian town of Khemenu, associated with the particular veneration of Thoth, Hermopolis, 'the city of Hermes'. The reason the Greek Hermes and the Egyptian Thoth became identified with one another was that they were both thought of as divine messengers and both inspired writing, which was a prized gift.

Since the Greeks had held power in Egypt under the Ptolemaic dynasty for centuries before the conquest of the Romans, the religion of the Egyptians had become assimilated into the similarly polytheistic worship of the Greeks. While the Greeks, and later the Romans, mocked the 'animal worship', as they saw it, of their subject land by the Nile, they recognised its vast antiquity and were in awe of the store of learning claimed by the priests. Gods were therefore adapted and amalgamated with Greek deities, resulting in beliefs such as those held by followers of Hermes Trismegistus. His writings, which comprised works on astrology, theology, philosophy, occultism, magic and alchemy, were believed by some to have been brought to Egypt by refugees when Atlantis was destroyed. One aspect of alchemy, the transmutation of metals, especially in order to manufacture gold, fascinated scholars and charlatans during the Middle Ages and the Renaissance, and it was thought that this body of writing from the classical world might contain clues to help them in achieving their aim.

A useful thought for modern students can be found in the works of Hermes Trismegistus: 'He who gets knowledge is good and pious; he is already divine.'

**SEE ALSO:** Athens

# HYDROPHORIA

The Hydrophoria was an annual festival that took place in ancient times in Athens to honour the spirits of the victims of the Flood of Deucalion. This great deluge was said to have been caused by Zeus in an effort to destroy the Bronze Age of man and all its works. Zeus despaired of humankind after a boy was sacrificed to him, a practice which was forbidden. Only two people were said to have survived the flood, Deucalion, who was a nephew of Atlas, and his wife Pyrrha. Both were said to have been spared because they were devout and pure of heart.

Deucalion was forewarned of the great destruction by his father, Prometheus. Deucalion constructed a chest and together he and Pyrrha were set adrift on the waters of the deluge for nine days and nights. Eventually, they settled on Mount Parnassus, where they left the safety of their chest, the only pair of humans to have survived the flood.

Thankful to Zeus for allowing them to live, they gave offerings and consulted the oracle at Delphi to ask how the earth might be populated again. They were instructed: 'With veiled heads and loosened robes throw behind you as you go the bones of your great mother.' Realising that the 'mother' in this case was the earth herself, Deucalion and Pyrrha picked up stones and cast them over their shoulders. Where Deucalion's stones fell men suddenly appeared, while Pyrrha's caused women to materialise where they landed. And so it was that the earth was rejuvenated.

The Hydrophoria was designed to placate the spirits of all those who perished, as well as to appease Zeus in case he should decide to unleash such fury again. Ignatius Donnelly described the festival in *Atlantis: The Antediluvian World*:

> Close to the temple of the Olympian Zeus a fissure in the soil was shown, in length but one cubit, through which it was said the waters of the Deluge had been swallowed up. Thus, every year, on the third day of the festival of the Anthesteria, a day of mourning consecrated to the dead — that is, on the thirteenth of the month of Anthesterion, toward the beginning of March — it was customary, as at Bambyce, to pour water into the fissure, together with flour mixed with honey, poured also into the trench dug to the west of the tomb, in the funeral sacrifices of the Athenians.

The connection with the deluge of Atlantis is clear, as are the parallels with the story of Noah's Flood. The fact that, according to the story, Deucalion was the nephew of Atlas is interesting, because Atlas, the son of Poseidon, was said to have been the first king of Atlantis, so the inference here is unmistakable: there is a distinct possibility that both Deucalion and Pyrrha were Atlanteans and that what is being described in the myth is the destruction of Atlantis itself, the subsequent scattering of her population and their gradual resettlement over the surface of the earth.

The novelist C.J. Cutcliffe Hyne certainly thought so, casting Deucalion as the protagonist of his fantastic Atlantis novel of 1900, *The Lost Continent*.

**SEE ALSO:** Atlas; Donnelly, Ignatius; Poseidon; Prometheus

# KIRCHER, ATHANASIUS

When we think today of the remarkable scholars of the Renaissance, it is Leonardo da Vinci who stands pre-eminent in our minds. The name of Athanasius Kircher has been largely forgotten, which is unfortunate, as he was a man of considerable talents and varied interests. Kircher was born, probably in 1602, in Geisa (part of modern Germany) and became a Jesuit priest in 1628. He studied various languages, including Hebrew, Greek and Syrian, and when he became interested in the hieroglyphic inscriptions of Ancient Egypt he learned Coptic, the language of Christian Egyptians, in his attempts to decipher the meanings of the symbols he studied.

He published over 40 books in his lifetime, several of them on the subject of Egypt. His *Prodromus coptus sive aegyptiacus* was the first book to detail the grammar of Coptic, then in 1643 he explained, correctly, in *Lingua aegyptiaca restituta*, that Coptic was a surviving remnant of the Ancient Egyptian language. His studies led him to speculate in *Oedipus aegyptiacus* that the figure known as Hermes Trismegistus was Moses, the Biblical prophet. Kircher also became fascinated by China and published an encyclopedia of China, containing maps of the country and his observations on Chinese writing. He came to identify Confucius with Hermes Trismegistus/Moses, believing them to have been the same person, a wise man and teacher.

Kircher taught ethics and mathematics at the university in Würzburg before moving to Avignon in France during a period of political instability in Europe. He was called to Rome in 1638 and after teaching languages and mathematics there for some years he devoted his life to study and to his publications. Unusually for a scientist at that time, he managed to support himself from the proceeds of his books.

One of Kircher's many interests was medicine and he was able to discern organisms in the blood of plague victims using an early microscope. He published his results in *Scrutinium pestis* (1658) and proposed that the disease was caused by parasites. Working from this premise, he advised measures, such as isolating victims and destroying clothing or materials that had been in contact with them, to try to combat the spread of the disease. He also proposed the wearing of masks by those tending to the sick, to prevent them picking up the infection.

Even for a man with an insatiable appetite for knowledge, one of the expeditions he made to investigate the geology of the earth sounds remarkably hazardous. In 1638, he travelled to the volcano Vesuvius, which was on the brink of an eruption, and had himself lowered into the crater to observe the activity inside. Unlike Pliny the Elder, whose curiosity about the activities of Vesuvius led to tragedy, Kircher was able to assimilate his geological findings into one of his most famous works, *Mundus subterraneus,* published in 1678.

In *Mundus subterraneus*, Kircher published a map showing the island of Atlantis, which he titles 'Site of Atlantis, now beneath the sea, according to the beliefs of the Egyptians and the description of Plato'. It is assumed that he copied the map from an older document, possibly in the archives of the Vatican in Rome, to which he would have had access. The map is unusual to modern viewers in that it has north at the bottom and south at the top. Africa is therefore shown above Spain and the continent of America and the Atlantic Ocean are on the right-hand side of the map. Atlantis is shown as an island in the Atlantic, beyond the Pillars of Hercules, outside the Strait of Gibraltar. If the map was originally an Ancient Egyptian one, this would explain its orientation, with south at the top. This was the convention in Egyptian maps, in which the Nile was always shown running from top to bottom, although it flows from south to north. By the same token, Upper Egypt was southern Egypt and Lower Egypt to the north. Comparisons have been made between the shape of Atlantis on Kircher's map and the continent of Antarctica on the Piri Reis Map, a sixteenth-century map that appears to depict in detail a continent that had not at that time been explored.

In Rome, he established the Museum Kircherianum, one of the

earliest collections of natural history and antiquities. When the sculptor Bernini relocated an Egyptian obelisk to surmount his *Fountain of the Four Rivers* in the Piazza Navona in Rome, Kircher assisted with the erection of the obelisk. After his death in 1680, his heart was buried in the church of Santuario della Mentorella, near Rome, which he had restored from the ruins of a church supposed to have been built by Constantine the Great.

**SEE ALSO:** Hermes; Pillars of Hercules; Piri Reis Map; Plato; Pliny the Elder

# LEMURIA

Lemuria is the name given to another lost land, similar to Atlantis, that is thought once to have existed somewhere in the Pacific Ocean. It is sometimes also used to refer to a legendary sunken land in the Indian Ocean.

The name Lemuria was introduced to the world by the zoologist Philip Sclater in the year 1864 and is derived from the small mammal the lemur. Because the fossilised remains of lemurs had been found in India and Madagascar but not in Africa, Sclater proposed that there must at one time have existed a large landmass, now beneath the waves, that had connected India with Madagascar. It was this hypothetical landmass that he named Lemuria.

The idea of Lemuria was for decades embraced by many scientists, until the arrival of the science of plate tectonics and continental drift sounded its death knell. It was then realised that if our understanding of continental drift was correct, Lemuria could not simply have disappeared without a trace.

Despite this, Lemuria made quite a splash in its day. The doyenne of the occult world, Madame Blavatsky, founder of the Theosophical Society, seized upon this legendary continent and claimed that it had been home to the 'Third Root Race', an ancient branch of humanity consisting of individuals who were less mentally developed than modern humans but spiritually more advanced, as well as being hermaphrodites who produced their offspring from eggs. They also possessed a physical 'third eye':

There were four-armed human creatures in those early days of the male-females; with one head, yet three eyes. They could see before them and behind them . . . When the Fourth [Root Race] arrived at its middle age, the inner vision had to be awakened, and acquired by artificial stimuli, the process of which was known to the old sages. The third eye, likewise, getting gradually petrified, soon disappeared. The double-faced became the one-faced, and the eye was drawn deep into the head and is now buried under the hair. During the activity of the inner man [meditation] the eye swells and expands.

According to Blavatsky, Lemuria had finally been destroyed by underground fires, probably volcanic in origin.

Not all the legends of Lemuria died when the theory of continental drift came to hold sway in the modern world. Today, some of the Tamil peoples of Southern India and Sri Lanka identify Lemuria with the fabled sunken land of Kumari Kandam, which, according to Tamil tradition, sat off the coast of the southern tip of India. Their legends tell that the land of Kumari Kandam was the ancestral home of all Dravidian peoples, of whom the Tamils are a branch. The implication is that if the Tamils and the other Dravidian peoples were the original inhabitants of Lemuria, this would make them among the oldest races in the world.

The Tamils today still mourn for the loss of their old homeland and their word 'kadatkol', which means 'devouring of the land by the sea', seems to underline their obsession with the ocean that surrounds them and the dangers that it can represent. In Tamil culture, the disastrous tsunami that struck the region in 2004 was not an unknown phenomenon.

The language of the Tamils is very ancient and is not based on the Indo-European family; it is unique. They also have a recorded history that goes back at least 2,000 years. So could it be possible that the relatively modern concept of Lemuria is actually founded in some truth and in fact relates to this fabled land of Kumari Kandam, which the Tamils certainly believe existed once and was their original home? Furthermore, is there any chance that rather than having existed off the coast of India, it was actually none other than that other great sunken land, Atlantis, and that, after the fall of that great nation, the survivors of the deluge found refuge as far away as the shores of Southern India and Sri Lanka?

**SEE ALSO:** Blavatsky, Madame

# LE PLONGEON, AUGUSTUS

**A**ugustus Le Plongeon was the first person, along with his wife, Alice Dixon Le Plongeon, to document the Yucatán Mayan sites of Chichen Itza and Uxmal. They were pioneers in their day, the first people to painstakingly excavate and photograph the ruins of Mayan culture. It was Le Plongeon's use of photography in particular that was groundbreaking.

Le Plongeon was born in 1826 on the island of Jersey. Having decided to sail to South America once his education was complete, he found himself shipwrecked in Chile. He taught there for a while, until in 1849 he heard about the gold rush in California, whereupon he left for San Francisco to become a surveyor. He spent a brief period in England learning photography before returning to San Francisco in 1855 to open a portrait studio. A few years later, in 1862, he moved his business to Peru, where he became interested in the ancient Inca ruins that were scattered across the country and began to photograph these, a task that would keep him occupied for the next eight years. During this time, he became interested in the writings of Charles-Étienne Brasseur de Bourbourg, who believed that civilisation had originated in the New World.

Then, in 1873, Le Plongeon met Alice Dixon, the woman with whom he would spend the rest of his life and who would become his greatest collaborator. The pair of them sailed to the Yucatán in Mexico in the same year and it was here that they began the work for which they would both be remembered. They spent more than ten years documenting and excavating Mayan ruins. It has been said that in that day and age anyone could become a Mayanist and an archaeologist, as long as they had the money to travel and the desire to explore. However, Le Plongeon's methods could almost be the envy of a modern archaeologist, so thorough was he. He even learned the language of the Yucatán natives, Yucatec Maya, in an effort to be able to decipher the inscriptions found on the monuments. It was at Chichen Itza that Le Plongeon found a statue of a reclining figure that he named a *chaacmol*, a word that has remained with us to this day, in the modified form of *chacmool*, as a designation for all such statues.

Le Plongeon's important work has often been overshadowed by the many theories that he promulgated while working in South America. It does seem now as if Le Plongeon travelled to the Yucatán with a desire to prove right the ideas he already possessed, a flaw that was to undermine all of his hard work in so meticulously documenting the remains of the Mayans. In fact, he even said as much, stating before he left for Mexico that he went there 'with the fixed intention of finding either proof or the denial of an opinion formed during my ramblings among the ruins of Tiahuanuco, that the cradle of the world's civilization is this continent on which we live'.

One of his most controversial ideas was that the Mayans had been responsible for founding the culture of Ancient Egypt, travelling first to South-east Asia and then working their way west to North Africa. At the time, it wasn't entirely clear that the Mayan culture was younger than those of the Middle East. However, when later it was proved conclusively that the Egyptians were far older than the Mayans, Le Plongeon not only stubbornly held on to his theories, he developed an entire new history to accommodate his ideas.

By the late 1880s, this had developed into a detailed chronology. He claimed that the Mayans were the original, founding civilisation of the modern world, that they had travelled east from Central America to Atlantis and from there to Egypt and the Middle East. Le Plongeon even invented a character, based on carvings and inscriptions he had found, called Queen Moo, who would star in his book *Queen Moo and the Egyptian Sphinx*. In this work, the queen herself, along with her brother, Prince Chacmool, are at the centre of many intrigues and, eventually, after Prince Chacmool is murdered by Prince Aac, Queen Moo leaves Central America and seeks refuge in Egypt, where it turns out that she is actually their long-lost queen, also known as Isis. Once in Egypt, she commemorates the life of her great love, Prince Chacmool, by erecting a giant feline statue with a man's head — the Sphinx that today sits at Giza.

Chacmool is said to mean 'power of the leopard', and so this giant statue honoured the dead prince. When Le Plongeon published this account of the origins of the Mayans and Egyptians in 1896, he was openly ridiculed, so we can see that it is not just today that his theories are greeted with scepticism.

Le Plongeon even used Ancient Egyptian hieratic writing to translate an inscription found on a pyramid at Xochicalco in the Yucatán, claiming that it read, 'A land in the ocean is destroyed and its inhabitants killed in order to transform them into dust.' He also, famously, translated the Troano Codex, claiming that it described the destruction of Mu, which he identified with Atlantis. However, his version of the text was again received with scepticism.

These theories have tended to colour many people's opinion of Le Plongeon and his painstaking work documenting many sites has often been overlooked. He had a highly systematic approach, often documenting buildings by photographing their entire facades, with not a single detail overlooked. This same method was applied to every object he came across. It is therefore a great shame that Le Plongeon did not apply this scientific rigour to his speculative theories; he could have been one of the world's greatest archaeologists if he had forsaken his bias. Instead of inspiring the academic community, he went on to influence other authors and researchers who devised their own fantastic claims, including James Churchward, who would bring the lost continent of Mu to the world's attention.

Le Plongeon himself remained intransigent to the last, writing towards the end of his life:

> I have been accused of promulgating notions on ancient America contrary to the opinion of men regarded as authorities on American Archaeology. And so it is, indeed. Mine is not the fault, however, although it may be my misfortune, since it has surely entailed upon me their enmity and its consequences. But who are those pretended authorities? Certainly not the doctors and professors at the head of the universities and colleges in the US; for not only do they know absolutely nothing of Ancient American civilisation, but, judging from letters in my possession, the majority of them refuse to learn anything concerning it.

**SEE ALSO:** Brasseur de Bourbourg, Abbé; Mu

# MINOANS

In 1900, Sir Arthur Evans excavated the ancient city of Knossos on Crete, where he discovered a vast palace complex dating to around 1500 BC, as well as an earlier structure on the same site dating to 2000 BC. The later palace, which is now thought to be a temple complex, consisted of a central rectangular court with rooms leading off from it. The complex was on several floors and proved to be highly sophisticated, containing drainage systems, toilets and bathrooms. The walls of the temple were wonderfully decorated with richly coloured frescoes depicting bulls, bull-leaping, dancers, fish and dolphins. These, together with the ceramics, jewellery and figurines found, displayed a high level of craftsmanship, suggesting an extremely refined and advanced society.

Since the discovery of Knossos, it has been argued by many that Crete was the location of Atlantis or at least that the Minoan civilisation was an 'echo' of the lost continent. The term 'Minoan' was coined by Sir Arthur Evans because of the abundance of bull depictions at Knossos and ancient Crete's link to King Minos and the legendary Minotaur. The identification of Crete with Atlantis pivots on a number of geographical and cultural factors, but Atlantologists have also searched for some hint of Atlantis in the ancient name for Crete. One possible name is the enigmatic Egyptian Haunebut, which translates literally as 'behind the islands' but could also be taken to have the sense of 'islands in the back of beyond'. The Egyptologist Eduard Meyer thought that Crete had to be the Haunebut mentioned in the Egyptian texts of the Hyksos period (1650–1550 BC), although this was not a theory that was generally accepted. An Egyptian queen, Ahhotep II, of the dynasty that followed the Hyksos, held the title 'Mistress of the Shores of Haunebut' but there is no further mention of this place. Most Egyptologists have associated the name with the Aegean islands, while some believe that this is simply a general term for a foreign, faraway location. However, alternative authors have attributed more significance to this name, stating that Haunabha is Sanskrit for 'People of the Haze' or 'People of the Pillar', and hence a name that resonates with Atlantis and the many pillars with which it is associated, including the ritual pillar in the Temple of Poseidon, described by Plato in *Critias*, on which the island's laws were inscribed. The name that most Egyptologists believe was used by the Egyptians, bearing in mind that it was often linked with 'the isles in the midst of the sea', was Keftiu. This is probably the Egyptian phonetic rendering of the name the Minoans used for themselves; the Akkadian name was Kaptara and the Hebrew one was Kaphtor. It has been suggested that Keftiu stems from the root word '*keft*', which may mean 'capital of a pillar'.

The significance of Crete and the Minoan civilisation was brought into the limelight in 1909 by an article published in *The Times* entitled 'The Lost Continent'. Writing anonymously, the author suggested that what Arthur Evans had discovered at Knossos was actually the remnants of ancient Atlantis. The author, later revealed to be K.T. Frost from Queen's University, Belfast, noted that: 'the Minoan realm, therefore, was a vast and ancient power which was united by the same sea which divided it from other nations, so that it seemed to be a separate continent with a genius of its own.' Further, he stated that: 'if the account of Atlantis be compared with the history of Crete and her relationship with Greece and Egypt, it seems almost certain that here we have an echo of the Minoans.'

In 1913, Frost expanded on his theory in an article published in the *Journal of Hellenic Studies*, Volume 33, entitled 'The *Critias* and Minoan Crete'. Frost set out his reasons for believing that Atlantis was 'reminiscent' of Minoan Crete, highlighting the cultural similarities between the two and stressing in particular the abundance of bull depictions and bull cults that existed on Crete. These he compared with Plato's account in *Critias* of the Atlantean ceremonies involving the hunting of bulls with 'no weapon of iron'. The Knossos frescoes depict the Minoan religious act of bull-leaping, which involved a male or female leaper diving between the bull's horns. To afford the leaper protection and ensure the bull kept its head lowered, a pair of helpers grabbed hold of its horns and held on to these. Once through the horns, the leaper somersaulted onto the back of the bull, vaulting over and landing on his or her feet behind it.

The 'divine leap' was usually performed from a block in the north-west corner of the bull court, the leaper being aided by helpers whose role it was to propel him or her over the bull's head. In support of Frost's theory regarding the bull-cult connection, Charles Pellegrino noted in *Unearthing Atlantis* that vessels found in Cretan tombs show

> scenes of bullfights engraved on their sides. The bulls were shown snared in ropes. Similar scenes were depicted on the palace walls of Knossos — scenes that differed from all other bullfights known though history in precisely the point Plato had emphasised: no weapons except ropes were used.

However, Peter James notes in *The Sunken Kingdom* that 'bull-cults were actually extremely common in the ancient Mediterranean' and writes that this connection is 'of no particular significance'.

In 1939, Professor Spyridon Marinatos, director of the Greek Archaeological Service, suggested that the island of Thera, to the north of Crete, had suffered a massive volcanic explosion in ancient times. Marinatos conjectured that, based on the size of the caldera (the flooded crater), which was a massive 80 sq. km, four times larger than the crater created when Krakatoa exploded in 1883, the impact on the area around Thera, and on Crete in particular, would have been catastrophic. Considering that the eruption of Krakatoa was audible 3,500 miles away, it is more than likely that this event was heard in Egypt. Marinatos stated that:

> the Egyptians must undoubtedly have learnt of an island becoming submerged and this was Thera, but being so small and insignificant they did not know of it. They transferred this event to Crete, the island so grievously struck and with which all contact was suddenly lost.

In the 1950s and '60s, the seismologist Professor Angelos Galanopoulos dated the Thera explosion to 1500 BC. This would have been during the Minoan New Temple Period, between 1700 and 1470 BC. At this time, Minoan civilisation was highly sophisticated, enjoying intricate architecture and high-quality frescoes and art; society was stratified and women had high status within the ceremonial sphere. It was during this period that the script known as Linear A was used on Crete; it is still to be deciphered, as it was written in an unidentified language. There is evidence that around 1500 BC Knossos and the rest of Crete suffered some form of devastation, probably an earthquake brought about by the eruption of Thera. Despite this, Knossos was repaired and continued in its role as the chief city of a highly successful state for another 100 years. It was at the very time when Crete was recovering from the devastation, though, that it fell under the influence of the Mycenaeans. The use of the Linear B script, a primitive form of Greek, from 1400 onwards attests to the Mycenaean influence and by 1400–1380 the Minoan civilisation had been eclipsed by Mycenaean culture. Whatever contact the Minoans had with Egypt up to 1500 would not, however, have been 'suddenly lost' as Marinatos suggested; it would have gradually declined.

Archaeological finds at the site of Akrotiri on Thera (often referred to as Santorini), a small island to the north of Crete, have proved to be spectacular and the material culture seems very similar to that found at Knossos. At Akrotiri, archaeologists discovered rows of houses two to three storeys high, exquisitely decorated with maritime scenes. The 'Minoan Pompeii', as it has been dubbed, revealed a sophisticated sewage system and extensive plumbing arrangements, to the extent that even individual buildings had running water, bringing to mind Plato's description of the hot and cold water supply enjoyed by the Atlanteans. Geographically, Thera has been described as looking remarkably similar to Plato's description of Atlantis, with its concentric rings of sea and land, reminiscent of Thera's appearance after the volcano erupted leaving the island with a large crescent-shaped lagoon with a circular island at its centre. However, given the fact that Thera is obviously much smaller than Atlantis would have been, and in order to fit the supposition that Egyptian descriptions of Atlantis were actually referring to Crete and Thera, theorists have decided that the Egyptians must have misunderstood the remains of Thera and, thinking Crete was also part of the original island, assumed the two had once been part of a much larger landmass.

Although the overall look of Thera fits the description of Atlantis, its dimensions do not. The island is much smaller than Atlantis is usually thought to be, making it difficult for Atlantologists to equate the two. In their book *Atlantis: The Truth Behind the Legend*, written in 1969, Galanopoulos and Edward Bacon got around this problem by reducing the stated dimensions of Atlantis by an order of ten to make their hypothesis fit. They concluded that the Egyptian priests had given Solon incorrect measurements as well as the wrong date for the destruction of Atlantis, which, according to their theory, was 900 rather than 9,000 years before Solon's visit. Similarly, Marinatos stated that by the time the priests of Sais related the story of Atlantis to Solon in 600 BC, 900 years after the eruption of Thera, the 'Saite priest projected tenfold into the abyss of the past'. Therefore, according to Galanopoulos and Bacon, despite being correct on all other details, the Egyptian priests had 'mistakenly multiplied some actual dates and linear measurements by ten'. As Peter James explains in *The Sunken Kingdom*, it is impossible to misinterpret the Ancient Egyptian hieroglyphs used for numerals, as each sign is different and it is not a simple matter of omitting a zero.

Another similarity often mentioned is the tricoloured stone of Thera, which corresponds to the stone quarried at Atlantis, which was 'white, another black and a third red'. However, as Peter James mentions, the geologist Dorothy Vitaliano has pointed out that this was not unique to Thera, as such coloured stones can be found elsewhere in the Aegean as well as in the Azores, another contender for the location of Atlantis.

Another problem with the Minoan theory for Atlantis is that Plato clearly stated that the continent of Atlantis was larger than Libya (North Africa) and Asia (the Middle East), which Crete clearly is not. It is also situated on the wrong side of the Pillars of Hercules, although, again, in order to make the theory of Crete/ Atlantis correspond with Egyptian accounts, K.T. Frost argued that, to the Egyptians, Crete may have seemed to be at the western point of their world. He speculated that when the Minoan civilisation was destroyed, the Egyptians 'invented the myth of an island that became submerged'. But James argues that Plato would have known about Crete and been aware of its geographical location, culture and traditions, and would not have passed on any misconceptions or incorrect information held by the Egyptian priests. Plato even wrote *Minos* about the Cretan king and would not have confused the island of Crete with the continent of Atlantis – unless he was writing a fictional account of a fictional continent.

According to Desmond Lee's 'Appendix on Atlantis' in his translations of *Timaeus* and *Critias*, Plato was not concerned with historical information but with the conflict 'between appearance and reality', between political 'principle and practice', and hence 'between what we think ought to be and what regrettably is'. Plato's *Republic* deals with this in relation to how the people should be governed, the principles around which society should be organised and the degeneration of society – in sum, the ideal and the reality – and it is believed that it could be these ideas which Plato is expressing when he describes Atlantis. In 1969, J.V. Luce, a lecturer at Trinity College, Dublin, wrote a book entitled *Lost Atlantis: New Light on an Old Legend*, in which he hypothesised that Plato's account of Atlantis actually detailed the fall of the Minoan civilisation. Whatever the motivation for Plato's recording of Atlantis, it is unlikely that Crete was that island. Even so, and despite the obvious discrepancies, Crete/Thera continues to be one of the main contenders for the location of the lost continent.

**SEE ALSO:** Crete; Critias; Pillars of Hercules; Plato; Santorini

# MU

Like Atlantis, Mu is a vanished continent, a lost land. It too is believed to have sunk beneath the waves, although Mu is said to have been located in the Pacific rather than the Atlantic Ocean.

It was the nineteenth-century traveller Augustus Le Plongeon who introduced the idea of Mu to the world. Le Plongeon and his wife spent many years extensively photographing and excavating Chichen Itza and other Yucatán Mayan sites. It was his belief that the Mayan culture predated that of Ancient Egypt. While translating a text known as the Troano Codex, Le Plongeon believed that he had found references that showed that Mayan culture was older not just than that of Ancient Egypt but also Atlantis. He went on to claim that the codex also told the story of a land called Mu. This continent had been situated in the Pacific and had experienced a disaster much like that which devastated Atlantis, the end result being that it sank beneath the ocean. It was the survivors of the destruction of Mu who founded the Mayan civilisations, Le Plongeon reported. It was later discovered that Le Plongeon's translations left much to be desired, but he would never concede that he was wrong and maintained his stance until his death.

The story of Mu was taken up by a later writer, Colonel James Churchward. He published a book in 1926 called *The Lost Continent of Mu*, in which he claimed that he had evidence that Mu had once existed in the Pacific Ocean and that it had been destroyed tens of thousands of years ago. He asserted that Mu had once been a huge landmass, reaching from Micronesia in the west all the way to Hawaii in the east.

Churchward also came up with a theory explaining the mechanisms by which both Mu and Atlantis sank. He believed that deep below the earth's surface there existed a series of vast underground caverns. He proposed that if these had once been filled with gas and were then suddenly vented, huge areas of land sitting above the caverns would be thrust below sea level.

Churchward had served in the British Army for 30 years and it was while he was serving in India, he claimed, that he met a priest who showed him ancient tablets written in an unknown language. The priest said that the lost language was called Naacal and he proceeded to teach Churchward how to read the tablets.

Churchward's Mu was certainly a remarkable place. Home to 64 million people, known as the Naacals, this civilisation flourished 50,000 years before our time and possessed technology far beyond that developed by either the Ancient Egyptians or the Mayans. Churchward even went so far as to claim that Mu was the site of the Garden of Eden.

Sceptics rail against Churchward, not least for his lack of scientific rigour. Worse still, his source material cannot be verified or checked, originating as it did from the so-called ancient tablets, which no one has seen since. Scientists point to the numerous coral atolls that are spread right across the Pacific and rightly remind us that these have taken millions of years to form. Furthermore, geologists claim that we can disregard the idea of there ever having been a landmass such as Mu in the Pacific for one very simple reason: continental landmasses are composed of lighter silicon/aluminium-type rocks which lie on top of the heavier silicon/magnesium rocks that make up ocean floors; studies into the Pacific basin show that it is devoid of any silicon/aluminium rocks, suggesting that Mu could never have existed in the region.

However, there is a sunken landmass on the edge of the Pacific that could be a candidate for Mu, although it is not where Churchward stated. Sundaland is the submerged continental shelf that surrounds Indonesia. At the time of the ice ages, it was exposed and above sea level. As the last ice age receded, Sundaland was once again lost under the sea. It has been suggested that Sundaland might have been home to a lost civilisation, and it was almost certainly the route by which Australia was first reached and inhabited.

Although there is no hard evidence for Mu, it has seeped into popular culture, inspiring many books, including several by H.P. Lovecraft, as well as films, video games and even music – the Justified Ancients of Mu Mu, who later became the chart-topping KLF, being the most notable example.

**SEE ALSO:** Le Plongeon, Augustus

# NEW ATLANTIS, THE

Sir Francis Bacon was a philosopher, writer, politician and lawyer who lived in England during the reigns of Elizabeth I and James I and VI. He published several books during his lifetime, but the work in which we are particularly interested, *The New Atlantis*, was published in 1627, the year after his death.

Francis Bacon was born in England in 1561 and educated at Trinity College, Cambridge, where he started to develop a mistrust of traditional Aristotelian philosophy. He studied law at Gray's Inn and became a barrister in 1582. Later in his life, he combined his career in the law with the roles of Member of Parliament and philosopher. Through his mother, he was related to Robert Cecil, the chief minister of Elizabeth I, and he used this connection to advance his position. A further opportunity for patronage developed as he became acquainted with Robert Devereux, Earl of Essex, who tried, unsuccessfully, to persuade Elizabeth to make Bacon Attorney General. In 1601, Essex led his rebellion against Elizabeth and was tried and executed for treason, with his erstwhile friend Bacon distancing himself from the taint of treachery. In 1604, to justify his part in the affair and emphasise his blameless conduct, Bacon published the *Apologie in Certaine Imputations Concerning the Late Earle of Essex*.

With the accession of James VI of Scotland to the English throne as James I in 1603, courtiers such as Bacon looked for opportunities to find advancement under the new regime. Robert Cecil was able to recommend Bacon for elevation to the knighthood, and from 1603 he became Sir Francis. An opportunity to pay tribute to the king came when he published *Advancement of Learning* and dedicated it to James. This book was unusual for a scholarly work at that time in that it was written in English. The compliment was repaid with his appointment as Solicitor General in 1607, crowning his legal career.

*Novum Organum* was published in 1620, a work on the correct way of acquiring knowledge of the world of nature, and this period represented the zenith of his public life. Just one year later, Sir Francis was charged with taking bribes and, after admitting to financial irregularities, he resigned his post and retired to continue writing. His death in 1626 was the result of his curiosity as to whether meat could be preserved by keeping it cool – he caught bronchitis and died after stuffing a chicken with snow!

There is debate as to when *The New Atlantis* was written, with dates of 1614 and 1623 being suggested. The novel describes a country that a group of travellers visit after a long journey, where they are told a story of Atlantis:

> At the same time, and an age after, or more, the inhabitants of the great Atlantis did flourish. For though the narration and description, which is made by a great man with you; that the descendants of Neptune planted there; and of the magnificent temple, palace, city, and hill; and the manifold streams of goodly navigable rivers same . . . yet so much is true, that the said country of Atlantis, as well that of Peru, then called Coya, as that of Mexico, then named Tyrambel, were mighty and proud kingdoms in arms, shipping and riches: so mighty, as at one time (or at least within the space of ten years) they both made two great expeditions . . . the same author amongst you (as it seemeth) had some relation from the Egyptian priest whom he cited. For assuredly such a thing there was.

The country visited by the travellers is called Bensalem and is portrayed as a utopian society. It is located near the Americas, and the idea of Atlantis being near the New World persisted in the work in the nineteenth century of Charles-Étienne Brasseur de Bourbourg and Augustus Le Plongeon.

**SEE ALSO:** Brasseur de Bourbourg, Abbé; Le Plongeon, Augustus

# OERA LINDA BOOK

The *Oera Linda Book* first entered the public domain in 1867, when it was handed to a local librarian in Friesland, a province in the north of the Netherlands, by Cornelis Over de Linden, who claimed that the book had been held safe within his family for generations – since AD 1256, in fact. Over de Linden had been charged with the care of the book, yet he could not read a single word of the text. The librarian, Dr Verwijs, spent four years translating the work after establishing that it was written in an ancient version of the Frisian language.

What was revealed once we were able to penetrate the language barrier and peer through the layers of time was an incredible story. The book tells the tale of the Frisian people and describes their origins. According to the ancient text, they had inhabited an island that was called Atland. However, around the year 2194 BC their homeland was subjected to a series of volcanic and geological assaults which ended in disaster. Here is how the original home of the Frisians came to be destroyed, as described in Chapter 22 of the *Oera Linda Book*, which is titled 'How the bad time came':

> During the whole summer the sun had been hidden behind the clouds, as if unwilling to look upon Irtha. There was perpetual calm, and the damp mist hung like a wet sail over the houses and marshes. The air was heavy and oppressive, and in men's hearts was neither joy nor cheerfulness. In the midst of this stillness Irtha began to tremble as if she was dying. The mountains opened to vomit forth fire and

flames. Some sank into the bosom of Irtha, and in other places mountains rose out of the plain. Aldland, called Atland by the navigators, disappeared, and the wild waves rose so high over hill and dale that everything was buried in the sea. Many people were swallowed up by Irtha, and others who had escaped the fire perished in the water.

The Frisians scattered and fled where they could, some seeking refuge in the Scandinavian lands while others headed for Britain. Further afield, other survivors of the catastrophe landed in the Mediterranean. The book mentions characters such as Nef Tunis and Nef Inka, who established their own kingdoms. Nef Tunis has been linked with the god Neptune, and some researchers have suggested that Nef Inka might have sailed west and landed in South America, the Inca naming themselves in his honour. This is only speculation, because the *Oera Linda Book* loses track of Nef Inka, but it is an interesting train of thought nonetheless. One other character is mentioned, a woman called Nyhellenia, also known as Minerva. She is said to have founded Athens and the inference is that she became a great goddess of the Greeks and the Romans in later years.

Such a story has clear similarities with the traditional tale of Atlantis that Plato left us. The *Oera Linda Book* contains many references that seem to be pointing to a shared origin for the two legends. For example, Nef Tunis and Nef Inka and the other founders of civilisations all share characteristics with figures such as Osiris and Quetzalcoatl, individuals who are said to have taught humanity valuable lessons and skills. Another interesting point is that some of the people of Atland are described as being tall and fair-skinned with blue eyes. We often find these attributes in other peoples connected with the legend of Atlantis, such as the Guanches of the Canary Islands and even the Mesoamerican god Quetzalcoatl himself.

A fascinating aspect of the *Oera Linda Book* is the account of the goddess of the people of Atland, Frya. The culture of Atland was clearly a matriarchal society and was ruled by a series of women who were known as earth mothers. These queens or priestesses were celibate and in the earliest sections of the *Oera Linda Book* we read how Adela refuses the honour because she wishes to marry and have a family. This worship of female deities echoes Plato's account of the land of Atlantis.

Though the book is said to date from AD 1256, it was actually composed from an original written in AD 803, with portions of the text dating from AD 560 and some even as early as 2194 BC. It is said to have been through a constant process of copying and preserving of the text down through the generations that the book has survived for so long.

This process is described in the book itself, and the text starts with an introduction, a letter from the author to his son, Okke:

> Okke, my son —
>
> You must preserve these books with body and soul. They contain the history of all people, as well as of our forefathers. Last year I saved them in the flood, as well as you and your mother; but they got wet, and therefore began to perish. In order not to lose them, I copied them on foreign paper. In case you inherit them, you must copy them likewise, and your children must do so too, so that they may never be lost.
>
> Written at Liudwerd, in the year 3449 after Atland was submerged — that is, according to the Christian reckoning, the year 1256.
>
> Hidde, surnamed Oera Linda — Watch!

The Frisian people today are generally described as a Germanic people. They occupy Friesland in the Netherlands and also live in parts of Germany and Denmark. It would seem obvious that their lost land of Atland couldn't have been far from Northern Europe, as so many of its former people settled in that region. So where exactly could Atland have stood? The *Oera Linda Book* is quite explicit and has this to say on the subject:

> Before the bad time came our land was the most beautiful in the world. The sun rose higher, and there was seldom frost. The trees and shrubs produced various fruits, which are now lost. In the fields we had not only barley, oats, and rye, but wheat which shone like gold, and which could be baked in the sun's rays. The years were not counted, for one was as happy as another. On one side we were bounded by the World Sea, on which no one but us might or could sail; on the other side we were hedged in by the broad Twiskland, through which Finda's people dared not come on account of the thick forests and the wild beasts.

Tyskland is a name for Germany in several Northern European languages, such as Norwegian and Swedish, so it would seem that the Atland that is being described here once comprised what is now known as the Netherlands, which border Germany, as well as large areas of the North Sea and possibly the British Isles too. Were all these regions once connected to one another and above water? Many geologists believe that Britain and the Netherlands were once joined and that just a delta separated the two landmasses. Did the catastrophic events described in the *Oera Linda Book* cause a collapse of a large tract of land into the North Sea, or did a flood of huge proportions simply bury this stretch of land beneath the waves? It is a fascinating prospect, and would explain why Britain has its own fair share of Atlantis myths and why in a few cases it has been chosen as a candidate for the site of Atlantis.

One of the many intriguing issues raised by the *Oera Linda Book* is the similarity between the Frisian language and English. If both countries once formed part of a much larger land known as Atland, these similarities would be explained. Of course, the Netherlands and Great Britain are separated only by the North Sea, so any similarities could simply be of the result of migration. However, the case put forward in the *Oera Linda Book* for a much larger, shared homeland should not necessarily be overlooked.

According to the book, those who settled in Britain brought with them the *Tex*, the earliest sections of what would later become the *Oera Linda Book* and upon which the legal system of Atland was based, handed down to the people of that land by their Goddess Frya. It is also thought by some researchers that in time this came to form the basis of Old English common law. There are many examples of this law in the *Oera Linda Book*, including the following:

> If our neighbours have a piece of land or water which it would be advantageous for us to possess, it is proper that we should offer to buy it. If they refuse to sell it, we must let them keep it. This is Frya's Tex, and it would be unjust to act contrary to it.

So does the *Oera Linda Book* really tell of the destruction of Atlantis and the diaspora of her people? There is evidence that seems to indicate that the paper upon which the book was written was produced in a paper mill around 1850. Yet other indicators point to the ink being very old, possibly from the thirteenth century, the date the book was claimed to have been compiled. And so the arguments sway back and forth.

One thing is certain, though: if the *Oera Linda Book* really is an original document that has travelled through time with generations of Frisians, then the history of Europe will have to be substantially rewritten. And if the book turns out to be a fraud, then whoever concocted it was very clever indeed, for when else did a fiction fit so perfectly with the outside world and mesh so neatly with recorded history that it filled in holes and elaborated where our knowledge of history was scant?

**SEE ALSO:** Athens; Canary Islands; Guanches; Plato; Quetzalcoatl

# PHOENICIANS

**T**he people known in the Bible as Canaanites were the early Phoenicians. They originally inhabited an area that today consists of Palestine, the Lebanon, Israel and part of Syria. Two millennia before the Christian era, they were exporting highly prized cedar wood to Egypt. Through their mastery of sailing, they were able to spread their trading links far and wide. The Phoenicians have been suggested as a possible source for the story of the lost continent of Atlantis, so what do we know about them?

The Phoenicians (meaning 'red people') founded many settlements around the Mediterranean Sea; Palermo, Marseilles and Cadiz were among their possessions. Spain, Sicily, Malta and Sardinia still show traces of their Phoenician (also known as Punic) connections and the Phoenicians also established trading posts on the Red Sea. One of the most famous cultures that owed its origins to the Phoenicians was that of the Carthaginians, in present-day Tunisia, who became early rivals for power with the Romans, who eventually defeated them.

The Hebrew, Greek and Roman alphabets had their origins in the writing system developed by the Phoenicians. They were among the very earliest people to realise that to facilitate commercial dealings of almost any kind, the skill of writing is very important, and before the development of their own system they used cuneiform script. They were among the great traders of the ancient world and were renowned for the quality of the artefacts they produced. The Phoenicians prospered greatly, especially by selling tin to the warlike Greeks. Greece had few or no deposits of this metal, which it needed to alloy with copper to make bronze armour for its warriors to use in their all-too-frequent local squabbles. The metal was also widely used to manufacture containers, statues, and so on. The Athenian poet Hermippos (c.350 BC) is quoted mentioning luxury goods in this fragment from Athenaeus, a slightly later writer: 'From Phoenicia the fruit of the palm and fine flour.'

The Persian kings relied heavily on Phoenician naval vessels in the Mediterranean. During 460 BC, the Athenians involved themselves in an Egyptian revolt against their Persian occupiers. The expedition ended in defeat, which the Athenians believed was due to the part the Phoenicians had played. Athens subsequently tried to push them out of Cyprus, which was an important Phoenician base. This too failed. It raises the question of whether the opportunistic Phoenician merchants continued trading with the Athenians and their allies during this time of conflict. Did the traders and their dependants suffer during this period? Did the Athenians have no dates or fine flour for their best bread and cakes?

During sea battles between the Athenian allies and the Persians, the usual method of combat was for the light, high, manoeuvrable Phoenician ships, each carrying 30 or more marines, to sail among the heavier triremes of the enemy and board them, killing the Greeks. This worked well at Artemision in 480, but in the confined waters of Salamis in the same year the Phoenician ships were rammed by the enemy and defeated. Strangely, however, at the sea battle of Eurymedon in 467, the Athenians employed their own marines and instead of the tactic of ramming the enemy with their ships they used their troops to win the victory. Hoplites, archers and javelin throwers were engaged. Even in the 430s, by which time the Athenians had belatedly decided that ramming was their best method of attack, not all Greek cities were using this effective method.

In 332 BC, Alexander the Great took the Phoenician naval bases from the Persians. With this power at his disposal, he was able to face an Athenian fleet at Amorgos, south-east of Naxos, and achieve victory. The Phoenicians no doubt had the satisfaction of seeing this as a long delayed revenge for their defeat at Salamis. However, from the time of Alexander in the Eastern Mediterranean they seem to have been assimilated into the Hellenistic culture of their neighbours and ceased to be a distinctive people.

An unusual aspect of the Phoenicians is that they seem not to have coveted other people's territories; they were simply peaceful traders, living for the most part in quite small settlements. (An exception to this was their great city of Sidon, which had very close links with Athens, tolerated by their overlords, the Persian kings.) The Phoenicians even paid rent for their occupation of Carthage for many years. Carthage was founded by emigrants from Phoenician Tyre, probably a little after 800 BC. Africans and Spanish tribes traded their metals for items that they prized, such as woven cloth and wine. The Carthaginians appear to have been more aggressive than their forefathers in the Eastern Mediterranean, as they tried to preserve their trading monopolies by destroying the shipping of rival states.

They found it necessary to build strong walls to defend their city, realising that their own belligerence was likely, at some time, to attract reprisals. Eventually, the emerging power of the Roman Republic found its interests clashed with those of the Carthaginians. The later stages of the hard-fought Punic Wars saw the famous Hannibal crossing the Alps from the Carthaginian territories in Spain and attacking Italy from the north, terrorising the Romans for many years. The final phase resulted in Roman victory in the year 146 BC. Carthage was destroyed. But Phoenician blood could not be eradicated, and today there can be no part of the Mediterranean area where the population has no genetic links to these people. The Romans were later to refound the city of Carthage.

Anthony Birley's excellent *Septimius Severus: The African Emperor* charts the rise of Septimius to hold the reins of power in the Roman Empire from 193 to 211 AD. His two sons briefly succeeded him as emperor. Septimius, from Lepcis Magna in Libya, came from Punic stock and probably spoke the Phoenician language as well as Latin, perhaps with an accent. A Phoenician became for a time master of the Mediterranean world and so proud of his origins was he that he spent a fortune on enhancing his native city and cultivating its civic pride. The remains of the city overlooking the sea may be seen and admired by visitors to the present day.

Diodorus Siculus, the Greek historian of the first century BC, claimed that the Phoenicians had access to an island in the west, beyond the Pillars of Hercules; it was large and bountiful, and they guarded the approach to it jealously. Since the Phoenicians seemed to sail to the four corners of the known world, if any people knew of lands unvisited by others, it would be them. Could this *terra incognita* have anything to do with Atlantis?

Some have suggested that the story that was told to Solon by the Egyptians and that made its way ultimately to Plato might have originated with Phoenician traders. As they were renowned for their seafaring abilities, this idea is certainly very plausible. Furthermore, it has also been claimed that the power that dominated the Mediterranean spoken of by Plato was not Atlantean in origin but Phoenician, and that the battles he describes were not between Athens and these mysterious Atlantean forces but between Athens and their old adversaries the Phoenicians.

It is now thought that the Phoenicians may have traded not just in the Mediterranean but as far away as the Americas. A geologist, Mark McMenamin, has found what he believes is a world map on a Phoenician coin from Carthage that was minted sometime between 350 and 320 BC. What he claims is a map seems to show Asia, Europe and the New World. Could the gods who arrived on the shores of Mesoamerica, the bearded, fair-skinned travellers who arrived in boats, actually have been Phoenicians?

All of these strands point to the possibility that it was the Phoenicians who inspired the story of Atlantis, that the Phoenician civilisation, with the grandeur of its culture and the great reach of its naval arm, was the one that Plato was describing.

**SEE ALSO:** Athens; Diodorus Siculus

# PILLARS OF HERCULES

The Pillars of Hercules, or Heracles, is the name given to a geographical feature found at the eastern end of the Strait of Gibraltar, generally accepted to refer to two promontories which form the entrance to the Mediterranean Sea. Heracles was the Ancient Greek name for the mythological hero who undertook twelve labours as penance for the killing of his wife and children. He is probably better known today as Hercules, which was how the Romans referred to him.

The earliest written reference to the Pillars of Hercules are to be found in the works of the Greek historian Herodotus, in the fifth century BC. However, it is their appearance in Plato's *Timaeus*, written in 360 BC, with which they are more usually associated:

> Our records tell how your city checked a great power which arrogantly advanced from its base in the Atlantic Ocean to attack the cities of Europe and Asia. For in those days the Atlantic was navigable. There was an island opposite the strait which you call (so you say) the Pillars of Heracles, an island larger than Libya and Asia combined; from it travellers could in those days reach the other islands, and from them the whole opposite continent which surrounds what can truly be called the ocean. For the sea within the strait we are talking about is like a lake with a narrow entrance; the outer ocean is the real ocean and the land which entirely surrounds it is properly termed continent.

The northern pillar is the Rock of Gibraltar and the southern one is usually identified with Monte Hacho in the Spanish enclave of Ceuta in Northern Africa. The other candidate often cited is Jebel Musa in Morocco.

According to Greek mythology, the pillars were created as Hercules completed one of his twelve labours. The tenth of these labours was to steal the cattle owned by Geryon and kept on the island of Erytheia in the western Mediterranean. On his way to the island, Hercules was confronted by a vast mountain that blocked his path. This peak had once been Atlas, the Titan having been turned into a mountain after Perseus showed him the head of Medusa. Rather than climb the great mountain, Hercules split it in two using his mace. With this one action, he changed the landscape of the area for ever and the waters of the Atlantic Ocean and the Mediterranean Sea rushed in and were joined, thereby creating the Strait of Gibraltar. One half of the original mountain became Monte Hacho and the other the Rock of Gibraltar. Ever after these were known as the Pillars of Hercules.

They even appear today on Spain's national flag, supporting the coat of arms. Intriguingly, the Latin motto on the flag, *Plus Ultra*, translates as 'there is more beyond'. It has been suggested that this is a reference to the Pillars of Hercules being seen as a gateway to the rest of the world, rather than as the entrance to the Mediterranean.

It is to Plato that we return next, as we find ourselves doing time and again. He mentioned the pillars further in *Critias*. It is clear from the following passage that they were viewed as dividing the known world of the Mediterranean civilisations from the outer, unknown world:

> We must first remind ourselves that in all nine thousand years have elapsed since the declaration of war between those who lived outside and all those who lived inside the Pillars of Heracles. This is the war whose course I am to trace.

In looking at the pillars in this context, we must ask whether, as well as delineating a geographical frontier, they also marked some spiritual boundary. Much has been written of the significance of pillars found inside temples – and later churches and cathedrals – all over the Mediterranean. What did sailors passing the Pillars of Hercules on their way into the outer world feel as they crossed over?

We can only guess at the emotions they must have experienced as they passed the northern and southern pillars, leaving the safety of their known world. But a clue is perhaps to be found in Dante's *Inferno*. In Canto 26, Dante meets Ulysses (the Greek warrior who ended the Trojan War by devising the idea of the wooden horse) in the eighth pouch of the eighth circle of hell. Dante is told that Ulysses passed through the Pillars of Hercules only to find Mount Purgatory. It is there that Ulysses' ship was caught in a whirlpool and the ship sunk with the loss of everyone on board.

This idea that purgatory lay outside the pillars is particularly interesting. There is plenty of indication in Dante's work that the Pillars of Hercules marked the boundary of man's permitted exploration:

> I and my company were old and slow
> When at that narrow passage we arrived
> Where Hercules his landmarks set as signals,
>
> That man no farther onward should adventure.
> On the right hand behind me left I Seville,
> And on the other already had left Ceuta.
>
> 'O brothers, who amid a hundred thousand
> Perils,' I said, 'have come unto the West,
> To this so inconsiderable vigil . . .'

Was this superstition also prevalent in Plato's time? How were the people of Atlantis viewed if their land existed outside the known borders of the world? We shall never know, yet we can at least be grateful that Plato left for future generations specific mention of the Pillars of Hercules so that we can continue the search for the true location of Atlantis.

**SEE ALSO:** Atlas; Plato

# PIRI REIS MAP

The Piri Reis Map has caused controversy in the world of cartography because it appears to show an Antarctica free of ice, with the continent's geographical features clearly mapped. Because today Antarctica is almost completely covered by ice that is up to 2.5 km thick in some places, it was only in the 1940s that scientists were first able to map the continent's coastline, deep below the ice.

So if the Piri Reis Map truly does depict Antarctica, this implies that it must have been drawn at a time before the ice advanced. Dates for an ice-free Antarctica vary but several researchers believe that it could have been free of ice between approximately 15000 and 6000 BC. To complicate matters, there is no known civilisation that is a candidate for completing such a map during that era. The question, then, seems to be: does the Piri Reis Map really show Antarctica? To answer that, let's start with the history of the map itself.

Piri Ibn Haji Mehmed was born in 1465 in Gallipoli. He became a privateer for the Ottoman Navy, fighting the Spanish, Genoese and Venetians, amongst others. He eventually joined the Ottoman Navy formally, at the invitation of the Sultan, and was given the rank of admiral, or *Reis* in Turkish, which is how we come to know him as Piri Reis.

During his escapades in the navy, Piri Reis collected as many maps as he could, as well as drawing his own charts of the coastlines he visited. These he compiled into a large volume, *Kitab-i Bahriye* (*Book of the Sea*), which was presented to Sultan Süleyman the

Magnificent. However, it is not for this book but for a single map that Piri Reis is most famous.

It was in the year 1513 that Piri Reis drew the map that now bears his name. Inscribed on a single piece of gazelle skin, the map we see today is only the left-hand half of a larger world map. The map contains 117 place names as well as 30 inscriptions. One of these inscriptions details the source maps and charts that Piri Reis used to compile his map. He numbers these at twenty, including eight Egyptian maps of Ptolemy, that he says date from the time of Alexander the Great, an Arabic map, four Portuguese maps and one by Columbus that contained details of the New World.

The Piri Reis Map has been praised for its detail, especially in its representation of the South American coastline. The interior of this continent is also shown and there are clearly rivers running down from the Andes and flowing to the coast. Remarkable as the finished map is, it is its depiction of a southern landmass that bears a strong resemblance to Antarctica that has brought the Piri Reis Map notoriety.

Antarctica was officially discovered in the 1820s, with the first landing taking place in 1821. So its appearance on a map of 1513 provokes a great deal of interest. Other maps of the period also show what scholars claim are imagined southern lands, the so-called 'terra australis', or 'unknown land of the south' (after which Australia was eventually named). However, what makes the Piri Reis Map special is the degree to which the southernmost continent marked on the map resembles Antarctica.

Charles Hapgood, author of *Maps of the Ancient Sea Kings*, initiated a survey into just how accurate the Piri Reis Map is. He contacted Harold Ohlmeyer, Commander of the Reconnaissance Technical Squadron of the US Air Force, who commented that, in his opinion, the Piri Reis Map corresponded remarkably with the results of a seismic profile of Antarctica made in 1949. He went on to say that he was at a loss to explain how this information could be present on a map made in 1513.

Hapgood put forward the idea that Antarctica had not always sat directly over the South Pole. He proposed that, through a process which he named 'crustal displacement', the earth's crust is able to shift in one piece, much like the loose skin of an orange. Originally, Hapgood stated that this process could occur very rapidly once the appropriate trigger events had taken place and many criticise Hapgood for this very point; however, what many people miss is that Hapgood later went on to alter his calculations, finally concluding that the process could take up to 5,000 years to complete. He states that the last time such a displacement concluded was 9500 BC, the result being that Antarctica ended up directly over the South Pole.

Hapgood goes on to declare that Piri Reis had access to maps that were drawn prior to this cataclysmic event – before 9500 BC – and that the mariners who had drawn the source maps had actually mapped the whole of the earth, including Antarctica. It was left to later authors to build upon this work and, in *When the Sky Fell*, Rand and Rose Flem-Ath put forward the idea that the lost land of Atlantis had actually once been Antarctica, before the continent had experienced the disastrous 30-degree crustal displacement detailed by Hapgood.

There were legends throughout the Middle Ages about *terra australis*, a southern land yet to be found, and critics of Charles Hapgood suggest that it is this that Piri Reis represents on his map, not Antarctica at all. However, if we ignore for a moment all the evidence laid out by Hapgood and accept the possibility that Piri Reis is showing us a mythical land, the question still remains: if such a legend of a southern land had always existed, where did such tales originate? Could these very legends have been started by sailors who had seen the old source maps?

What we will never know is which parts of the map were culled from which charts. Elements in the north-west section seem to indicate that they were copied from Columbus's own map, as the same mistakes are present on both, yet we cannot so clearly trace every feature to its source map.

However, on Columbus's map there is no Antarctica, yet it exists on the Piri Reis Map. Remember that Piri Reis tells us himself that he used source maps that had once been held at Alexandria in Egypt. The Library of Alexandria was destroyed in antiquity and what maps it may once have contained we can only imagine in our wildest dreams. Could it have been from maps once held there that the continent thought to be Antarctica was drawn?

Eventually, the debate boils down to one question: did Piri Reis stumble across a map that contained detailed accounts of the geography of Antarctica and did he incorporate these elements into his own map, or is he merely depicting a legendary southern land that had yet to be navigated? The definitive answer is still to be discovered.

**SEE ALSO:** Hapgood, Charles

# PLATO

Plato (c.427–c.347 BC) came from a distinguished Athenian family and was much influenced by the life and death of his mentor Socrates, whom he greatly admired. He left Athens for a while after the condemnation and death of Socrates, disgusted with the way the city was then governed. He believed that there would not be good governance until either philosophers became rulers or rulers became philosophers. For some years, he travelled, certainly to Italy and Sicily, where he tried and failed to introduce his ideal of the philosopher king, and to other places, which may have included Egypt.

Plato was without doubt the most famous philosopher of the ancient world. He produced a huge number of literary works over a period of around fifty years, most of which appear to have survived. In two of these works, *Timaeus* and *Critias*, he introduces the subject of the lost land of Atlantis. In these works, Plato was either preserving the legend of a long-lost continent or starting one of the greatest wild-goose chases in history. When candidates for the location of Atlantis are proposed today, it is to Plato's descriptions that writers turn, to compare his description of the canals and the city of Atlantis with the geography under examination.

His writings include the *Publications*, all of which we have, comprising 25 dialogues and the *Apology*, a vindication of Socrates. There are also 13 letters, about which there is much controversy since some scholars do not believe them to be genuine. The early dialogues aim at giving pen portraits of people. His description of Socrates, without which we would know nothing of that great philosopher, is of a physically ugly man with a brilliant, argumentative mind, strong, stubborn and determined. Plato and his exemplar believed that virtue is knowledge, but what this knowledge should be is only vaguely described. It may mean that an individual should be alive to the goodness and happiness he possesses. Virtue can be taught and consequently, in Plato's account of Socrates' teaching, he expresses surprise that those who rule cities do not ensure that it is taught to their sons. Real knowledge ensures that people do not willingly do wrong and as a result happiness ensues.

Socrates apparently annoyed people who questioned him by destroying their assumptions that they had knowledge. He would ask them questions of his own, each of which was designed to elicit a particular response. Ultimately, it would often become clear that the preconceived ideas of those who came to seek answers from Socrates were incorrect. Since no one enjoys the experience of being proved foolish or wrong, this did not make Socrates at all popular and led ultimately to his being sentenced to death on spurious charges. Plato was so greatly influenced by Socrates' trial and its outcome that it informed his own philosophy.

One of the results of the trauma of seeing his friend and mentor hounded to death in what passed for a democracy was that Plato believed that good government needed to be conducted by experts totally unanswerable to the people governed and uncontrolled by a rigid constitution. The rule of law is useful only in the absence of expertise. Next in line come a benevolent monarchy, law-abiding aristocracy and democracy, lower still is lawless democracy, then rule by oligarchs and tyrants. It may be seen at once that this proposal has practical flaws in that the 'experts' in government would have to be very exceptional humans indeed not to take advantage of unfettered power. Yet in his *Republic*, Plato points out that, in his opinion, 'Democracy passes into despotism.' An ideal form of government is extremely elusive, to the extent that if it actually existed we would all want to live under it. In his own time, Plato was not without opposition; for instance, Isocrates criticised him for being impractical, for not really dealing with things of importance. Isocrates believed that usefulness should be at the heart of education. In *Helen*, Isocrates wrote:

> There are some who are very proud of their ability to formulate an absurd and impractical proposition and then make a tolerable defence of it. There are men who . . . [say] it is impossible to make or deny a false statement . . . They

should remember that it is much better to be able to form
a reasonable judgement about practical affairs than to have
any amount of precise but useless knowledge, and that it is
better to have a marginal superiority in affairs of importance
than to excel in detailed knowledge of no consequence.

In his *Euthydemos*, Plato made fun of the eponymous Sophist, who
can demonstrate to Socrates that Socrates' father, Sophroniskos,
is not his father merely by playing with questions and statements
which cannot be denied. The more down-to-earth Isocrates felt that
the exercise was of little or no value whatsoever.

When in Athens, much of Plato's teaching was done at the
Academy, within a gymnasium, in a grove of trees very near a
sanctuary dedicated to the hero Hekademos, who gave his name to
the area.

Plato had an unflattering view of his homeland, Attica. In *Critias*,
he claims Attica is like 'the skeleton of a body wasted by disease;
the rich soft soil has all run away leaving the land nothing but skin
and bone'.

Visitors to Greece today will find that, over two millennia
later, the soil still supports sufficient vegetation to make the place
attractive. Equally, those who read Plato's writing in our own day
cannot fail to be struck by the author's ability to vary his style; he
can write narrative expressing humour or sadness, he can describe
great events with passion or solemnity.

Plato's philosophy did not remain a thing of its own time. The
thinkers of the Roman Empire were fascinated by his ideas, among
them the great Marcus Tullius Cicero (106–43 BC). Cicero in turn
exerted an influence long after his death on early Christian writers
such as saints Jerome and Ambrose. Controversy arose as to whether
virtue came from the grace of God or from human efforts. In Verona
in the year 1345, Cicero's letters were rediscovered, and the scholar
Petrarch copied them and based much of his own thinking on them.
Other humanist writers followed suit. In *Who's Who in the Ancient
World*, Betty Radice points out: 'The continuity of Greek thinking
through Rome and western civilization could hardly have been
maintained if Cicero had not transmitted it.' This 'Greek thinking',
of course, is largely synonymous with Plato's thinking.

Plato did not only influence the Christian world, however. The
great Islamic sages such as Al-Farabi (*c*.878–*c*.950 AD) and Averroës
(1126–98 AD) were familiar with the thinking of Greek philosophers
such as Plato himself and also Aristotle, his great pupil. Clearly, to

Muslims, Plato's belief that philosophers make the best rulers is totally compatible with their belief in the precepts of Mohammed, teacher and ruler. Jewish philosophy has also been influenced by the teachings of Plato, as well as those of Aristotle and the Islamic philosophers, although, to Jewish thinkers, Aristotelian philosophy was most worthy of study.

This revival of Platonism, which became hugely important to thinkers of the pagan world of the third century AD, has been given the name Neoplatonism. Along with Plato's own philosophy, it takes elements of the precepts of Pythagoras and Aristotle, and also includes Stoic beliefs. Although the Emperor Justinian suppressed the pagan schools which remained in the year AD 529, the impact of the Greek philosophers was far too potent to be lost to the world. Plotinus (c.204–270 AD) is usually thought of as the founder of Neoplatonism, although the term itself was only used from the early nineteenth century and Plotinus would have thought of himself simply as a Platonist. In Renaissance times, Giovanni Pico della Mirandola (1463–94 AD), an Italian nobleman and author of *Oration on the Dignity of Man*, gave a new impetus to philosophy and particularly to humanism, which accepted that religious truth might be at least partially understood by both Christians and non-Christians. For Pico, the philosophy of Plato and his school was valuable, and during the Renaissance period it gained renewed currency. Pico wished to test the value of all forms of philosophy and religion to Christian thought.

It has been said of the poetry of Homer that to try to understand it is rather like trying to peel an onion, each layer having another layer beneath. This is equally true of the works of Plato. His own thoughts and teachings were heavily influenced by others, especially his hero Socrates. In the dialogues, since Socrates is apparently the main participant, it is argued by some that the historical Socrates' views are being represented, rather than being mediated by Plato. It is also unclear exactly what Plato himself believed, since he implies much but is not particularly explicit about his views. His philosophy was added to and amended by his pupil Aristotle, and since then by scholars and thinkers of the succeeding centuries. The theologies of some of the world's great religions owe a debt to Plato, who was the first great thinker to argue that the soul is immortal because it was created by God. While disease can destroy the body, the soul, emanating from God, is incorruptible.

The *Encyclopaedia Britannica* sums up Plato's work thus:

# PLATO

The influence of Plato can be traced throughout Western culture from Aristotle through St Augustine, from Pascal to A.N. Whitehead, an eminent twentieth-century metaphysician who declared: 'The safest general characterisation of the European philosophical tradition is that it consists of a series of footnotes to Plato.'

**SEE ALSO:** Athens; Critias; Timaeus

# PLINY THE ELDER

**G**aius Plinius Secundus (*c*.23–79 AD), known to us as Pliny the Elder, to distinguish him from his nephew and adoptive son Pliny the Younger, was commander of the Roman fleet at Misenum, Italy, in August 79. For some time, he had been observing signs of disturbance in Vesuvius, the huge volcanic cone which he could clearly see from across the Bay of Naples. By night, he noticed a red glow; by day, increasing plumes of smoke. He was fascinated and kept the situation in mind as he attended to his daily duties.

As a friend of the Emperor Vespasian (ruled 69–79 AD), he was a powerful and influential figure, but it was not as a politician that he had made his mark on Roman history. He was a man of the equestrian class (a knight, in other words), a little below senatorial rank, who had, it appears, a fairly comfortable station in life, with no financial problems. A Roman of his rank generally embarked on a military career or chose the law or administration to make his way. He went into the army, at one time being captain of a squadron of cavalry, yet he was not a man to waste his leisure time lounging about the officers' mess. While campaigning in Germany, he embarked upon a history of his country's military exploits against the Germans and a monograph concerning methods of fighting using cavalry armed with javelins (which at this time was generally done by auxiliary troops from the provinces, not by citizens). He was also the biographer of his friend and patron Pomponius Secundus, with whom he had much in common.

By AD 58, he had returned home to Italy and was leading a quiet life out of the limelight. It is believed that he had little respect for the Emperor Nero and the government of the time and so kept his head down. He may have done some law work but generally seems to have devoted his time to scholarly pursuits. After Nero's suicide in AD 68 and the accession to the throne of three short-lived claimants, the legions in the east declared their support for Vespasian, who was campaigning against the Jews who were once again revolting against Roman rule in Palestine. Vespasian left his eldest son, Titus, to finish the work there and made his way to the city of Rome to take up the role of emperor. Titus and Pliny had served together in Germany, and Pliny therefore had a connection with the new ruling family, which may have been the reason for his appointment to senior administrative positions, including those in Spain, Gaul and Africa.

Vespasian, a very down-to-earth and practical emperor with a sense of humour, was, presumably, more to Pliny's taste than Nero. He clearly gave satisfaction in his posts and was appointed to the imperial council. Pliny's relaxation included writing a history comprising 31 books, which were only published after his death. He dedicated another work, which is the only one still available to us, his *Historia Naturalis* (*Natural History*), to his old comrade Titus. His other writings are mentioned by Pliny the Younger, some of which suggested ways in which public-speaking techniques might be improved.

The *Historia Naturalis*, in 37 books, ranges widely over subjects such as botany, zoology, medicine and aspects of geology, art and architecture. He can be criticised for not discriminating between the probable and the improbable; some of his statements were, even in his day, known not to be true, and even if some had been believed in days gone by, some were plainly ridiculous. However, he was not trained in scientific methods and despite this many of his observations were of value and of great interest. For example, he tells us of some of the petty deceits of society, such as how freedmen and even slaves wore gold-plated iron rings on their fingers to give others the impression that they were, like Pliny himself, of equestrian rank.

One of the most fascinating aspects of the culture of the Roman Empire is that the elites of societies who were not Italian were able to appreciate and participate in events and customs which were traditionally Roman. Britons, Africans, Greeks, Gauls, Iberians and others were assimilated in this way. Pliny saw this cultural colonisation as a duty given to the Romans by the gods, the task of civilising other peoples. Pliny was displaying an old-fashioned and traditional view of Roman superiority, an attitude that was instrumental in the building of the Empire and in its longevity. More modern empire builders have taken a similar view of their own natural superiority, though not usually with such lasting success.

Pliny was clearly a man of great enthusiasm with a massive curiosity concerning the world around him. Imagine, then, his reaction as the eruption of Vesuvius unfolded before his eyes. He ordered his fleet to prepare to sail the short distance across the water to help and hopefully to rescue some of the inhabitants, whose lives were clearly now at risk. The air was filled with the stench of sulphur; a huge cloud of expelled gases and debris rose and discharged its contents upon the heads of the poor souls below. Tremendously hot thermal currents rolled down the sides of the volcano, hideously incinerating all in their path. The citizens of Herculaneum had little chance of escape, though those at Pompeii who were alert and nimble enough managed to do so.

Pliny could scarcely credit what was happening but his curiosity was such that he had to get as close as he could in order to observe the phenomenon. A brave man, he gambled his life – and lost, when he was overcome by the choking fumes and died at nearby Stabiae. His memory lives on, however, through his surviving great work.

In the *Historia Naturalis*, Pliny states that a king of Numidia, North Africa, named Uba, had had plans for farming the sea-snail murex, which yielded a valuable dye, at Atlantis. The mucus extracted from these creatures could be transformed into the famed Tyrian purple. Pliny describes the whole process, from harvesting the molluscs using mussels as bait through the extraction and manufacture of the dye to the actual dyeing process. He places Atlantis about 12,000 km from Cadiz in Spain. In addition, Pliny mentions another island which is reported to be 'also called Atlantis' off the coast of Africa.

# PLUTARCH

At the time of the Renaissance, it was the re-emergence of the *Lives* of Plutarch which inspired many to undertake a study of classical literature and culture. Since the collapse of the Western Roman Empire, the Eastern, so-called Byzantine Empire, which survived in some form until AD 1453, had preserved much of the knowledge of the ancient world, as had the emerging Islamic states. It was the Byzantines who kept alive many of the works of Plutarch, in particular a monk named Maximus Planudes (*c*.1260–*c*.1310 AD), born near modern Izmir, in what is today Turkey.

Mestrius Plutarchus, generally known as Plutarch, lived in Chaeroneia in Greece about 32 km from the great Temple of Apollo at Delphi, famous for its oracle. The temple stands on the slopes of Mount Parnassus, high above extensive olive groves, which are still to be seen. He acted as co-priest there for the final 30 years of his life. He was rich enough to own an estate, which was visited by people anxious to meet this man of letters, and was fortunate in having his talent recognised during his lifetime. Plutarch also found time to serve as a local politician, an activity expected of a man of his standing, and he served as mayor of his town.

He wrote and gave lectures, visiting not only nearby Athens but also Italy and Egypt. Such was the distinction of his thinking that his fame spread throughout the Roman Empire. Just below the temple in which he served is a spring that is the source of water which, if drunk, is said to impart the gift of wisdom. If true, and if Plutarch drank there, perhaps it explains the quality of his mind. His overriding interest seems to have been studying the pattern of people's lives. He produced dialogues, 78 essays and other works.

The *Moralia* is the title given to all the extant works apart from Plutarch's monumental *Lives*. Some of its contents are short essays, derived from earlier writers such as Aristotle and Plato or from Stoic and Epicurean works, philosophising on the question of morals. He comes over as a warm personality, well placed to write advice to a young man just entering a political career. Plutarch uses the wisdom he has gained during his own life and adds to it the moral conclusions he has come to as a result of his historical research. He favoured couching his work in the form of a dialogue, creating conversations through which his philosophical views were revealed. It was a common method not only in his day but also in earlier works. His Pythian dialogues, as they are known, are not only concerned with philosophy but also with religious attitudes and beliefs, and are based largely on his experiences as a priest of Apollo.

Some of the titles might raise a smile today. He asks the question whether water animals are more intelligent than those who live on land. However, the emphasis is not so much on answering the question one way or another but rather on philosophising around the issues raised by the subject in a rational way.

His philosophy was based on Plato's teachings. As he was a Platonist, it was probably inevitable that Plutarch should mention Atlantis in his *Lives*. His life of Lycurgus brings us the conception of the ideal commonwealth, a utopian state. He also writes, in *Parallel Lives*, on Solon:

> Plato, ambitious to elaborate and adorn the subject of the lost Atlantis, as if it were the soil of a fair estate unoccupied, but appropriately his by virtue of some kinship with Solon, began the work by laying out great porches, enclosures and courtyards, such as no story, tale or poesy ever had before. But he was late in beginning, and ended his life before his work. Therefore the greater our delight in what he actually wrote, the greater is our distress in view of what he left undone. For as the Olympieium in the city of Athens, so the tale of the lost Atlantis in the wisdom of Plato is the only one among many beautiful works to remain unfinished.

Plutarch belonged to the Roman Empire and while the language of the day was Latin for matters pertinent to the national government, in the Greek-speaking parts Latin was much more of a second language. Conversely, fluency in Greek was increasingly becoming the mark of learned men, even in Rome itself, and this tendency increased over time. Plutarch was one of the pragmatic Greeks of his day who accepted that while his people held power through their learning, military power belonged to the Romans, and reasoned that the two, with their different strengths, would gain more from cooperating than they would from being antagonistic. This is one of the main reasons why Greek cities vied with one another for the honour of being granted permission to erect and maintain temples dedicated to the genius of Roman emperors; rather that than smart as subject people under the yoke of an oppressor.

In return, for very many years after the conquest of Greece, the Roman administration was happy for its subject people to retain their old customs and laws and even to mint their own local currency, provided only that these activities did not subvert Roman authority and interests. Local coinages, even the billon tetradrachms of Alexandria, Egypt, ceased to be issued in AD 296 under the great Diocletian and his associates. On the other hand, as the Western Roman Empire struggled vainly to maintain its sovereignty, the eastern part of the empire increasingly became the stronger one, and Greek language, culture and attitudes began to dominate the 'Roman' world.

Plutarch's *Lives*, of which more than three-quarters of a million words survive, compared the lives of pairs of men, one Roman and one Greek, who had certain experiences in common. The emphasis throughout is on the peculiarities of human nature. Clearly, the research necessary for exploring the lives of men who had lived centuries before must have been very time-consuming and difficult. This was long before the days of the printed, mass-produced book. Among the Greeks, Athenians Theseus (the ancient king and national hero), Pericles and Nicias (both politicians and generals), appear, as do the Spartans Agis and Agesilaus (both kings) and Lycurgus (founder of the constitution), as well as Pelopidas, the energetic Theban statesman, general and patriot. Romans thought worthy of inclusion were that phenomenon Julius Caesar and his kinsman, the consul and general Gaius Marius, as well as politician and lawyer Cicero and the legendary Coriolanus. The *Oxford Classical Dictionary* has this to say of the *Lives*:

> Tantalizing and treacherous to the historian, Plutarch has
> won the affection of the many generations to whom he has

been a main source of understanding of the ancient world by his unerring choice of detail, his vivid and memorable narrative, and his flexible and controlled style.

**SEE ALSO:** Athens; Plato; Solon

# POPOL VUH

The *Popol Vuh* is a sacred book of the Quiché kingdom, a Mayan civilisation based in Guatemala. *Popol Vuh* means 'Book of the Community', although some have translated it as 'Book of Written Leaves'. It is been popularly known as the 'Mayan Bible'. Essentially, the book contains a Mayan creation story and tells the tale of the origins of the Maya, how they came to live in Mesoamerica and how the Quiché kingdom was founded.

The book was discovered – or, more accurately, rediscovered – in the mid-1800s by Dr Carl Scherzer. It had had a convoluted life. It seems to have been based on a Mayan-language copy of a much older book, written using western letters, as writing in the old Mayan script was outlawed after the Spanish conquest. This was found in 1702 by a Spanish priest called Fransisco Ximénez in a Guatemalan town. Instead of following the usual practice of destroying what were considered heathen books, Father Ximénez instead made a copy of it and even translated it into Spanish. This version of the *Popol Vuh* was sent to a library in Guatemala City, where it became hidden amongst many other documents and lost for over a hundred years. It was Dr Scherzer, along with Brasseur de Bourbourg, who rediscovered the book in 1854.

The *Popol Vuh* is divided into four volumes and the first few chapters, in which we learn that the first humans were made of wood, deal with the creation of the earth. However, the gods destroyed these creatures because they had no soul and could not honour their creator:

A flood was brought about by the Heart of Heaven; a great flood was formed which fell on the heads of the wooden creatures. Of tzité [a berry tree], the flesh of man was made, but when woman was fashioned by the Creator and the Maker, her flesh was made of rushes. These were the materials the Creator and the Maker wanted to use in making them.

However, these creatures too were destroyed:

But those that they had made, that they had created, did not think, did not speak with their Creator, their Maker. And for this reason they were killed, they were deluged. A heavy resin fell from the sky. The one called Xecotcovach came and gouged out their eyes; Camalotz came and cut off their heads; Cotzbalam came and devoured their flesh. Tucumbalam came, too, and broke and mangled their bones and their nerves, and ground and crumbled their bones. This was to punish them because they had not thought of their mother, nor their father, the Heart of Heaven, called Huracán. And for this reason the face of the earth was darkened and a black rain began to fall, by day and by night.

Finally, humans were created and they gathered in a place called Tulan. However, they faced many challenges and eventually the language of the tribes became divided, so they decided to take part in one final migration. It was under the leadership of the god Tohil that they attempted this and, finally, after many hardships, they crossed the sea. It is said that the sea parted before them:

It is not quite clear, however, how they crossed the sea; they crossed to this side, as if there were no sea; they crossed on stones, placed in a row over the sand. For this reason they were called Stones in a Row, Sand Under the Sea, six names given to them when they [the tribes] crossed the sea, the waters having parted when they passed.

Is it possible that the 'stones in a row' were in fact islands that the tribes used to reach their new homeland? It is an intriguing thought and no other satisfactory explanation comes to mind, except perhaps the intervention of the gods themselves.

At one point, the *Popol Vuh* tells of how some tribes fled east while others went west; those who travelled to Central America became the Quiché people. Interestingly, this relates closely to what is written in the *Oera Linda Book* of the Frisian people of northern Europe, which recounts the story of the followers of Nef Tunis and Nef Inka, who travelled east and west respectively after the destruction of their home, Atland.

Other Mesoamerican myths tell of this great migration: the Aztecs have a legend that tells how they arrived in Central America from a place called Aztlan after travelling across the sea. Many other tribes tell similar stories, of surviving a great flood and finally landing in their new home. One aspect of this original homeland that the *Popol Vuh* alludes to is that this place where humankind was born once contained people of all races, who seem to have lived side by side as one: 'There they were then, in great number, the black men and the white men, men of many classes, men of many tongues, that it was wonderful to hear them.'

Although the copy of the *Popol Vuh* that we have in our possession was written sometime in the sixteenth century, it documents events that seem to date far back into prehistory. Lewis Spence published in 1908 the first English translation of the sacred book of the Quiché. He believed that the *Popol Vuh* had been handed down from generation to generation via oral tradition and that the myths contained in it had been kept alive in this way:

> That the Mayan civilisation was of very considerable antiquity is possible, although no adequate proof exists for the assumption. This much is certain: that at the period of the Conquest written language was still in a state of transition from the pictographic to the phonetic-ideographic stage, and that therefore no version of the 'Popol Vuh' which had been fixed by its receiving literary form could have long existed. It is much more probable that it existed for many generations by being handed down from mouth to mouth – a manner of literary preservation exceedingly common with the American peoples. The memories of the natives of America were and still are a matter for astonishment for all who come into contact with them. The Conquistadores were astounded at the ease with which the Mexicans could recite poems and orations of stupendous length, and numerous instances of Indian feats of mnemonics are on record.

So it would seem that we have an ancient tale in our hands, one that echoes other accounts of the land we have come to know as Atlantis. Surely all these independent accounts must be speaking of a common homeland, an origin for the many civilisations founded by those who fled its ravaged shores and made new homes in both east and west?

**SEE ALSO:** *Oera Linda Book*; Brasseur de Bourbourg, Abbé

# POSEIDON

Arguably the best ancient site to visit in order to gain an impression of the territory of the great god Poseidon, whose realm was the sea, is Cape Sounion. There, a short trip away from Athens, lie the remains of his temple, overlooking the waves far below from their elevated position. The great bronze statue of Poseidon which once stood there is now safely housed in the National Museum in the Greek capital, but for the visitor with imagination his presence may still be felt not only by the ruins of the temple but also across the great expanse of water from which, according to his followers in the ancient world, he would occasionally rise up into view.

As Greece is a land of mountains and islands the sea was, and still is, a highway. Even mainland cities only a few miles apart but with precipitous mountains between them might as well have been on different planets. Modern road- and tunnel-building techniques have solved some of the communication problems but in some places the boat is still the quickest and easiest way to go from place to place and, where an island does not have an airport, virtually the only way to reach it. On a calm, sunny day the prospect of a boat trip is inviting; but when Poseidon becomes angry, which can occur quite suddenly in the Mediterranean Aegean area, a safe harbour is something to pray for.

Poseidon, in consequence, was a powerful figure, who needed to be cultivated and often placated, as a seafarer's life depended as much on the god's goodwill as on the skill of the sailors and the reliability of their craft. In his *Critias*, Plato describes a shrine to

Poseidon within the palace of the city of Atlantis. The temple was described as:

> a stade in length, three hundred feet wide and proportionate in height, although somewhat outlandish in appearance. The outside of it was covered all over with silver, except for the figures on the pediment, which were covered in gold . . . It contained gold statues of the god standing in a chariot drawn by six winged horses, so tall that his head touched the roof.

Fish of all varieties was a major source of protein for the Ancient Greeks and the many fishermen would clearly have been among Poseidon's devotees. His status in the pantheon of gods was high; he had the honour of being one of the gods worshipped at the Erechtheum, which stands next to the Parthenon on the Acropolis in Athens. This is an unusual temple, since it was not dedicated to just one deity. Poseidon's companions are Athena, the protector of the city, and Erechtheus, the legendary king. This king, in the very early days of Athens, had a palace on the summit of the Acropolis, it is said. At this time, Poseidon was attempting to impress the people of the city sufficiently to be able to rule them. According to some, he killed King Erechtheus; others claim that the greatest god, Zeus, Poseidon's brother, did the deed with his thunderbolt. After his death, Erechtheus's palace was converted into a temple and he was worshipped as a god. The Erechtheum, which was finished c.406 BC and still stands, was built to please three deities, namely the god-king himself, Athena and Poseidon.

The Romans knew Poseidon as Neptune and, like the Greeks, they regarded him as a powerfully built man who not only held sway over the sea but was also responsible for earthquakes. He was, all in all, a very dangerous character, who, like the gods generally, was not to be trusted too much and above all never crossed. Depictions of Poseidon usually show him clutching a trident, a three-pointed spear, and he is often surrounded by sea creatures both real and mythical. However, it is hard to positively identify images of Poseidon since there were many other sea-gods in the Graeco-Roman world, including Oceanus, who can easily be confused with him. Plato once likened the Greeks to frogs sitting round a pond, referring to his people's dependence on the water which surrounded them. Naturally enough, these 'frogs' believed that many of their gods had associations with water. Poseidon had, in very early times, been a god of water generally, but gradually he metamorphosed into a saltwater god.

Poseidon was also the god of horses. It seems to be generally agreed that he fulfilled this duty even before he became ruler of the sea. In his *Critias*, Plato writes that the kings of Atlantis made sacrifice of horses to Poseidon by night. The association with horses may stem from the story of how Poseidon's mother, Rhea, decided to protect him from his father, the great god Cronos, who had the unpleasant habit of swallowing his children as soon as they were born. Being, apparently, much brighter than Cronos, she gave him a young foal, which was duly gobbled up in place of their son. Hence the baby survived and eventually grew to assist his siblings who had escaped the same fate in deposing their father. Poseidon was declared ruler of the sea, Zeus of the sky and Hades of the underworld. It should be noted that there are several variations of this tale.

Some surviving illustrations and models of Poseidon show him driving a horse-drawn chariot, as described by Plato. He is an imposing sight, and one calculated to strike fear into the bravest heart. He could be a merciless enemy. One who offended him was the wily Odysseus. Homer tells us at the beginning of the *Odyssey*: 'But all the gods pitied him, except Poseidon; he remained relentlessly angry with godlike Odysseus, until his return to his own country.' Odysseus's problems in crossing the wine-dark sea to return home to Ithaca following the end of the Trojan War form the basis of the epic tale.

Poseidon once tried to impress the Athenians by challenging their goddess, Athena, to a contest to prove which of them would be most valuable to the people of the city, or so the story goes. Poseidon hit the earth with his trident and out flowed brackish water. Unimpressed, the goddess plunged her spear into the ground and an olive tree bearing fruit appeared on the spot. Since olives are valuable to people, whereas salty water generally is not, she was the accepted winner.

The inhabitants of Rhodes travelled to the volcanic island of Thera (also known as Santorini) to erect a temple to Poseidon Asphalios, or Poseidon, Giver of Safety. The siting of this temple clearly had to do with the god's function as the creator of earthquakes and the wish of those living in the area to keep his goodwill. It is interesting that this island, according to doctors Angelos Galanopoulos and Spyridon Marinatos, was where Atlantis was situated until it was destroyed in an enormous volcanic eruption around one and a half millennia BC.

Despite Athena having been chosen over him as supreme god of Athens, Poseidon's valuable consolation prize was to be the protector of the Corinthians. The people of Corinth also worshipped Helios, a solar deity, but they were in sufficient awe of Poseidon the earth-shaker to wish to cultivate his patronage. It was believed that Pegasus, the winged horse, was one of the offspring of Poseidon and Medusa, and for many years the coins of Corinth featured Pegasus on the reverse. Poseidon was in the top rank of the gods of the pagan world. It may be hard to believe today that there were those who believed in his actual existence, but the Thessalian and Messenian royal families claimed him as an ancestor in order to impress their contemporaries. No doubt future generations will look at some of the many and various religious ideas of our day and find it incredible that even the gullible could ever have believed them.

**SEE ALSO:** Athens; Atlas; Critias; Plato; Santorini

# PROCLUS

Proclus Lycaeus was a Greek philosopher born around AD 412. He is most famous for his commentaries on Plato's works. At the time Proclus was writing, much of Plato's work was misunderstood, and Proclus analysed and restored Plato's great philosophies.

There is an interesting passage in Proclus's *Memorandi* in which he states that 300 years after Solon's voyage to Egypt, Crantor, another celebrated Greek philosopher, travelled to the town of Sais in the north-western Delta. He was taken to the temple of Neith, the local deity, goddess of the hunt and of war. There he was shown a column covered with hieroglyphs that recounted the history of Atlantis. Crantor obtained a translation from Egyptian scholars, who told him that their account was in exact accordance with that of Plato.

Neither the column nor the temple of Neith survive in Egypt today, so we are totally dependent on ancient sources for our information. Plutarch gives another account of the temple of Neith, writing that the temple bore the inscription:

> I am All That Has Been, That Is, and That Will Be. No mortal
> has yet been able to lift the veil that covers Me.

That sounds very much like a fitting epitaph for the lost island of Atlantis itself.

**SEE ALSO:** Crantor; Plato; Plutarch; Sais

# PROMETHEUS

In order to understand the connection between Prometheus and the Atlantis mystery it is necessary to appreciate the fact that legend, myth, folk memory and religion were inextricably entwined in the ancient world.

The Greeks were conscious that there had been cataclysmic happenings in the past and had developed beliefs which were essentially attempts to explain what had happened and why it had occurred. For instance, like many of their contemporaries, they believed that the earth had been subject to a terrible flood. In the story of Noah and his ark, or in the Sumerians' Gilgamesh Epic (in which we learn the story of Utnapishtim, which has parallels with the Atlantis legend), and in myths from other cultures, including pre-Columbian America, Scandinavia, China and India, similar traditions are to be discovered.

The Greeks had their own legends of Atlantis, including one according to which the Athenians, the last bastion of defence, had successfully driven off the previously all-conquering Atlantean invaders, forcing them to return to their homeland. In the aftermath of their defeat, the vanquished Atlanteans and their country disappeared beneath the waves as a result of an earthquake. Like Noah's Flood, this was alleged to have occurred long ago in the mists of antiquity. One version describes the Atlanteans as giants or Titans.

In those early days of mankind, the Greeks believed, there were gods – supremely powerful, and fickle, creatures with whom one should keep on good terms if possible – and humans – weak and frail for the most part and subject to the vicissitudes of life. Between the two fairly clearly defined groups of human and divine beings, there were others who were demigods or superhumans, often the result of interbreeding between humans and deities, who were able to interfere in both the realms of the gods and of the mortals. To some extent, perhaps, the Christian concept of angels is a parallel. God, it is believed, sent the angel Gabriel as a messenger to a human, Mary, announcing the part she would play in the Christian story. Gabriel was not a god, but neither was he a human. There are other parallels, such as the old Christian ideas concerning Satan: he was not a god, but could visit and tempt humankind, although he was not one of them.

The lyric poet Pindar (c.518–c.438 BC) claimed that when Zeus, Poseidon and Hades divided, respectively, the sky, sea and earth among themselves to be their realms, Helios, who became god of the sun, was not present and when it was realised that he had no kingdom, he chose to rule the 'plot of land', so valuable to men, which he observed rising from the depths of the ocean.

Helios married a nymph and with her had seven sons. This raises interesting questions concerning Greek gods. How near divinity is a nymph, how near human or god is the son of a god and a nymph? What of his offspring? How many generations later will the progeny become purely mortal? An example of the strange relationship between humans and gods is the fact that a hero who begins as a mortal, such as Hercules, son of a god, might perform such wonderful deeds that he becomes a god himself and is worshipped as such. After Greece became absorbed into the Roman Empire, the Greeks were generally quite happy to erect temples to the divinity of the emperors. This was something the Romans themselves were not at all keen to do, at least during the lifetimes of the rulers, although to acknowledge the 'genius', or attendant spirit, of the emperor was a rather different, political matter.

A race known as Titans, or *Titanes*, who had been deities before the takeover of Zeus and his brothers, were ousted by the new Olympian gods. Titans were giants and they had ruled very well. Humankind had been the creation of the Titan Prometheus, who had smiled upon them and encouraged them to live peacefully, sharing the earth's bounty. When the Olympian gods appeared on the scene, the Titans were understandably unwilling to relinquish their realm to the newcomers. After a struggle lasting a decade, the defeated Titans were banished to Tartarus (meaning a deep hole, or hell). If they were immortals, had they enough spirit and cunning left to return again to walk the earth?

The wily but generally benevolent Prometheus (whose name means 'forethought') dared to offend the mighty Zeus on more than one occasion. He was the son of Iapetos and Clymene, an ocean nymph famed for her attractive ankles! Among their other sons was Atlas, condemned by Zeus to hold up the heavens. Prometheus, described by the very early poet Hesiod as 'subtle and wily', was condemned by Zeus to be chained to a pillar to which came an eagle to eat his liver. As he was immortal, this did not kill the unfortunate Titan, who grew a new liver each night only to have it pecked away during the following day, this torment to continue for eternity, or according to some versions for a mere 30,000 years. The hero Hercules was responsible for chasing off the eagle, however, and freeing Prometheus. Zeus forgave Hercules, a son whom he favoured, on the grounds that this deed would add to his fame, and Prometheus he left at liberty.

What had Prometheus done to anger Zeus? Quite apart from being a despised Titan, he once attempted to cheat the great god when an animal had been sacrificed. It was the practice, unless the whole of an animal was being burnt as an offering (the original meaning of the word 'holocaust'), for the carcass to be divided into the god's portion and the parts to be eaten by the celebrants present. What Prometheus tried to get Zeus to accept consisted of just bones wrapped in fat, which, apart from the nutritious marrow, was of little use to anyone else. Hesiod, in his *Theogony*, explains that this was the origin of the custom adopted by mortals since that day whereby the inedible parts of a sacrifice were offered to the gods. Zeus forbade the use of fire by men as a consequence of this offence. Prometheus, however, stole fire, hiding it in a reed, to give the precious gift to mankind. Zeus avenged this deed by making a beautiful woman, Pandora, from whom all females since then are descended, so that women became

> a great curse to mortal men with whom they live, no help in accursed poverty and ready enough to share wealth. They are like drones which are fed by the bees in their roofed hives and are their partners in crime. For the bees are busy all day till the sun goes down and build white honeycombs, while the drones stay at home in the safety of the hive, filling their bellies with the toil of others. High thundering Zeus made woman to be a similar curse to mortal men, and partner in vexation.

It must be recalled that Hesiod, one of the very oldest Greek poets, lived long before the time of women's liberation and political correctness. Hesiod went on to explain that a man who tries to avoid this curse by not marrying will have no support in his old age, which is not entirely logical if women are really to be considered to be so worthless to their menfolk.

It is not clear which of Prometheus's two offences merited the punishment involving the chains and the eagle. Hesiod claims that it was the deception over the sacrifice, but, according to the Athenian playwright Aeschylus (if, as is generally thought, Aeschylus is indeed the author of *Prometheus Bound*), it was the theft of fire. Aeschylus also claims that Prometheus knew the secret of Thetis, which was that she would bear Zeus a son greater than his father, and revealed the fact to Zeus as the price of his liberty. In other versions, it is Themis, who was an oracle, who reveals this secret, whereupon both Zeus and Poseidon decided they would be better off not having children by Thetis, as they had intended, and give her instead to the adventurer Peleus, as most deserving her. Greek myths and legends are often contradictory and complicated, and there is often more than one version of a given story.

The Roman Ovid (43 BC–17 AD) states in *Metamorphoses* that when Prometheus created man, he made him from water and earth, which we should probably understand as clay. He chose to make man in the image of the gods, 'to stand erect and turn his eyes to heaven'. The legend goes that, after the people were created, Prometheus's rather dim third brother, Epimetheus, was tasked with giving all forms of life abilities: to some he gave speed, strength or ability to use weapons; to others flight; some he gave tolerance of living below ground, and so on. Not all creatures were given the same abilities or the same dietary needs. Epimetheus, however, had only considered the survival of animals, so, realising that men were a very special case, Prometheus endowed them with the ability to create things themselves to improve their quality of life. He stole artistic skills from Hephaestus, the lame god of metalworking, and from the great goddess of wisdom, Athena. To this he added the stolen fire, which got him into so much trouble. We may see fire as representing knowledge, like the apple taken by Eve in the Garden of Eden. Prometheus, then, was the friend of the humans and suffered for his kindness.

**SEE ALSO:** Deluge Myths

# PUNT

**P**unt was a land described by the Ancient Egyptians, known also
to them as Ta Netjer, which means 'God's Land'. However, the
only details we have of this legendary land have come down to us
solely from the records of the Egyptians. Furthermore, despite the
fact that the pharaohs are said to have made several expeditions
to the Land of Punt, we still have no idea where this fabled land
actually was. The conservative viewpoint is that Punt was probably
located in eastern Africa, perhaps near where Sudan and Eritrea, or
possibly Somalia, are located today.

However, the Land of Punt is of interest to us because it has
been suggested that, far from being a country within Africa, it
was in fact Atlantis itself. Certainly, all of the expeditions of which
we have details were conducted by sea rather than by land. This
in itself does not rule out Africa, because it would have taken
an immense amount of effort to carry all of the spoils from Punt
back across Africa, so a fleet of ships would have been by far the
easiest method. In order to answer the question of whether Punt
was Atlantis, we need to examine first the descriptions given of the
Land of Punt by the Egyptians who ventured there.

The first expedition was mounted during the reign of King Sahure,
probably sometime around 2480 BC, and it is documented that this
voyage returned to Egypt with myrrh, malachite and electrum,
among other materials. The next reported mission to the Land of
Punt, during the rule of King Montuhotep II, roughly around 2000
BC, yielded more incense, as well as perfumes and gum, all of which

were used in Egyptian religious rituals as well as in the process of mummification.

The most famous and well-documented expedition to Punt was made in the reign of Queen Hatshepsut during the fifteenth century BC. Hatshepsut sent five large ships, which departed from the Red Sea. When they returned, they were laden with every form of produce imaginable:

> . . . loading of the ships very heavily with marvels of the country of Punt; all goodly fragrant woods of God's-Land, heaps of myrrh resin, with fresh myrrh trees, with ebony and pure ivory, with green gold of Emu, with cinnamon wood, khesyt wood, with two kinds of incense, eye-cosmetics, with apes, monkeys, dogs, and with skins of the southern panther, with natives and their children. Never was brought the like of this for any king who has been since the beginning.

Queen Hatshepsut's temple at Deir el-Bahri is full of reliefs detailing the expedition and also documenting the Land of Punt itself. The chieftain of Punt, Parakhu, is shown with his large, and some believe disfigured, wife, Aty. Two races are seen to occupy the Land of Punt, a darker race like the West Africans and another that looks very similar to the Egyptians themselves.

James Henry Breasted, the American Egyptologist, believed that these depictions at Deir el-Bahri were some of the most impressive reliefs in the whole of Egypt. In *A History of the Early World*, he wrote:

> These are undoubtedly the most interesting series of reliefs in Egypt, and form almost our only early source of information for the land of Punt. They are as beautiful in execution as they are important in content. They record an important expedition of the queen thither, which was successfully concluded just before her ninth year.

It has been suggested by some researchers that Queen Hatshepsut's incredible mortuary temple complex was itself built to a design obtained from Punt and that it recreated a style of architecture found in that land. Certainly, nothing like Deir el-Bahri existed in Egypt either before or after Queen Hatshepsut and it truly is a unique monument. Furthermore, nothing even faintly like it has ever been found anywhere else in Africa. Rather, it does seem to bear a resemblance to a building we might expect to find in the city of Atlantis as described by Plato. However, we do not have inscriptions attesting to the existence of such buildings in the Land of Punt and the reliefs at Deir el-Bahri show only what appear to be wooden huts in the region.

Despite the appeal of the idea that the Land of Punt might be Atlantis, the truth is that there is no evidence at all to suggest that this was the case. We don't, for example, have any indication that Punt ever underwent a great catastrophe such as befell Atlantis. There is no record of a deluge striking Punt, no mention of it falling beneath the waves. What's more, at the time of Dynastic Egypt, it is clear that Punt had not been destroyed; on the contrary, the country was yielding up unending treasures, if the accounts of the Pharaohs can be believed.

However, there is a very odd story that has been left to us from Ancient Egypt. Known as 'The Tale of the Shipwrecked Sailor' and dating from sometime around the year 1900 BC, it concerns a mariner who is washed up on an island and after three days is shaken by a noise as loud as a clap of thunder:

> The trees shook, and the earth was moved. I uncovered my face, and I saw that a serpent drew near. He was thirty cubits long, and his beard greater than two cubits; his body was as overlaid with gold, and his colour as that of true lazuli. He coiled himself before me . . . Then he smiled at my speech, because of that which was in his heart, for he said to me: 'You are not rich in perfumes, for all that you have is but common incense. As for me, I am prince of the land of Punt, and I have perfumes. Only the oil which you say you would bring is not common in this isle. But, when you shall depart from this place, you shall never more see this isle; it shall be changed into waves.'

We do not know for sure that the island itself was called Punt, the serpent merely says that he was a prince from that land; but the connection is fascinating, because here we have a legend from Egypt that mentions both a sinking island and Punt in the same breath.

Could it be that Punt was not in Africa but was in fact the lost kingdom of Atlantis, rich in natural treasure, as described by Plato? It certainly is a possibility. However, it remains much more likely that Punt was in the region of modern-day Somalia or Sudan. As for the title 'God's Land', that too is a mystery that we still have not solved. One inscription at Deir el-Bahri, rather than clearing up the issue, simply throws up more questions. It details Queen Hatshepsut herself offering all the treasures of Punt to the god Amun:

> [Amun] entrusted me with establishing for him Punt in his house. I made for him Punt in his garden . . . Her majesty herself offers the marvels of Punt to Amun . . . The likes of which was never brought by any king since the beginning of earth . . . such a thing never happened for the other kings who appeared on this earth.

So it would seem that Queen Hatshepsut, as well as bringing much needed precious commodities back to Egypt, also brought many of the animals and plants of Punt so that she could reconstruct the so-called God's Land in Egypt for Amun's satisfaction. This does not answer the question of why Punt was thought of as God's Land, but it does seem to confirm the importance of the place in the ancient world.

As an interesting footnote, in 1998 a region in the north-east of Somalia became a semi-autonomous state and the leaders of this new province announced that from then on it would be called Puntland. Many believe that Somalia was the location for the legendary Land of Punt and the government of the region obviously agrees.

**SEE ALSO:** Atlantis, City of; Plato

# QUETZALCOATL

Quetzalcoatl is the name of a Mesoamerican god. The word means 'feathered serpent' or 'plumed serpent'. He was a major deity of the Olmecs, Toltecs and Aztecs in particular, and his story is a complex one.

Across the cultures in which he was worshipped, he was given many roles and several different versions of his origins and life can be found. He bore many gifts and bestowed much knowledge upon the people he came into contact with. For example, it was Quetzalcoatl who is said to have been responsible for inventing the advanced calendar that the Mayans used, with which they calculated the day that would mark the end of the world.

Quetzalcoatl is often described as light-skinned and bearded, and as such was very different in appearance from the native people of Middle America, who were free of facial hair. Ironically, it was this image of their god that led to the downfall of the Aztecs. When the Spanish conqueror Hernán Cortés landed on the coast of the Americas in 1519, he was greeted as the return of Quetzalcoatl incarnate, such was his resemblance to the god of their numerous legends. The Aztecs were so in awe of Cortés that their leader, Moctezuma, sent gifts to the Spaniard that included many treasures linked to Quetzalcoatl, and in particular the headdress from a statue of the god.

If, instead of welcoming Cortés with open arms, the Aztecs had quelled the Spanish invasion as soon as it had landed, before the foreigners had had time to gain the assistance of other local tribes, then the outcome of the campaign could have been very different and the destruction of the Aztec nation might have been avoided. Cortés landed with a mere 500 soldiers and it is hard to imagine him suppressing the Aztecs had he been greeted with hostility instead of hospitality.

The Toltec version of the story of Quetzalcoatl tells how the god returned after a long period of absence to teach them about the arts and science. In *An Introduction to the Study of Maya Hieroglyphics*, scholar Sylvanus Griswold Morley describes Quetzalcoatl's legacy:

> The great God Kukulkan, or Feathered Serpent was the Mayan counterpart of the Aztec Quetzalcoatl, the Mexican god of light, learning and culture. In the Maya pantheon he was regarded as having been the great organizer, the founder of cities, the former of laws and the teacher of the calendar. Indeed his attributes and life history are so human that it is not improbable that he may have been an actual historical character, some great lawgiver and organizer, the memory of whose benefactions lingered long after death, and whose personality was eventually deified.

Parallels have been drawn between Quetzalcoatl and the Osiris of Egyptian myth. According to Egyptian legend, Osiris left his throne early in his reign as the first king of Egypt and travelled the country teaching and educating the general populace. He was especially known for imparting knowledge of agriculture. Similarly, Quetzalcoatl is said to have introduced humankind to maize. Furthermore, Osiris was connected with corn and was worshipped at both sowing and harvesting times.

Osiris was the god of the dead and was also connected with rebirth and renewal, having been briefly brought back to life by Isis. So too Quetzalcoatl was seen as a symbol not only of resurrection but also of death. As well as having these roles, Quetzalcoatl was seen as the inventor of the calendar and measurement of time, and of writing and books, roles that in Egypt we see attributed to Thoth. Quetzalcoatl, according to the Toltecs, had an opposite, known as Tezcatlipoca, a dark, evil force, who sent Quetzalcoatl into exile. It was at this time that Quetzalcoatl was said to have left Mesoamerica on a raft of snakes, vowing to return one day. There are strong similarities between this story and that of the conflict between Osiris and his brother Seth.

So is it possible that Osiris and Quetzalcoatl were actually the same god? Or were they both Atlanteans who had arrived in

Egypt and Mesoamerica to teach the same skills and values? It is a fascinating possibility.

The physical appearance of Quetzalcoatl certainly adds weight to this argument. His fair complexion and his beard seem to indicate that he could be of Cro-Magnon descent, the race identified as the most likely candidates for the population of Atlantis. Another race sometimes said to be survivors from Atlantis's fall, the Guanches of the Canary Islands, bore an uncanny resemblance to the description of Quetzalcoatl and it has been suggested that they shared the same origins.

As well as sharing attributes with Osiris, Quetzalcoatl also seems to mirror the idol of the Incas, Viracocha. Here we also have a tale of a god who was fair-skinned, red-haired and bearded. According to legend, Viracocha rose from Lake Titicaca in Peru and created mankind from stones. Just like Quetzalcoatl, he is said to have taught his people everything they knew before sailing away.

In Mesoamerican culture, Quetzalcoatl had many names: Kukulkan, Itzamana, Nacxit, Gukumatz. Are these all references to the same man or is it possible that many men of the same race as the original Quetzalcoatl figure landed in the area, all from the same place and all with the same agenda: to share their knowledge with the local population? In *Fingerprints of the Gods*, Graham Hancock mentions traditions held by the Mayans that seem to indicate that this was the case:

> Certain myths set out in the Ancient Mayan religious texts known as the Books of Chilam Balam, for instance, reported that the 'first inhabitants of Yucatan were the "People of the Serpent".' They came from the east in boats across the water with their leader Itzamana, 'Serpent of the East', a healer who could cure by laying on hands and who revived the dead . . . 'Kukulkan,' stated another tradition, 'came with nineteen companions, two of whom were gods of fish, two other gods of agriculture, and a god of thunder.'

So it seems that there are multiple traditions of white, bearded men arriving to teach the locals how to live more benevolent, fruitful lives. However, when their task was done, they left the shores of Mesoamerica and returned to wherever they had come from. Whether this was Atlantis or another place, we will never know for sure.

What is intriguing is a text which describes Quetzalcoatl leaving

Mesoamerica on a 'raft of serpents'. If Quetzalcoatl was really an Atlantean arriving in the Americas to teach the natives and pass on all the knowledge that he possessed, it is clear that he would have travelled by boat, very possibly on a ship with sails. Note the term 'raft of serpents'. Is a 'serpent' exactly how these ships appeared to the locals and was it their term for this new craft of which they may have had no knowledge? It seems very likely. In that case, it would appear obvious that the natives gave Quetzalcoatl his name after the ship he travelled in. A plumed or feathered serpent is merely a ship with a sail. That would be a very simple explanation of how Quetzalcoatl came to gain his title – he was named after the vessel in which he arrived.

According to legend, Quetzalcoatl's departure from Mesoamerica took place at a place called Coatzacoalcos. It turns out that this name means 'the hiding place of the snake' and, according to Graham Hancock, 'serpent sanctuary'. If the plumed serpents were the vessels in which Quetzalcoatl arrived, then this place name seems to describe a port or harbour where those ships were anchored.

**SEE ALSO:** Canary Islands; Guanches

# SAIS

Although little, indeed virtually nothing, remains today at the Ancient Egyptian site of Sais (Ancient Egyptian name Zau), it was once a very important Egyptian town, dating back at least to the 1st Dynasty (3050–2850 BC), as attested by ivory labels which state that King Horaha built the temple to Neith at Sais. Between 727 and 715 BC and 664 and 525 BC, Sais reached its zenith when it became the seat of power for the 24th Dynasty and the 26th Saite Dynasty pharaohs. Situated in the north-western Delta region, its patron deity was the war-like goddess Neith. According to Plato's *Timaeus* and *Critias*, it was from the priests of the Temple of Neith at Sais that Solon, the Greek law-giver and founder of Athenian democracy, learned of the story of Atlantis and its demise some 9,000 years prior to his visit in around 565 BC.

Spyridon Marinatos, professor of archaeology at the University of Athens, has suggested in *Some Words about the Legend of Atlantis* (1971) that the account Solon was told of Atlantis by the priests of Sais may actually have been confused in part with a popular Egyptian tale entitled 'The Tale of the Shipwrecked Sailor'. Dating to the Egyptian Middle Kingdom (2061–1786 BC), it relates how a sailor was shipwrecked on a mysterious island inhabited by an enormous serpent. The serpent, however, was extraordinary, as not only did it talk but it was enormous, bearded, its body overlaid with gold and its eyebrows made of lapis lazuli. Grabbing the sailor from out of the sea, the serpent took him back to its abode. However, the creature had no desire to hurt the sailor but instead informed him that he had been brought to the 'island of the spirit' by the grace of

196

god. It explains that the island is full of everything anyone desires, in fact 'there is nothing that is not in it, it is full of all good things' (*Ancient Egyptian Literature*, Vol. 1, Miriam Lichtheim). The serpent recounts how the island had once been the home of his brothers and their children but that all apart from him had been burned to death by a star that fell onto the island. It foretells that the sailor will be rescued in four months by his countrymen and gives him many precious gifts to take home with him upon his rescue. The serpent adds, however, that once the sailor has departed, the island will vanish under the sea, never to be seen again.

Marinatos has speculated that this tale illustrates that the Ancient Egyptians were familiar with the concept of a blissful, utopian island whose remarkable inhabitants were destroyed and which eventually disappeared under the sea. As such, Marinatos states that the Egyptian tale 'could have been confused with other traditional accounts concerning Atlantis because they contain similarities'. However, 'The Tale of the Shipwrecked Sailor' is clearly allegorical, pertaining to death and rebirth, and the intelligence and wisdom of the priests must surely suggest that they would have known the difference between a familiar, and by then ancient, parable and the Atlantis legend.

Interestingly, in *The Rise and Fall of Athens*, Plutarch (*c*.46–126 AD) mentions the two priests from whom Solon received some form of instruction and with whom he discussed philosophy: one was Psenophis of Heliopolis and the other was Sonchis of Sais. Plutarch described these as 'the most learned Egyptian priests'. It is, therefore, highly likely that the aforementioned Sonchis of Sais was among those who reported the Atlantis legend to Solon, given that he would undoubtedly have been familiar with the ancient written records of the temple.

Although Plato does not tell us the form taken by the Egyptian 'sacred records' that documented every 'great or splendid achievement or notable event', Proclus (412–485 AD) states in his *Commentary on the Timaeus* that these were actually written on columns within the Temple of Neith, as attested to by Crantor, a student of Plato's philosophy. Unfortunately, none of Crantor's writings have survived to validate and elaborate upon this statement. With little remaining to be studied at the site of Sais, and without any reference to these pillars so far found in the Egyptian record, it is unlikely that we will ever be able to confirm or deny the existence of such pillars and hence the history of Atlantis, or Predynastic Egypt and its environs, as recorded by the Ancient Egyptians.

One classical author who did record details of his visit to Sais and the Temple of Neith was Herodotus, who travelled to Egypt in around 454 BC. Herodotus notes in his *Histories* that the temple at Sais was 'a vast building, well worthy of notice'. He was particularly impressed by the gateway to the temple, 'which is an astonishing work, far surpassing all other buildings of the same kind both in extent and height, and built with stones of rare size and excellency'. Although he mentions seeing the temple with its courts, obelisks, sacred lake and 'pillars carved so as to resemble palm-trees', Herodotus makes no reference to any pillars carved with hieroglyphs that relate the legend of Atlantis. However, he did write about a structure in Sais that he most admired of 'all these wonderful masses', namely a chamber hewn from a single block which had taken the Egyptians three years to transport from a quarry in the south of Egypt to Sais – a journey that normally took just 20 days. Today, all the great and wonderful buildings of Sais have disappeared. This is in part due to the re-use of the stone blocks during the Middle Ages for local buildings, as well as the use, over time, of the remaining mud bricks for fertiliser.

The account of Atlantis as written by Plato relates that the priests of Sais welcomed Solon, happily instructing him on the history of Atlantis and Athens. Plato affirms that the Egyptians were 'very friendly to the Athenians and claim some relationship to them'. In his *Library of History*, written around 30 BC, Diodorus Siculus referred to an old tradition that colonists from Sais founded Athens. Furthermore, he also mentions another, conflicting tradition – that Sais was actually founded by people from Rhodes and Athens – highlighting Greece's actual, or desired, ties with Ancient Egypt.

**SEE ALSO:** Crantor; Critias; Diodorus Siculus; Plato; Plutarch; Proclus; Solon; Timaeus

# SANTORINI

**S**antorini is a group of islands that sit in the Aegean Sea, just north of the Mediterranean. The islands that we see today are the remains of what was once a much larger, single island. In effect, what exists above sea level today is just a caldera, the remnants of the volcano Thera, which dramatically blew itself to pieces when it erupted sometime around the year 1500 BC. The final eruption of Thera is said to have been at least twice as large as the eruption of Krakatoa that took place in the Sunda Strait between the Java Sea and the Indian Ocean in 1883, with dramatic consequences. Thera's explosion is also said to have been roughly 40 times larger than the 1980 eruption of Mount St Helens.

This catastrophic event had disastrous consequences for many of the Mediterranean cultures that were growing up on the shores of the sea, all of them within reach of the spiteful clutches of the volcano. A huge tidal wave swept the region, devastating towns and reaching far inland. Plumes of boiling ash and pumice were ejected high into the sky only to fall on the surrounding lands. Tens of thousands of people, if not more, would have died in the first few days of the eruption. But that was not the end of the disaster. Crops buried under tons of ash would have failed and the effects on the weather systems of the Mediterranean would have been felt for many years afterwards. We will probably, and thankfully, never know what the full death toll was, how many lives Thera claimed.

However, we do have some idea what it must have been like to have lived through that period of destruction, because the awful effects of the eruption were recorded in historical accounts, myths and legends across the region and remembered with dread for centuries afterwards. Many researchers believe that Euripides, the Greek playwright, described the huge tidal wave that was generated by the explosion of Thera in his play *Hippolytus*:

> Just there an angry sound,
> Slow-swelling, like God's thunder underground
> Broke on us, and we trembled. And the steeds
> Pricked their ears skyward, and threw back their heads.
> And wonder came on all men, and affright,
> Whence rose that awful voice. And swift our sight
> Turned seaward, down the salt and roaring sand.
> And there, above the horizon, seemed to stand
> A wave unearthly, crested in the sky;
> Till Skiron's Cape first vanished from mine eye,
> Then sank the Isthmus hidden, then the rock
> Of Epidaurus. Then it broke, one shock
> And roar of gasping sea and spray flung far,
> And shoreward swept, where stood the Prince's car.
> Three lines of wave together raced, and, full
> In the white crest of them, a wild Sea-Bull
> Flung to the shore, a fell and marvellous Thing.
> The whole land held his voice, and answering
> Roared in each echo. And all we, gazing there,
> Gazed seeing not; 'twas more than eyes could bear.
> Then straight upon the team wild terror fell.

The association between the tidal wave and the sea-bull in this passage is an intriguing footnote given that the Minoans – who held the bull sacred and central to their culture – had colonised Santorini and that their entire culture was destroyed by precisely this event.

Some researchers have linked the eruption of Thera with the biblical plagues that afflicted Egypt just prior to the exodus of Moses and the Jews from Egypt to their eventual new homeland in Palestine. Indeed, it would seem that many of the phenomena associated with a volcanic eruption of such magnitude do echo what we see in the plagues of Egypt. In the Bible, in the book of Exodus, we find the following passage:

> Then the Lord said to Moses and Aaron, 'Take handfuls of
> soot from a furnace and have Moses toss it into the air in the

presence of Pharaoh. It will become fine dust over the whole land of Egypt, and festering boils will break out on men and animals throughout the land.' So they took soot from a furnace and stood before Pharaoh. Moses tossed it into the air, and festering boils broke out on men and animals.

The biblical account of the Exodus would have us believe that it was God who created these afflictions in an effort to convince the Egyptians to free the enslaved Jews, but in the form of the volcano Thera we have a much more down-to-earth culprit, and one certainly capable of producing the same horrific conditions.

The Nile Delta of Egypt is a little over 800 km from Thera. However, the Smithsonian Institution has apparently discovered a layer of ash in the Nile Delta that seems to have come directly from Thera. If this is indeed correct, it would indicate that the eruption of Thera was large enough to have devastating effects in Egypt itself. Again, from the book of Exodus:

> The fire ran along upon the ground . . . There was hail, and fire mingled with the hail, very grievous . . . Then the Lord said to Moses, 'Stretch out your hand toward the sky so that darkness will spread over Egypt – darkness that can be felt.' So Moses stretched out his hand toward the sky, and total darkness covered all Egypt for three days.

Additionally, we have accounts from Egypt itself that seem to speak of the same series of events. We find a series of lamentations, written by an Egyptian sage named Ipuwer, preserved on a single papyrus that was found at Memphis and is now held in Leiden in Holland. Here are some extracts:

> Indeed, the land turns around as does a potter's wheel . . . Towns are destroyed and Upper Egypt has become an empty waste . . . Indeed, everywhere barley has perished and men are stripped of clothes, spice, and oil; everyone says: 'There is none.' The storehouse is empty and its keeper is stretched on the ground.

The papyrus describes events that had never before occurred in Egypt and that were obviously catastrophic, resulting in a complete breakdown in living conditions and civilisation itself.

The Papyrus of Ipuwer is said to have been written sometime

during the thirteenth century BC, but appears to relate to events that occurred sometime between the nineteenth and sixteenth centuries BC, when there was great turmoil in Egypt, a period during which several dynasties were squabbling for power in Egypt. It is possible that this instability and the multiple claims to the throne were caused by the extreme hardships brought about by the eruption of Thera. Some even suggest that this is the period when the Hyksos, hordes of foreign invaders, swept into Egypt and took control of the country without a fight.

Comparisons have been drawn between the Papyrus of Ipuwer and the book of Exodus itself, and there are certainly many correspondences. For example, Exodus states 'There was blood throughout all the land of Egypt', while the Papyrus of Ipuwer says 'Plague is throughout the land. Blood is everywhere.' Another passage in *Exodus* tells us that 'All the waters that were in the river were turned to blood', while Ipuwer's document states 'The river is blood.' Many more passages seem to be speaking of the same disaster, so here we clearly have the same series of events described not only in the holy book of the Jews, but in the words of the Egyptians themselves.

There is one final plague that is mentioned both in Exodus and the Papyrus of Ipuwer and this is the tenth plague. In the Bible, it is described as the death of the firstborn of everyone in Egypt, including the Pharaoh. However, some researchers have argued that this 'plague' must refer to the death toll resulting from a cataclysmic event which struck Egypt. In his book *Ages in Chaos*, Immanuel Velikovsky equates this final plague with an earthquake that took many lives. 'According to the Haggadic tradition, not only the firstborn but the majority of the population in Egypt was killed during the tenth plague.' The Papyrus of Ipuwer seems to describe this event: 'Indeed, the children of princes are dashed against walls.' Exodus says: 'And Pharaoh rose up in the night, he, and all his servants, and all the Egyptians; and there was a great cry in Egypt: for there was not a house where there was not one dead.' Is it possible that an earthquake struck Egypt days after Thera had erupted? The evidence for such an occurrence is certainly compelling.

Having examined many of the catastrophic events that appear to have occurred at this time in Egyptian history, it is clear that it may even be possible that the exodus of Moses was itself brought about by the destruction that was wreaked by Thera. The long-term effects of the eruption would have meant that food was scarce and people would have died in their thousands as crops failed and the sun disappeared from the sky. Was this the catalyst that forced Moses to lead his people from Egypt? Was he simply attempting to escape such dire conditions and find a land free of such afflictions? It is certainly a possibility.

Returning to Santorini, we discover that the single island that once existed became the several islands we find today, the mere bones of a much larger landmass. The largest of the islands of Santorini is still called Thera, but now there is also Therasia and Aspronisi, and, in the centre, Nea Kameni and Palea Kameni. This transition from single island to a group of separate islands did not happen overnight and since the extraordinary eruption of 1500 BC the islands have undergone constant evolution. A further eruption in 230 BC split the islands of Thera and Therasia from each other. Palea Kameni rose from the sea in 196 BC and, in more recent times, in 1570, a major collapse of Thera saw a significant portion of the main island slide into the sea.

Excavations on Santorini have revealed that the Minoans from Crete had also populated Santorini. The most well-known of their settlements on the island is the port of Akrotiri, where incredible finds have been discovered. Vibrant and detailed wall paintings have been found amongst the remains, depicting Minoan saffron gatherers and ancient fishermen. At Akrotiri, the earliest examples of water-carrying pipes in the world have been discovered and, incredibly, it has been found that these pipes always ran in pairs, suggesting that the inhabitants of the town had access to hot and cold water supplies. The size and sophistication of the buildings at Akrotiri demonstrate how important and wealthy the port once was and it has been suggested that it was one of the most significant urban centres in the Aegean.

The town was buried below tons of ash and pumice in the death throes of Thera and was only discovered again in the late 1800s, not being finally uncovered until the 1960s. However, the lack of bodies in the layers and also the absence of metal objects or, for that matter, any other portable objects, seems to indicate that the inhabitants had some warning that Thera was going to explode with devastating effect and that they left the town well before the fateful day. In fact, the lowest layer of pumice at the site indicates that it was exposed to the atmosphere for as long as two years before being covered over by a much deeper layer. So it is very likely that the inhabitants of Akrotiri experienced an earlier and much smaller eruption and it was probably this event that inspired them to leave the island for good, before the more destructive explosion.

Santorini was called Strongyle by the Minoans, which means 'the circular one', a reference to its perfect round shape before the volcano marred its appearance for ever. Prior to this, the island was called Kalliste after a sea nymph. Legend states that her father was the god Triton, who gave a clod of earth to the Argonaut Euphemos, which eventually formed the island of Santorini. The tale is recounted in the *Argonautica* as told by Apollonius of Rhodes, the Greek poet of the third century BC.

> Euphemos, after committing his dream to memory, told it to Jason. The dream reminded Jason of an oracle of Apollon's himself, exclaiming: 'My noble friend, you are marked out for great renown! When you have thrown this clod of earth into the sea, the gods will make an island of it, and there your children's children are to live. Triton received you as a friend with this little piece of Libyan soil. It was Triton and no other god that met us and gave you this.'
>
> Euphemos heard Jason's prophecy with joy and did not make it void. He threw the clod into the depths of the sea, and there grew up from it an island called Kalliste, the sacred Nurse of his descendants.

After the devastation of Thera, the islands of Santorini were uninhabited for a time. The Greeks colonised Crete, once home of the Minoans, but Santorini itself remained deserted, possibly because the Greeks feared the fury and violence of Thera. It was inhabited again by the Phoenicians around 1200 BC and the first recorded account of their living on the islands can be found in the Greek historian Herodotus's epic *Histories*:

> Now, there were on the island now called Thera and that same previously Calliste, descendants of Membliareus, the son of Poeciles, a Phoenician man. For Cadmus, the son of Agenor, in looking for Europe, touched at the land now called Thera and, when he had touched, either probably the country pleased him or maybe for another reason he wished to do that following action; for he left down on that island others of the Phoenicians and, in particular, of his own kin, Membliareus. Those inhabited the land called Calliste for eight generations of men before Theras went from Lacedaemon.

Christianity reached Santorini early and in the fourth century AD a church was established and the island was ruled by the Byzantine Empire, which was becoming ever more Christianised. Later still, during the 1200s, Santorini became part of the Catholic Duchy of Naxos and it was at that time that the islands were given their modern name, in honour of a chapel of Santa Irene – a Christian martyr who was burnt at the stake – that was founded on the island.

The destruction of Thera has been seen by many as the antecedent of Plato's story of Atlantis, the seed that flourished into the vivid tale he presented to the world. With the eruption of Thera, we see not only the destruction of the island itself, but also that of many of the neighbouring islands in the Mediterranean. It is now believed that the Minoan culture that had once flourished on Crete was destroyed by the fury of Thera, perhaps not overnight as might be inferred from Plato, but certainly within a few decades. Furthermore, part of Thera did fall beneath the waves after the eruption, so here perhaps we find another element responsible for Plato's tale.

Plato says that the story of Atlantis came from the Egyptians. So is it possible that in the archives of Ancient Egypt the tale of the destruction of Thera and the culture of the Minoans of Crete was preserved by the Egyptian scribes, but that over time the details of the story were lost and altered, so that the location Plato gives for this land he named Atlantis is outside the Mediterranean? Many believe this is the case, presenting as it does a rational explanation for the story of Atlantis that does not involve sunken continents in the Atlantic Ocean.

The volcano of Thera that still lies at the heart of Santorini is far from quiescent. It may be dormant but it is merely biding its time, waiting to erupt yet again. It is possible that the next major explosion of Thera may not be for many thousands of years but the unpredictability of volcanoes means that it could erupt with devastating consequences once again very soon. Next time, it could be our own, modern culture that feels the wrath of Thera.

**SEE ALSO:** Crete; Minoans; Phoenicians; Plato

# SOLON

It is Plato who introduces us to Solon. In his works *Timaeus* and *Critias*, he tells us that it was through Solon that the story of Atlantis came to be revealed to the world. Solon was born around 638 BC and is famous for writing the constitution of Athens and hence becoming the architect of the first democracy in the world. Athens was said to be a city rife with avarice and greed in Solon's day and he set out to devise laws that would ease the lives of all the inhabitants, not just the wealthy. According to Plutarch, Solon considered himself a poor man, but he did not desire to be rich, as the lawgiver explains in this poem:

> The man whose riches satisfy his greed
> Is not more rich for all those heaps and hoards
> Than some poor man who has enough to feed
> And clothe his corpse with such as God affords.
>
> I have no use for men who steal and cheat;
> The fruit of evil poisons those who eat.
>
> Some wicked men are rich, some good men poor,
> But I would rather trust in what's secure;
> Our virtue sticks with us and makes us strong,
> But money changes owners all day long.

It is said that after devising the laws of Athens he went on a tour of the Mediterranean for ten years, not only to remove himself from all the tedious questions that he was becoming embroiled in concerning the new laws but also to allow enough time to pass to see how the new constitution suited the country.

It was during this leave of absence that he found himself in Egypt, the guest of the priests of the temple of Neith in Sais, on the edge of the Nile Delta. At the time of Solon's visit, Sais was the capital of Egypt, the seat of power for the 26th Dynasty and King Amasis II. It was a time of great turmoil in the region and the Greeks were aiding Egypt in her fight with the Babylonians, whose advance they had managed to push back. However, only a few years after Solon's visit, the Egyptians were overrun by the Persians.

In *Timaeus*, Plato tells us that Solon recounted to Plato's grandfather, Critias, the history of Atlantis that he had uncovered in Egypt:

> Listen then, Socrates. The story [of Atlantis] is a strange one, but Solon, the wisest of the seven wise men, once vouched its truth. He was a relation and close friend of Dropides, my great-grandfather, as he often says himself in his poems, and told the story to my grandfather Critias, who in turn repeated it to us when he was an old man. It relates the many notable achievements of our city long ago, which have been lost sight of because of the lapse of time and destruction of human life. Of these the greatest is one that we could well recall now . . .

In Egypt, according to Plutarch, Solon was taught many things by the priests Psenophis of Heliopolis and Sonchis of Sais, but it was in the temple of the goddess Neith that Solon was told details of the country called Atlantis and its history. Plato explains that at the time Neith was considered the founder of the Egyptian capital and that her Greek equivalent was the goddess Athena. This has since been found to be untrue; it is possible that Plato thought this was so because they are both goddesses associated with war.

According to *Timaeus*, Solon found a hospitable welcome in Sais and was told that the Greeks were in some way related to the Egyptians and hence shared the same history. The priests also told Solon that he and the other Greeks knew hardly anything concerning ancient history and proceeded to tell him many tales from the ancient world, of past deluges and disasters and, finally, of the lost kingdom of Atlantis:

> On this island of Atlantis had arisen a powerful and
> remarkable dynasty of kings, who ruled the whole island,
> and many other islands as well and parts of the continent;
> in addition it controlled, within the strait, Libya up to the
> borders of Egypt and Europe as far as Tyrrhenia.

The tale that Solon heard concerned the foundation of Athens
by the goddess Neith 9,000 years prior to Solon's visit and the
subsequent war between Athens and invaders from Atlantis, who
were attacking the whole Mediterranean. Solon was then told that,
after a great battle, Athens eventually became the victor. It is then
said that, not long after Athens had freed all those who had been
subjugated by Atlantis, there was a series of violent earthquakes
and 'in a single day and night of misfortune' Atlantis sank below
the sea. So it was that the tale of Atlantis that has haunted us ever
since was passed down from Solon to Critias, then finally to Plato
and, thanks to his *Timaeus* and *Critias*, on to us.

One question that has puzzled many scholars is why Solon didn't
make more of the story; why, for example, he did not turn the epic
tale into a long poem. He was known as a poet as well as a lawmaker,
after all. Plato himself comments on this in *Timaeus*:

> And one of the clansmen, either because he thought so
> or out of politeness to Critias, said that he thought that
> Solon was not only the wisest of men but also the most
> outspoken of poets. And the old man – I remember it well
> – was extremely pleased, and said with a smile, 'I wish,
> Amynander, that he hadn't treated poetry as a spare-time
> occupation but had taken it seriously like others; if he had
> finished the story he brought back from Egypt, and hadn't
> been compelled to neglect it because of the class struggles
> and other evils he found here on his return, I don't think
> any poet, even Homer or Hesiod, would have been more
> famous.'

It does indeed seem a shame that Solon did not make his great tale
into a poem, because it would surely have rivalled the *Odyssey* and
the *Iliad*. Upon such a missed opportunity hangs a question: why
didn't Solon tell the great story in his own words? Having obtained
the tale of Atlantis from the Egyptians after much travelling, why
didn't he write the story up with all the drama that it deserved?
We do know that when Solon returned to Athens after his ten-

year sojourn he was almost at the end of his life. He is said to have returned from his travels sometime during the 560s BC and he died in 559, so he would not have had a great deal of time in which to complete what would surely have been a lengthy work. And, as Plato says, Solon returned to find Athens in turmoil and had much work to do.

Is this the reason why it was left instead to Plato to tell Solon's story of Atlantis? Or, as some have suggested, did Plato make the whole thing up? Only Plato and Solon knew the answer to that for certain.

**SEE ALSO:** Athens; Critias; Plato; Plutarch; Sais; Timaeus

# SPANUTH, JÜRGEN

Spanuth was born in Leoben, Austria, in 1907. He became a pastor in Germany, in Bordelum, Friesland. It was here that he became exposed to Frisian myths, including the *Oera Linda Book*, which speaks of a land that could once be found in the region called Atland, which sank long ago. After much research, in 1953 Spanuth published his controversial new theory on the location of Atlantis in a book called *Atlantis of the North*.

Atlantis, according to Spanuth, had once been located in the vicinity of what is now Heligoland, a German archipelago situated just off the coast in the North Sea. He put forward the idea that most of the island sank sometime during the twelfth century BC, leaving only the small group of islands that we see today.

Spanuth found evidence that a collection of Norse poems known as the *Eddas*, recorded in AD 1200 but likely to have originated long before that date, refer to a northern land called Attland and a surrounding sea called Atle's path. This corresponds with the Atland that we find in the *Oera Linda Book*. Atle, according to Spanuth, was an ancient sea king who ruled the whole area and who gave his name to the Atlantic Ocean itself. The similarity between the name Atle and that of Atlas, the first king of Atlantis, is striking.

The Greeks had a legend of a mythical race of people called the Hyperboreans, who lived to the north of Greece. It was this land of the Hyperboreans that Spanuth associated with the Attland of the *Eddas*. The Greek belief that the Hyperboreans lived in a land where the sun rose and set just once in a year points to the conclusion that in fact they were referring to a kingdom in the far north. Beyond the Arctic Circle, the sun does in fact shine for six months in the summer, while in the winter it is eternal night. Furthermore, the land of the Hyperboreans was said to be opposite the land of the Celts, which refers probably to Britain, and this is also in accordance with a landmass that might once have sat where Attland is proposed to have existed.

Spanuth, along with others, believed that it was this land of Attland, situated near today's Heligoland, that was the original birthplace of a sea people who invaded the Mediterranean around 1200 BC, after their own homeland sank in a catastrophe brought about by a comet which passed close to the earth. Details of this invasion have been recorded on the walls of the Egyptian temple at Medinet Habu, Thebes (modern Luxor), amongst other places.

To search for evidence to back up his theories, Spanuth undertook a series of expeditions into the North Sea, using his own money as well as sponsorships. He aimed to discover proof of the lost kingdom that he felt sure had once existed in the region. He claimed that there had always been reports of sunken buildings around the island of Heligoland and he proposed an expedition to try to determine once and for all if they were the ruins of Atlantis. In 1953, he found what he claimed were the remains of a sunken city at a depth of 14 m some 8 km south of Heligoland. What clinched it for Spanuth was the fact that he seemed to have discovered parallel walls constructed from rock of three different colours: red, black and white. According to Plato, these were exactly the three colours of stone that were used to build the walls that surrounded the city of Atlantis:

> One kind of stone was white, another black, and a third red
> . . . Some of their buildings were simple, but in others they
> put together different stones, which they intermingled for
> the sake of ornament, to be a natural source of delight.

There is one major problem with Spanuth's ideas. Plato gives the date of the Mediterranean invasion of the sea people from Atlantis and the war between the Atlanteans and the Athenians as 9,000 years before his own time. This is clearly not 1200 BC. However, many researchers believe that Plato became confused over this issue and actually meant 900 years before. If that was the case, we are indeed talking roughly in the region of 1200 BC, the time that we do indeed see recorded accounts of an invasion of the Mediterranean. So for Spanuth's theory of a northern Atlantis to work, we have to agree that Plato made such a mistake. Is it possible that the timespan of 9,000 years that Plato mentions had somehow become corrupted in the telling of the story, as it was handed down through the years? It is; but we cannot rely on that alone to back up this tale of Attland and an Atlantis sitting near Heligoland.

So only further diving and more expeditions can confirm whether this was the true location of Atlantis. If Atlantis really did sit just off the coast of Germany, and if it did sink as late as 1200 BC, there should surely exist the tangible remains of such a culture and we should be able to reclaim enough relics to substantiate Spanuth's claims. The answer, as always with Atlantis, seems to be somewhere on the bottom of the sea – the North Sea, on this occasion.

**SEE ALSO:** Atlas; Celts; *Oera Linda Book*

# STEINER, RUDOLF

Rudolf Steiner was an Austrian philosopher born in the mid-1800s. He was a unique thinker and developed many new concepts that were ahead of their time, including biodynamic agriculture, the scientific discipline of anthroposophy and his own brand of education, known today as Waldorf education. Steiner believed that Atlantis existed long ago in history and he wrote a book in 1904 titled *Cosmic Memory: Prehistory of Earth and Man*, setting out the full spectrum of his beliefs.

His views were very controversial, especially because he claimed to have obtained his ideas about Atlantis not through conventional research but directly from the Akashic records, that body of knowledge that is said to exist in the spiritual plane rather than in the physical world as such. The Akashic records (a term coined by the Theosophists) are said by those who claim to be able to access them to contain details of all that has happened on the earth and in the universe and are accessible, in theory, to everyone; furthermore, everyone in their own way contributes to this all-encompassing library. Steiner detailed his acquisition of knowledge from this source in a collection of essays which were released under the title *From the Akasha Chronicle*.

Quite obviously, this whole area is fraught with difficulty for most Atlantis researchers. While the Akashic records sound a perfect place to conduct research, who can tell if what the individual 'receives' is accurate information or just a figment of the imagination? So, while he provides an interesting account of

Atlantis, what Steiner has put forward clearly does not represent a body of information that we can verify.

We have to add that, if the Akashic records do actually exist, they are themselves likely to be highly ambiguous. Every person has their own world-view and experiences life in a different way; we have only to look at current world events to appreciate that history is not a black-and-white matter, but is coloured by the biases and prejudices each individual holds and by their belief system. If such a vast library does exist, it is likely to hold contradictory information, and people 'browsing' the Akashic records will probably, and quite naturally, receive information that backs up their own theories and ideas. So such a tool, if it truly does exist, can only ever be the ultimate double-edged sword.

But what exactly did Steiner say of Atlantis? Well, the underlying theme is that the mind of the ancient Atlantean was substantially different from that of modern man:

> Our Atlantean ancestors differed more from present-day man than he would imagine, whose knowledge is confined wholly to the world of the senses. This difference extended not only to the external appearance but also to spiritual faculties. Their knowledge, their technical arts, indeed their entire civilisation differed from what can be observed today. If we go back to the first periods of Atlantean humanity we find a mental capacity quite different from ours. Logical reason, the power of arithmetical combining, on which everything rests that is produced today, were totally absent among the first Atlanteans. On the other hand, they had a highly developed memory. This memory was one of their most prominent mental faculties. For example, the Atlantean did not calculate as we do, by learning certain rules which he then applied. A 'multiplication table' was something totally unknown in Atlantean times. Nobody impressed upon his intellect that three times four is twelve. In the event that he had to perform such a calculation he could manage because he remembered identical or similar situations. He remembered how it had been on previous occasions.

Steiner also pointed out that this ancient race of man did not use speech but instead communicated via telepathic images.

It was this difference in the Atlanteans' mode of thought to which

Steiner attributed the greatness of Atlantis itself and he took many of the underlying concepts and used these to create a new method of educating children. This is probably Steiner's greatest legacy. His methods are still practised in many select schools throughout the world, under the guise of Steiner or Waldorf education. In the Waldorf schools, a child's growth is split up into three distinct phases: the Physical Body, which the child possesses between birth and the age of seven; the Etheric Body, between the years of seven and fourteen; and finally, the Astral Body, which begins at fourteen and ends when the child becomes twenty-one.

During the first stage of development, the Physical Body, the child is to be engaged in creative activities – knitting, physical exercise and painting, for example. It is also said to be important not to expose the child to reading before the age of seven, so reading and writing are not permitted during this vulnerable stage of development. Once the child reaches the Etheric Body stage, reading is developed and writing is taught, as well as mathematics and humanities such as history. Creative activities are still encouraged but become more focused, with storytelling becoming an important area. Only when the child approaches the final stage of development, the Astral Body, at year fourteen, are sciences introduced.

The main consideration in a Steiner or Waldorf school is that the child be thought of first and foremost as a reincarnated soul in human form and therefore educated in a sympathetic and appropriate manner. As the child progresses through the school, the onus is placed on the individual to gradually seek out for him or herself the truth present in the world and follow their own unique pathway for the rest of their life.

This ties in with the science of anthroposophy, which Steiner founded and which he applied to the greater understanding of the whole universe. On the meaning and purpose of his new science, Steiner said:

> Anthroposophy is a path of knowledge, to guide the spiritual in the human being to the spiritual in the universe. Anthroposophists are those who experience, as an essential need of life, certain questions on the nature of the human being and the universe, just as one experiences hunger and thirst.

The method of education begun by Steiner is certainly of great interest to many people and is growing in popularity. Studies indicate that children who attend these schools are behind students of similar ages from non-Waldorf schools up until the age of about eight (largely as a result of the prohibition on reading and writing until the age of seven under the Waldorf model) but that after this they soon catch up and then overtake the majority of students from conventional schools. Waldorf methods are apparently catching on in other areas of child education, even if the whole curriculum is not adhered to. For example, some psychologists are beginning to believe that the practice of teaching under-fives to read and write in an effort to give those children a 'head start' is actually detrimental to the long-term development of the child.

Steiner's adherence to his belief in Atlantis is still of importance to us today simply because his history of Atlantis is actually taught in a number of Waldorf schools, so many children are exposed every day to Steiner's ideas and thoughts about the lost island.

It is worth noting that, like many around him at the turn of the twentieth century, including Madame Blavatsky and the Theosophists, Steiner was a firm believer in the concept of the 'Root Races', the idea that humankind's history could be broken down into the existence of certain ethnic types. This is a very controversial area, and since the events of the Second World War – after which the fruits of racial dogma could be clearly seen by everyone – it has been a taboo subject.

Steiner has been accused of being a racist himself, and although it is claimed by his supporters that he never said that any one race was radically superior, some of his comments are considered today to be, let's say, 'unsavoury', and at the very least leave him open to such accusations. His main claim was that although all of the current races were in decline, the white race was declining at a lesser rate and was most suitable to succeed in the present day and age. Obviously, this has caused a great deal of controversy because children are still being taught in Waldorf schools today and the fear is that racism could become entrenched in such an environment. However, a report carried out in 1995 in the Netherlands declared that Waldorf schools were not teaching racist views, although certain practices were put in place to monitor the situation more closely.

Overall, Steiner's ideas on Atlantis are an interesting diversion but they cannot be taken seriously by academics and historians trying to piece together a definitive account of the lost island and its people because of Steiner's insistence on using the Akashic records as his primary source. However, he did inspire many people and his book on Atlantis certainly ensured that the topic of the lost continent was once again brought to people's attention. One person in particular whom he is said to have influenced was Edgar Cayce, who himself claimed to use the Akashic records.

**SEE ALSO:** Blavatsky, Madame; Cayce, Edgar

# STRABO

S trabo was of principally Greek extraction, hailing from Amaseia in Pontus (now part of Turkey) on the Black Sea. Coming from a well-to-do family, he had sufficient funds to allow him to travel in search of knowledge. He received a good education of the sort approved in his day, studying among other subjects grammar, geography and philosophy, and had little time for the religions commonly practised at the time, following the Peripatetic (wandering) School of philosophy, so called, it seems, because its founder Aristotle walked as he taught in Athens. Strabo also became attracted to the allied philosophy of the Stoics, sometimes regarded as a branch of the Peripatetics, who taught not dissimilar doctrines. The Stoics, who got their name because the philosophy of Stoicism was first argued in the porch, or *stoa*, in the Athenian *agora* (the marketplace), believed that all human emotions came from faulty judgements and that the truly wise might achieve happiness through nothing more than virtue. Only the wise man is truly free, those who do not have wisdom are merely slaves, slaves to their emotions. A true Stoic feels neither pain nor pleasure.

Strabo, who lived from around 63 BC until at least AD 21, is best known for his writings. Those contained in the 17 books on the geography of the Roman Empire, *Geographica*, are largely extant but, sadly, the even longer *Historical Studies* is almost entirely lost to us, unless a lucky excavation in the future brings it back to light. Perhaps the city of Herculaneum, buried under volcanic mud in the terrible eruption of Vesuvius in AD 79, may yield more papyri to add to those discovered in the library there in the eighteenth century. Some of Strabo's works might be among them, or perhaps they are awaiting discovery in a deposit somewhere in Alexandria, Athens or elsewhere.

Long before the time of Strabo, a geographer, Eratosthenes of Cyrene (c.275–c.194 BC or, according to some sources, c.284–202), was head of the great library of Alexandria and tutor to the children of the pharaoh Ptolemy III Euergetes I. Eratosthenes believed that the world was a sphere and Strabo too adopted this view. The idea that in ancient times it was universally acknowledged that the earth is flat is quite wrong. It should be added, though, that Strabo did not approve of all of Eratosthenes' conclusions, contained in the latter's *Geographica*. This work was the foundation of mathematical geography and Eratosthenes had the distinction of devising a method of measuring the circumference of the earth.

Strabo's work attempts to modernise that of Eratosthenes. It is fair to say that Strabo is subjective in what he chooses to include in his work, and his knowledge in some areas is patently lacking. However, as the *Oxford Classical Dictionary* points out, 'his work is a storehouse of information, an historical geography and a philosophy of geography'. It would be unfair, of course, to expect that geographical knowledge of this period would bear a close resemblance to the discipline as it is practised today, with all our modern advantages, but it is true to say that at times in Strabo's work mythology and geography go strangely hand in hand.

One example of Strabo's idiosyncrasy is that he was a passionate admirer of Homer and used him as a source of geographical information, while he tended to disregard, for instance, Herodotus, on whom he might have done better to rely. It is only by way of Strabo's writing that we have access to Eratosthenes' Homeric geography. Eratosthenes' admiration of Homer was something he was able to instil in others, perhaps best illustrated by the fact that Pharaoh Ptolemy IV Philopator of Egypt, who had been taught by Eratosthenes, had a temple built which was dedicated to Homer and in Alexandria a cult was dedicated to the ancient poet.

Evidently an admirer of the Roman world, Strabo settled in the city of Rome in 29 BC, when he was in his mid-30s, having already studied there when he was younger. His travels took him to Egypt, Arabia Felix (the province known as 'Arabia the Blessed' because it was the most fertile of those regions) and Ethiopia.

Strabo wrote that Aristotle, who had been Plato's pupil, had claimed that his teacher had invented the idea of Atlantis merely to illustrate a point in his teaching. Unfortunately, we only have

Strabo's word for this, as anything that Aristotle himself might have had to tell us on the subject is no longer available to us.

Strabo writes in the *Geographica*:

> Concerning Atlantis, Plato says that Solon, after having inquired of priests of Egypt, reports that Atlantis once existed but disappeared; an island no smaller in size than a continent; and Poseidonius believes that it is better to deal with the matter in this way than to say about Atlantis, 'Its inventor made it disappear just as the Poet did to the Achaean wall.'

This is just one of Strabo's references to Homer's *Iliad*.

In his great work, Strabo largely acts as a critical compiler of earlier works. In this way, he gives us a snapshot of the state of geographical science in his time, pointing out the strengths and weaknesses of his sources. His is our only complete source of information for the wide range of countries and populations which were known to the Graeco-Roman world in the Augustan Age. The first two books define his view of geographical knowledge through a critique of past authors. The next four describe Iberia, Gaul and Italy, again drawing on previous writers. Book VII covers the Danube and European Black Sea areas, and in the next three, covering Greek territory, he draws heavily on Homer and those who had commentated on the poet. Books XI to XIV deal with the Asian Black Sea areas, the Caucasus and Asia Minor. He goes on to describe Troy, India and Persia (drawing on accounts of Alexander the Great's conquests) and by Book XVI he is in the realms of Mesopotamia (most of which is now Iraq), Syria, Palestine and the Red Sea. In writing about these, he had the advantage of modern reports of expeditions dispatched by Mark Antony and Augustus as well as the works of Ancient Greek authors. In the final Book XVII, Strabo describes the North African Mediterranean sea coast, including Egypt, for which he makes use not only of earlier writers but also of his own personal knowledge, as he does in covering those other areas he has visited. His first-hand experience, though, forms only a small part of the foundation of his *Geographica*.

His information largely relates to conditions prevailing when his sources were writing but he must be given credit for the wide scope of his compilation. He mentions distances, frontiers, agriculture, industry, political matters, religion and ethnography. Myths, legends, geological features and historical subjects are also included.

While it has its deficiencies, Strabo's *Geographica* is a valuable work, well worthy of a place in the bookcase of the student of the Graeco-Roman world.

**SEE ALSO:** Athens; Plato

# TARTESSOS

The *Encyclopaedia Britannica* describes Tartessos as 'semi-historic, semi-legendary'. Spelled 'Tartessos' by the Greeks, known as 'Tartessus' to the Romans, this region may well be the Tarshish of the Bible. It is situated in southern Spain (perhaps having been centred on modern Seville) around the lower and middle reaches of the Guadalquivir River, which was known in Roman times as the Baetis. There is evidence that the Minoans visited in very early times and it was populated by Phoenicians for a while. Samian and Phocaean Greeks knew of Tartessos, which became renowned for its wealth, gained through trade with Carthaginian and Phoenician merchants. The people of Tartessos traded in tin — a prized commodity in the ancient world, perhaps imported from the mines of Brittany and Cornwall — as well as in gold, silver and copper from the Rio Tinto. Agriculture and animal rearing were other sources of wealth for the people of the area.

The town may have gained more fame through being situated near the famous Pillars of Hercules, which that hero, legend had it, had erected to mark the boundaries of Africa and Europe. It was also where the sun god unharnessed his horses after a hard day's work, at least in the imaginations of the ancient poets. Tartessos was regarded by the Romans as an extremely remote place situated in the far west. The Tartessians had their own writing system, which cannot at the present time be deciphered, and were ruled by a hereditary monarchy.

It was probably the Carthaginians who were responsible for the destruction wrought in Tartessos around 500 BC. It has been suggested that loans made by the Tartessians to the Phocians, who needed to pay for fortifications of their city to defend it from their Persian enemies, were the cause of the aggression. By that time, it seems, the Phoenicians had challenged the commercial importance of Tartessos and taken the trade for themselves. Probably, too, the increasing use of iron rather than softer metals in artefacts led to the economic decline of the area.

The town has sometimes been confused with Gades (Cádiz, Spain), which, according to Dr J. Lemprière in his *Classical Dictionary*, was near a settlement also named Tartessos, which was situated on a small island. Poets of later times began to refer to the whole of Spain or even the entire western area of Europe as Tartessos. Rainer W. Kühne, in *Antiquity*, June 2004, claims that near the mouth of the Guadalquivir River, south-west of Seville, 'where the town of Tartessos was thought to have been located', might be the site of Plato's Atlantis, citing other scholars who have posited this theory. He states, 'it is not without interest that large structures have been identified from recent satellite photos in this part of the lower Guadalquivir basin.' One of these could be the remains of a temple to Poseidon of similar dimensions to those given in *Critias*.

Another feature might have been the Temple of Cleito and Poseidon. Poseidon and the sea nymph Cleito were, according to legend, the parents of five pairs of twins who became the first kings of Atlantis. Cleito was the daughter of Evenor and Leucippe, who lived on a mountain on the island of Atlantis. She was a mortal who was chosen by the god Poseidon to be his wife.

In his conclusion, Kühne further states that:

> Plato's war between Atlantis and the Eastern Mediterranean countries finds echoes with the activities of the Sea Peoples around 1200 BC . . . there is a possibility that the city and society of Atlantis may refer to either Iron Age Tartessos or a Bronze Age culture in the same area of south-west Spain.

**SEE ALSO:** Critias; Minoans; Phoenicians; Pillars of Hercules; Plato; Poseidon

# TIMAEUS

**T**he Greek Pythagorean philosopher Timaeus is said to have hailed from Locri in Italy. Although he is a chief speaker in Plato's *Timaeus*, we have no external evidence of his existence. It is perfectly possible that he was a fictional person invented for the part by Plato. It should be borne in mind, however, that in one of his other works, *Critias*, with which *Timaeus* is associated, the eponymous Critias is a genuine historical character. This Timaeus should not be confused with the friend of Alexander the Great or with the Sicilian historian of the third century BC, who both had the same name.

Plato's *Timaeus* takes the form of a conversation between Timaeus himself, the philosopher Socrates, Critias and one Hermocrates, who may also have been a fictional character. Socrates and Critias were both people known to history, however, so again it is possible that this Hermocrates was better known in Plato's time.

In the work, Plato gives his version of the formation of the universe, clearly awed by its order and loveliness. It is governed by the laws of mathematics and was created by a benevolent hand. It creates a model which people would do well to consider. *Timaeus* was written late in Plato's life and he had intended that the unfinished *Critias* would further explain his views on cosmology, physics and biology. The character Timaeus speaks as an astronomer, which was, in the fourth century BC, a much wider discipline than most present-day astronomers would recognise. *Timaeus* commences with an account of the brave Athenians standing up to and defeating the kings of Atlantis in their aggressive pursuit of world domination.

The dialogue also deals with Platonic ideas of a universe consisting of an ascending ladder of Forms, or a 'great chain of being'. *Timaeus* suggests that the element water can condense to become stone and earth; when melted these become air, inflamed air becomes fire and extinguished fire becomes air again. Condensed air becomes cloud and mist, which can become flowing water to complete the cycle. While this is by no means the modern concept of the elements, it persisted into Renaissance times. It establishes that Forms are not stable, change is constantly occurring. At the Creation, we are told, God made beautiful and good things out of Forms which were not beautiful or good. However, Plato's Forms were not simply material elements; there was also a place to which the intelligence could gain access where his Forms might be found. For instance, there was the Form of Beauty – absolute perfect beauty. Common objects considered beautiful would all have some defect or imperfection or a contradictory characteristic. Such concepts are difficult to understand and it is, perhaps, comforting to know that even Plato himself realised these difficulties and did not feel himself able to explain his ideas fully in this respect.

In *Timaeus*, Plato describes the Creation by the Craftsman/Creator. Unlike in later, Christian theology, the universe was not created from nothing at all, but from unformed elements comprising water, earth, fire and air. Everything that we have experience of is composed of these four elements, according to those who followed Plato's teachings. He continues with arguments ranging over physics, astronomy, biology and chemistry. *Timaeus* has the distinction of being the only part of Plato's large body of writing which deals with the subject of natural science. His ideas were tremendously influential on thinkers throughout the Middle Ages.

Plato suggests that there is a part of the human soul that the Creator infuses with divinity, and a mortal part, influenced by inferior gods. It is the latter which is likely to lead the soul astray, bringing it to punishment in the afterworld and reincarnation in this one. The Creator therefore cannot be blamed for man's imperfections. These come from the elements of impiety and unruliness which man has inherited from the Titans, themselves having been good in early days, but who became evil. Perhaps this is parallelled by human nature; think, for example, of Christ's exhortation to become like little children.

Along with *Critias*, *Timaeus* contains the first written account of the lost civilisation of Atlantis. It might be dismissed as a mere artifice constructed by a master philosopher to strengthen his argument. It might, however, be an account of actual catastrophic happenings that occurred long before Plato's time. If so, the question is whether Plato's description comes anywhere near the truth.

**SEE ALSO:** Critias; Plato

# TUATHA DÉ DANAAN

The faerie people known as the Tuatha dé Danaan (pronounced 'Tootha day dannan') once ruled Ireland, being the fourth wave of invaders of that land. They brought with them the spear of Lug, which always hit its target; the cauldron of the Dagda, which never ran short of food; the invincible sword of Nuadu; and the stone of Fál, which cried out when the true king of Ireland set foot upon it.

Their name translates from Old Irish as 'the family of Danu'. The myths and folklore which attach to these godlike spirits are mainly to be found in the *Book of Invasions*, or *Lebor Gabála Érenn* ('book of the taking of Ireland'), which dates to the twelfth century AD. This writing was an attempt to give the Irish people a history which might be compared with the Israelite legends of their origins, compiling both Gaelic and pre-Gaelic pagan myths but adding a veneer of reinterpretation in the light of Christianity. In it, we find a people enslaved, an exodus, a wandering and a promised land. However, the pagan elements in this 'history' were not completely expunged, hence we find that some of the Tuatha dé Danaan goddesses married Gaels after the Gaelic conquest of Ireland. The *Book of Invasions* brings in wizards and sorcery, battles and gods, supernatural beings and a genealogy for the Irish nation stretching back to no less a person than Noah.

Elements appear borrowed from other histories in the compilation of the Tuatha dé Danaan story, including from the writings of the rhetorician Timagenes of Alexandria, who was taken to Rome in 55 BC. His account of Gaulish ancestors being driven from their eastern European homelands by wars and floods (some of which may be found in *The Later Roman Empire* by the soldier and the last of the great Roman historians, Ammianus Marcellinus) bears a recognisable resemblance to the dé Danaan legend. Other stories had appeared before the *Book of Invasions*, both written down and in the bardic, or spoken, tradition, on which it draws.

Lady Jane Francesca Speranza Wilde, in her *Ancient Legends of Ireland*, published in 1887, describes the horses of the Tuatha dé Danaan, which, like their owners, could live for over a century. The last of these was allegedly auctioned in Connaught and bought by a member of the British administration. The groom who attempted to ride the animal was thrown and killed. Lady Wilde writes:

> The breed of horses [which the Tuatha dé Danaan] reared could not be surpassed in the world – fleet as the wind with the arched neck and broad chest and the quivering nostril, and the large eye that showed they were made of fire and flame and not of dull, heavy earth. And the Tuatha made stables for them in the great caves in the hills, and they were shod with silver and had golden bridles, and never a slave was allowed to ride them. A splendid sight was the cavalcade of the Tuatha-de-Danann knights. Seven-score steeds, each with a jewel on his forehead like a star, and seven-score horsemen, all the sons of kings, in their green mantles fringed with gold, and golden helmets on the head, and golden greaves on their limbs and each knight having in his hand a golden spear.

The courtly riders described are much like the Seelie Court of Scottish legend and may themselves have become the Irish equivalent, the Daoine Sidhe (pronounced 'theena shee').

The Tuatha were renowned for their skill in magic, poetry and music, and as builders. Their reputation as magicians is perhaps especially interesting, since one legend concerning their origins has them emigrating from Persia, a land whose population had a reputation for such knowledge in the ancient world.

In early days, Ireland was populated by the Fir Bolg, which may translate as 'men with spears', against whom the Tuatha dé Danaan fought when they arrived in Ireland. They were not the only inhabitants, however; there were also the Fomors, who may have been similar to the Greek Titans from before the time of the gods proper. The Fomors might be described as spirits of the wild, whereas the Tuatha dé Danaan were divinities of civilisation, who finally overcame their rivals.

The Tuatha dé Danaan were defeated by the Milesian Celts when the latter arrived in Ireland, and their descendants became known as the Daoine Sidhe, the faerie people (*sidhe* being the Irish word for 'faerie'). They now live beneath the hollow hills, or raths, and are known by various titles, among others, Davana, Hill People, Áes Si, Áes Sidh, Áos Sidhe and the Children of Danu.

The Milesians, believed to be Celtic people from Spain, invaded Ireland and it was they who wrested supremacy from the Tuatha dé Danaan. The Dagda, the all-powerful high king of the Tuatha, was not strong enough to defend his clan from these Celtic people and in defeat led his followers into the Sidhe hills. Though the Tuatha dé Danaan had long ago been giants, after their defeat by the Milesians, having lost their status as rulers of Ireland, they also lost their stature and became much smaller. Occasionally since then they have emerged to defend justice, with flaming lances and magic shields, defended by invisibility. One of their number, Etain, appears as the beautiful heroine of the love story 'Midhir and Etain', of which there are several versions, involving witchcraft, winds and warfare. It also features Tir-na-n-oge, the Land of the Young, lying westward across the sea, to where some of the Tuatha fled after their defeat by the Milesians. Tir-na-n-oge is the timeless paradise, a kind of Eden, where fighting takes place but the slain return to life to fight again the next day! There is no old age, no sickness, no death.

It has been suggested that the Atlantis legend may have its origins in the Tuatha dé Danaan, who came flying into Ireland, and that Ireland itself may have been the land where the Atlantean culture had its being.

Today, the most prominent of the Daoine Sidhe is Finvarra, high king of all the Irish faerie folk. He is sometimes thought of as the King of the Dead, dwelling underneath the mound of Knockma. In *Faeries* by Brian Froud and Alan Lee, it is said that as well as being fighters and skilful players of the Irish sport of hurling, the Daoine Sidhe are masters of the chessboard and that unwise mortals have lost their possessions to Finvarra after betting they could beat him.

To many people, the word 'faerie' conjures up a vision of a tiny creature with wings, wearing flowing garments and perhaps carrying a wand, but for generations past it had much more serious connotations. Man has for long explained natural happenings by reference to gods, magic or spirits beyond human powers to control. In ancient times, local gods were believed to exercise good or malign influences according to their whims, and people sacrificed and prayed to them to try to influence their mood. The weather, the harvest, the chances of accident or loss, sickness or health, all were matters of concern that lay in the hands of unseen forces. With the coming of Christianity to Europe, this concept never quite went away and the pagan faeries, often well disguised, sometimes strange to behold, beautiful or hideous, almost always capricious, lived on. By Renaissance times, they had become the subject of literature and drama. They are supernormal beings, described by Robert Kirk, a Gaelic scholar and minister of the Episcopal Church, in his *Secret Commonwealth* of 1691 as 'of a middle nature between Man and Angel'.

**SEE ALSO:** Ammianus Marcellinus

# TWENTY THOUSAND LEAGUES UNDER THE SEA

One of the most popular books to discuss the submerged land of Atlantis was Jules Verne's *Twenty Thousand Leagues under the Sea*. The fantastic novel about undersea adventures was published in 1869. The book concerns the adventures of one Professor Pierre Aronnax, who is taken aboard a fabulous submarine, the *Nautilus*, operated by Captain Nemo. A popular misconception is that the title refers to the depth of the world's oceans, when in fact it describes the distance the *Nautilus* travelled during her adventures.

Nemo was a recluse from civilisation who spent his life engaged in scientific exploration of the undersea world in his submarine. Nemo takes Arronax to many underwater locations, including the coral reefs of the Red Sea, beneath the ice of Antarctica and to recover treasure from the sunken wrecks of the Battle of Vigo Bay. A highlight of the book is when, deep below the middle of the Atlantic, Captain Nemo shows Professor Aronnax a ruined city, close to a still-active underwater volcano, that he says is Atlantis itself:

> What lightning flashed through my mind! Atlantis, that ancient land of Meropis mentioned by the historian Theopompus; Plato's Atlantis; the continent whose very existence has been denied by such philosophers and scientists as Origen, Porphyry, Iamblichus, d'Anville, Malte-Brun, and Humboldt, who entered its disappearance in the ledger of myths and folk tales; the country whose reality

has nevertheless been accepted by such other thinkers as Posidonius, Pliny, Ammianus Marcellinus, Tertullian, Engel, Scherer, Tournefort, Buffon, and d'Avezac; I had this land right under my eyes, furnishing its own unimpeachable evidence of the catastrophe that had overtaken it! So this was the submerged region that had existed outside Europe, Asia, and Libya, beyond the Pillars of Hercules, home of those powerful Atlantean people against whom ancient Greece had waged its earliest wars!

Professor Arronax explains how that region of the seabed was wracked with convulsions and lined with deadly volcanoes. So dangerous was that part of the Atlantic that ships were said to be able to hear the devastation that was being wreaked below on the seabed. He also speculates as to whether those same volcanoes would cause Atlantis to rise again some day. Arronax tells us what Atlantis looked like, sunk far below the waves:

In fact, there beneath my eyes was a town in ruins, demolished, overwhelmed, laid low, its roofs caved in, its temples pulled down, its arches dislocated, its columns stretching over the earth; in these ruins you could still detect the solid proportions of a sort of Tuscan architecture; farther off, the remains of a gigantic aqueduct; here, the caked heights of an acropolis along with the fluid forms of a Parthenon; there, the remnants of a wharf, as if some bygone port had long ago harboured merchant vessels and triple-tiered war galleys on the shores of some lost ocean; still farther off, long rows of collapsing walls, deserted thoroughfares, a whole Pompeii buried under the waters, which Captain Nemo had resurrected before my eyes!

Verne was certainly ahead of his time and wrote in detail about many technologies that were either as yet unknown or at a very early stage in their development. For example, the vessel that Captain Nemo commands in *Twenty Thousand Leagues under the Sea*, the *Nautilus*, was likely named after the world's first successful submarine, which was commissioned by Napoleon Bonaparte, First Consul at the time, and launched in 1800. While it shared the same name as Captain Nemo's extraordinary vessel, that is where the similarity ends. Instead of the electric power source of the fictional *Nautilus*, the real-world equivalent was powered by hand, the propeller having to be turned manually by the crew. Furthermore, rather than being a vessel that could provide comfortable habitation for many men during a long journey, the real *Nautilus* could only stay under water for some six hours.

Verne's incredible tale must certainly have inspired writers such as Ignatius Donnelly who were to write non-fictional accounts of the lost land. *Twenty Thousand Leagues under the Sea* must have fuelled people's desire to discover more about the secrets of Atlantis and the land that Nemo shows to Professor Arronax. Verne's description of Nemo just before he leaves the underwater ruins seems to sum up the sense of mystery and intrigue that Atlantis stirs in those who search for it, and it also touches upon that ineffable emotion – the desire sometimes to live in an age other than our own, an age when the world was perhaps a simpler place.

> As I mused in this way, trying to establish in my memory every detail of this impressive landscape, Captain Nemo was leaning his elbows on a moss-covered monument, motionless as if petrified in some mute trance. Was he dreaming of those lost generations, asking them for the secret of human destiny? Was it here that this strange man came to revive himself, basking in historical memories, reliving that bygone life, he who had no desire for our modern one? I would have given anything to know his thoughts, to share them, understand them!

**SEE ALSO:** Donnelly, Ignatius

# BIBLIOGRAPHY

Allan, D.S. and Delair, J.B., *Cataclysm! Compelling Evidence of a Cosmic Catastrophe in 9500 BC*, Bear & Co., 1997

Ashe, Geoffrey, *Atlantis: Lost Lands, Ancient Wisdom*, Thames & Hudson, 1992

Bacon, Francis, *The New Atlantis and The Great Instauration*, Harlan Davidson, Inc., 1989

Bahn, Paul G., *The Enigma of Easter Island*, Weidenfeld Illustrated, 1997

Baines, John and Malek, Jaromir, *Atlas of Ancient Egypt*, Time Life Books, 1990

Bauval, Robert and Hancock, Graham, *Keeper of Genesis*, Arrow, 2001

Bellamy, H.S., *The Atlantis Myth*, Faber & Faber, 1948

Benest, D. and Duvent, J.L., 'Is Sirius a Triple Star?', *Astronomy and Astrophysics*, No. 299, 1995

Berlitz, Charles, *Atlantis: The Lost Continent Revealed*, Macmillan, 1984

Berlitz, Charles, *Atlantis: The Eighth Continent*, Faucett Books, 1984

Berlitz, Charles, *The Mystery of Atlantis*, Souvenir Press, 1969

Bierhost, John, *The Mythology of Mexico and Central America*, William Morrow & Co., 1990

Birley, Anthony R., *Septimius Severus: The African Emperor*, Yale University Press, 1989

Blavatsky, H. P., *The Secret Doctrine: The Synthesis of Science, Religion and Philosophy*, Theosophical Publishing, 1888

# BIBLIOGRAPHY

Braghine, A., *The Shadow of Atlantis*, Turnstone Press, 1986

Bray, Warwick, *Everyday Life of the Aztecs*, B.T. Batsford, 1968

Bro, Harmon H., *Edgar Cayce: A Seer Out of Season*, Signet Books, 1990

Brown, Hugh Auchincloss, *Cataclysms of the Earth*, Twayne Publishing Inc., 1967

Cameron, Ian, *Kingdom of the Sun God: A History of the Andes and Their People*, Guild Publishing, 1990

Campbell, Joseph and Moyers, Bill, *The Power of Myth*, Doubleday, 1988

Castleden, Rodney, *Atlantis Destroyed*, Routledge, 1998

Castleden, Rodney, *Minoans: Life in Bronze Age Crete*, Routledge, 1993

Cayce, Edgar, *Edgar Cayce on Atlantis*, Warner Books, 1968

Churchward, James, *The Lost Continent of Mu*, BE Books, 1988

Churchward, James, *The Sacred Symbols of Mu*, BE Books, 1988

Clark, R. T. Rundle, *Myth and Symbol in Ancient Egypt*, Thames & Hudson, 1959

Coe, Michael D., *Breaking the Maya Code*, Thames & Hudson, 1992

Comyns Beaumont, William, *The Riddle of Prehistoric Britain*, Rider & Co., 1946

Concepción, José L., *The Guanches, Survivors and their Descendants*, Ediciónes Graficolor, 1984

Cutcliffe Hyne, C.J., *The Lost Continent*, Fontana, 1972

Dalley, Stephanie, *Myths from Mesopotamia: Creation, The Flood, Gilgamesh, and Others*, Oxford Paperbacks, 1991

Dante, *The Divine Comedy, Volume I: Inferno*, Penguin Books, 1971

Davis, Nigel, *The Ancient Kingdoms of Mexico*, Penguin Books, 1990

Derry, Douglas, 'The Dynastic Race in Egypt' in *Journal of Egyptian Archaeology*, No. 42, 1956

Desmond, Lawrence Gustave and Messenger, Phyllis Mauch, *A Dream of Maya: Augustus and Alice Le Plongeon in Nineteenth-Century Yucatan*, University of New Mexico Press, 1988

Dieterlen, G. and de Ganay, S., *Le Génie des eaux chez les Dogons*, Librairie Orientaliste Paul Geuthner, 1948

Donnelly, Ignatius, *Atlantis: The Antediluvian World*, Marston & Co. Ltd, 1882

Donnelly, Ignatius, *The Destruction Of Atlantis: Ragnarok, or the Age Of Fire and Gravel*, Whittim, 1883

Douglas, J. D., *The New Bible Dictionary*, Inter-Varsity Press, 1962

Ellis, Richard, *Imagining Atlantis*, Alfred A. Knopf, Inc., 1998

Emery, Walter B., *Archaic Egypt*, Penguin Books Ltd, 1991

Faulkner, Raymond O., *Ancient Egyptian Book of the Dead*, British Museum Press, 1989

Faulkner, Raymond O., *Ancient Egyptian Pyramid Texts*, Aris & Phillips, 1985

Feuerestein, Georg; Kak, Subhash; and Frawley, David, *In Search of the Cradle of Civilisation*, Quest Books, 1995

Fix, William R., *Pyramid Odyssey*, Mayflower Books 1978

Flem-Ath, Rand and Rose, *When The Sky Fell*, Stoddart, 1995

Flem-Ath, Rand and Wilson, Colin, *The Atlantis Blueprint*, Dell, 2002

Forsyth, Phyllis Young, *Atlantis: the Making of Myth*, McGill-Queen's University Press, 1980

Frankfort, H., *Kingship and the Gods*, University of Chicago Press, 1978

Frazer, J.G., *The Golden Bough*, Macmillan, 1963

Frost, K.T, 'The *Critias* and Minoan Crete' in *Journal of Hellenic Studies*, Volume 33, 1913

Froud, Brian and Lee, Alan, *Fairies*, Pavilion Books, 2002

Galanapoulos, Professor Angelos and Bacon, Edward, *Atlantis: The Truth Behind the Legend*, Thomas Nelson & Sons Ltd, 1969

Gill, Christopher, *Plato: The Atlantis Story*, Bristol Classical Press, 1980

Gordon, Cyrus H., *Before Columbus: Links Between the Old World and Ancient America*, Crown Publishers, 1971

Graves, Robert, *The Greek Myths, Volumes I & II*, Penguin Books, 1984

Hancock, Graham, *Fingerprints of the Gods*, Crown, 1995

Hapgood, Charles H., *Earth's Shifting Crust: A Key to Some Basic Problems of Earth Science*, Pantheon Books, 1958

Hapgood, Charles H., *Maps of the Ancient Sea Kings: Evidence of Advanced Civilization in the Ice Age*, Turnstone Books, 1979

Hapgood, Charles H., *The Path of the Pole,* Chilton Books, 1970

Hawkins, Gerald S., *Beyond Stonehenge*, Arrow Books, 1977

Herodotus, *The History*, University of Chicago Press, 1987

Hope, Murry, *The Ancient Wisdom of Atlantis*, Thorsons, 1995

James, Peter, *The Sunken Kingdom: The Atlantis Mystery Solved*, Jonathan Cape, 1995

Joseph, Frank, *The Atlantis Encyclopedia*, Career Press Inc., 2005

Joseph, Frank, *The Destruction of Atlantis: Compelling Evidence of the Sudden Fall of the Legendary Civilization*, Inner Traditions Press, 2002

Kirch, Patrick V., *The Evolution of the Polynesian Chiefdoms*, Cambridge University Press, 1984

# BIBLIOGRAPHY

Kühne, Rainer W., 'Location and dating of Atlantis', in *Antiquity*, Vol. 78, No. 300, June 2004

Lemprière, Dr J., *Classical Dictionary*, Bracken Books, 1984

Leonard, Cedric, *The Quest of Atlantis*, Manor Books, 1979

Le Plongeon, Augustus, *Queen Moo and the Egyptian Sphinx*, Paul Trench, Truebner, 1896

Lichtheim, Miriam, *Ancient Egyptian Literature Volume 1: The Old and Middle Kingdoms*, University of California Press, 1905

Luce, J.V., *Lost Atlantis: New Light on an Old Legend*, HarperCollins, 1969

Mackenzie, Donald, *Egyptian Myth and Legend*, Gresham Publishing Co., 1907

Marinatos, Spyridon, *Some Words about the Legend of Atlantis*, Deltion Publications, 1971

Menzies, Gavin, *1421: The Year China Discovered America*, William Morrow & Company, 2003

Michell, John, *The New View over Atlantis*, Thames & Hudson, 1983

Milton, Joyce; Orsi, Robert; and Harrison, Norman, *The Feathered Serpent and the Cross: The Pre-Columbian God-Kings and the Papal States*, Cassell, 1980

Mooney, Richard, *Colony: Earth*, Souvenir Press, 1974

Morton, Chris and Thomas, Ceri Louise, *The Mystery of the Crystal Skulls*, Element, 1997

Muck, Otto Heinrich, *The Secret Of Atlantis*, Collins, 1978

Nash, Daphne, *Coinage in the Celtic World*, Spink & Son, 1987

O'Brien, Christian and Barbara, J., *The Shining Ones*, Collectors Books, 2001

Oliver, Frederick, *A Dweller on Two Planets*, Poseid Publishing Company, 1920

Pellegrino, Charles, *Unearthing Atlantis: An Archaeological Odyssey*, Random House, 1991

Plato, *Timaeus and Critias*, trans. Desmond Lee, advisory ed. Betty Radice, Penguin Books, 1977

Plutarch, *The Rise and Fall of Athens: Nine Greek Lives by Plutarch*, Penguin Books, 1973

*Popol Vuh*, trans. Dennis Tedlock, Simon & Schuster, 1985

Radice, Betty, *Who's Who in the Ancient World*, Penguin Books, 1973

Roberts, Anthony, *Atlantean Traditions in Ancient Britain*, Rider & Co., 1975

Ryan, William and Pitman, Walter, *Noah's Flood: The New Scientific Discoveries about the Event that Changed History*, Simon & Schuster, 1999

Santillana, Giorgio de and Dechend, Hertha von, *Hamlet's Mill*, David R. Godine, 1977

Sarmast, Robert, *Discovery of Atlantis: The Startling Case for the Island of Cyprus*, Origin Press, 2003

Schwaller de Lubicz, R.A., *Sacred Science: The King of Pharaonic Theocracy*, HarperCollins, 1982

Scrutton, Robert, *Secrets of Lost Atland*, Spearman, 1978

Sitchin, Zecharia, *The Lost Realms*, HarperTorch, 1990

Spanuth, Jürgen, *Atlantis of the North*, Sidgwick & Jackson, 1953

Spence, Lewis, *The History of Atlantis*, University Books Inc., 1968

Spence, Lewis, *The Mysteries of Britain*, Senate, 1905

Spence, Lewis, *The Problem of Atlantis*, Rider & Sons, 1924

Steiger, Brad, *Atlantis Rising*, Berkeley Books, 1981

Steiner, Rudolf, *Cosmic Memory: Prehistory of Earth and Man*, Harper & Row, 1969

Stobbart, Lorainne, *Utopia – Fact or Fiction?: The Evidence from the Americas*, Alan Sutton, 1992

Sugrue, Thomas, *There is a River: The Story of Edgar Cayce*, ARE Press, 1988

Taylor, Thomas, *Proclus' Commentary on the Timaeus of Plato*, The Prometheus Trust, 1998

Temple, Robert K.G., *The Sirius Mystery: New Scientific Evidence for Alien Contact 5,000 Years Ago*, Destiny Books, 1998

Thompson, J. Eric, *The Rise and Fall of Maya Civilization*, Pimlico, 1993

Tomas, Andrew, *Atlantis: From Legend To Discovery*, Robert Hale, 1972

Tomas, Andrew, *We Are Not the First*, Souvenir Press, 1971

Tompkins, Peter, *Secrets of the Great Pyramid*, Harper, 1971

Velikovsky, Immanuel, *Ages in Chaos*, Doubleday, 1952

Velikovsky, Immanuel, *Worlds in Collision*, Doubleday, 1950

Verne, Jules, *Twenty Thousand Leagues under the Sea*, Scholastic, 1982

Wallis Budge, E.A., *Osiris and the Egyptian Resurrection*, The Medici Society, 1911

Walters, Frank, *Book of the Hopi*, Penguin Books, 1963

Warren, William F., *Paradise Found: The Cradle of the Human Race at the North Pole*, Houghton, Mifflin & Co., 1885

West, John Anthony, *Serpent in the Sky: The High Wisdom of Ancient Egypt*, Quest Books, 1993

Whishaw, E.M., *Atlantis in Spain*, Adventures Unlimited Press, 1997

# BIBLIOGRAPHY

Wilde, Lady Francesca Speranza, *Ancient Legend, Mystic Charms and Superstitions of Ireland*, Ward & Downey, 1887

Wilson, Colin, *From Atlantis to the Sphinx*, Virgin, 1997

Zangger, Eberhard, *The Flood from Heaven: Deciphering the Atlantis Legend*, Pan Macmillan, 1993

Zapp, Ivar and Erikson, George, *Atlantis in America: Navigators of the Ancient World*, AUP, 1998